DUNERA LIVES

To the memory of Amirah Inglis

Dunera Lives

Volume 1
A Visual History

KEN INGLIS, SEUMAS SPARK
AND JAY WINTER

WITH CAROL BUNYAN

Kenneth Stanley Inglis
7 October 1929 – 1 December 2017

Photograph: Nicholas Nazari

© Copyright 2018 Ken Inglis, Seumas Spark and Jay Winter

All rights reserved. Apart from any uses permitted by Australia's Copyright Act 1968, no part of this book may be reproduced by any process without prior written permission from the copyright owners. Inquiries should be directed to the publisher.

Second printing, 2018.

Monash University Publishing
Matheson Library and Information Services Building
40 Exhibition Walk
Monash University
Clayton, Victoria 3800, Australia
www.publishing.monash.edu

Monash University Publishing brings to the world publications which advance the best traditions of humane and enlightened thought.

Monash University Publishing titles pass through a rigorous process of independent peer review.

www.publishing.monash.edu/books/dlv1-9781925495492.html

ISBN: 978-1-925495-49-2 (paperback)
ISBN: 978-1-925495-50-8 (PDF)
ISBN: 978-1-925495-52-2 (ePub)

Series: Australian History
Series Editor: Sean Scalmer

Design: Les Thomas

Front cover painting by Emil Wittenberg, painted at Tatura on 23 May 1941. Copyright Martin Burman.

Back cover photograph by Henry Talbot, *Dunera* boys reunion, Melbourne, 1963. National Library of Australia. Copyright: Lynette Anne Talbot.

All royalties from the sale of this book will be donated to the Ken Inglis Historical Fund at Monash University.

 A catalogue record for this book is available from the National Library of Australia

CONTENTS

Acknowledgements ix
Authors' notes. xvi
General introduction. xvii

Section 1	The beginning of the end 1
Section 2	Havens? Britain and Singapore, 1939–1940. 26
Section 3	Enemy aliens in Britain, 1940: Adrift, arrested, interned, deported. 41
Section 4	At sea: Aboard the *Dunera* and the *Queen Mary* 65
Section 5	Hay, Tatura, Orange: Lassitude, solidarity, resilience 108
Section 5A	Internment: Hay, 1940–1941 114
Section 5A.1	The physical environment. 114
Section 5A.2	Waiting for freedom 126
Section 5A.3	Adaptation. 144
Section 5A.4	Learning and living 163
Section 5A.5	The landscape of internment 180
Section 5A.6	Farewell to Hay. 191
Section 5B	Internment: Tatura, 1940–1941. 194
Section 5B.1	*Dunera* internees at Tatura, 1940–1941 194
Section 5B.2	*Queen Mary* internees at Tatura, 1940–1941 201
Section 5C	Internment: Orange, 1941 208
Section 5D	Internment: Tatura, 1941–1945. 225
Section 5D.1	Between bitterness and hope 226
Section 5D.2	Dreams and reflections on living in limbo. 233

Section 5D.3	Landscapes and longing	246
Section 5D.4	Filling time	257
Section 5D.5	Seeking God	274
Section 5D.6	Tatura portraits	279
Section 5D.7	Hermann Valentin: Trees and Tatura	289
Section 5D.8	To the end	297

Section 6	**After internment**	**303**
Section 6A	Returners	307
Section 6B	Fruit-picking and the 8th Employment Company	320
Section 6C	Civilian life	367
Section 7	**Toward the future**	**387**
Section 8	**Between memory and history**	**452**
Section 8A	Australian faces	457
Section 8B	Commemoration	467
Section 8C	Legacies	488

Conclusion: Images of injustice and its aftermath 510

Appendix 1: The end of internment 515

Appendix 2: Ships on which *Dunera* internees returned to Britain, 1941–1945 518

Appendix 3: Name changes 519

Index 544

About the authors 550

ACKNOWLEDGEMENTS

We have incurred many debts in the writing of this book and in the collection of materials published here. Many of the images have never been seen before, let alone published. For providing us with drawings, photographs, paintings, and other objects, we are grateful to many people and institutions. For giving us permission to reproduce them, we are additionally indebted, and make such acknowledgement in the list of credits.

The term '*Dunera* boy' is a locution widely adopted in the 1980s by the subjects themselves and in general parlance. We wish to thank the following '*Dunera* boys', *Queen Mary* passengers, and their families for giving us their time and insights in interviews, conversations, and access to objects or images in their possession. 'D' denotes a '*Dunera* boy', 'QM' a *Queen Mary* passenger.

Mary-Clare Adam
Sara Adams
Karin Altmann
Anna Armstrong-Smith
Janet Arndt
David Baer
Herbert Baer (D)
Annette Baier
Muriel Barber
Barney Barnett (D)
Sharon Barnett
Miriam Baruch
Monica Behrend
Chris Bell
Ilse Blair (QM)
Frankie Blei
Bern Brent (D)
Michael Brent (D)
Adrian Bruch
Max Bruch (D) and Nora Bruch
Michi Bryant
Christopher (Kit) Buchdahl
Gerd Buchdahl (D) and Nancy Buchdahl
Hans Buchdahl (D) and Pamela Buchdahl
Joseph Buchdahl
Nicholas Buchdahl
Roger Buchdahl
Martin Burman and family
Alicia Byrne
Carmen Byrne
Belinda Castles
Frank Castles

Stephen Castles
Maxine Cooke
Eileen Cunningham
Michael Danby
Eva de Jong-Duldig (QM)
Reinhold Eckfeld (D)
Tonia Eckfeld
David Eckstein
Nicholas Eckstein
Jeanette Eforgan
Erwin Fabian (D)
Peter Felder
Tom Firestone
Walter Firestone
Rosemary Fisher
Steb Fisher and Wendy Wright
Loretta Forsey (QM) and Sid Forsey
Walter Freiberger (D)
David (Lord) Freud
Klaus Friedeberger (D) and Julie Friedeberger
Walter Fuerst (D)
Ian Gabriel
Paul Gabriel
Michael Gordon
Henry Graupner
Nina Greenwood
David Gruen and Jenny Wilkinson
Nicholas Gruen
Herta Guttman
Steven Guttmann
Paul Haarburger
John Haim
Leslie Heine
Michael Heine
Peter Herbst (D)
Colin Heymann
Ernest Hirsch (D) and Anne Hirsch
Heine Hirsch (D) and Sonia Hirsch
Frank Hofmann
Gerry Hofmann
Jacquie Houlden
Walter Kaufmann (D)
Danny Lamm
Erwin Lamm (D) and Ilse Lamm
Karl Liffman
Kurt Liffman
Anthony Lipmann
Bryan Lipmann
Ed Lippmann
Klaus Loewald (D) and Uyen Loewald
Tonio Loewald
Monica Lee Lowen
Jocelyn Lowen
Tanya Makin
Debbie and Leon Mandel and family
Linda Mannheim
Gary Max
Elaine Mayer
Esther Meir-Glitzenstein
Karin Morrison
Greta Hofmann Nemiroff
Rosemary Newall
Caroline Philipp
Franz Philipp (D) and June Philipp
Helen Philipp

ACKNOWLEDGEMENTS

Max Pietruschka
Susanne Platt
Kathy Radok
Stephanie Radok
Ron Reichwald
Valerie Reynolds
Ernest Rodeck (D) and Sheila Rodeck
Christian Routh
Jonathon Jodi Routh
Gabriela Schonbach
Frank Schumacher
Selma Seknow
Rebecca Silk
Ruth Simon (QM)
Clive and Fran Sondheim
Mike Sondheim (D)
Steve Sostheim
Edith Spira
Anton Stampfl
Andrew Stocky
Julius Stocky
Lynette Talbot
Betty Teltscher
Sue Teltscher
Wendy Teltscher
Roy Thalheimer (D)
Rosemary Thomas
Tanya Tintner
Joseph Weidenbaum
Felix Werder (D) and Vera Werder
Geoff Winter
Andrew and Anna Wolf
Ilse Wolfsohn

We hope we have done justice to their stories, their memories, and their interpretations.

Among academic colleagues, we have incurred many debts. The greatest is to Carol Bunyan, an independent scholar and researcher originally from Hay, who has created a unique database on all the internees sent to Australia on the *Dunera*. Carol is a source of wisdom on all matters *Dunera*, and we could not have written the book without her.

Another academic debt is to Elisabeth Lebensaft, a Viennese scholar who has been unfailingly generous in sharing her knowledge of *Dunera* internees from Austria. In enriching our understanding of many aspects of the *Dunera* story, Elisabeth has helped shape this book.

Monash University has funded this project over many years, and deserves both our respect and our gratitude in upholding the finest traditions of a research university. We acknowledge wholeheartedly our debt to Rae Frances, former Dean of the Faculty of Arts at Monash University, and to fellow historian Bruce Scates. Together with Corrie McKee in the Dean's Office, they provided support of all kinds in seeing this project through.

We thank the Bachrach Charitable Trust for its generous financial contribution to this project. The Trust is named after Hans Bachrach, who came to Australia on the *Dunera*.

Nathan Hollier and his staff at Monash University Publishing – Sarah Cannon, Laura McNicol Smith, Joanne Mullins, Les Thomas and Duncan Fardon – were exemplary in their patience and commitment to an unusual and challenging project. Kara Rasmanis, of the Faculty of Arts at Monash University, worked on many of the images that appear in this book, providing us with high quality digital files for publication. She also produced the two maps that appear at the start of the book. We acknowledge her skill and patience. Our thanks also to Robert Dare, for his detailed and constructive reading of the manuscript; to Kate Garrett and Rachel Stanyon who translated documents from German to English with care and precision; to John Colwell and Helen Spark, our eagle-eyed proofreaders; and to Russell Gray for assistance with photography.

The committee and members of the Dunera Association have provided unfailing assistance in the production of this book. We are grateful for their support and encouragement. Special thanks to Rebecca Silk, Anna Wolf and the late Mike Sondheim.

In this book we reproduce many images from the collection of the Jewish Museum of Australia, Melbourne. Working with the museum and its friendly and helpful staff is a pleasure. We offer particular thanks to Peta Cook, Susan Faine, Juliette Hanson, Lauren McAlary and Clare Saunder.

It has also been a pleasure to work with Eva de Jong-Duldig, Stefan Damschke and Melinda Mockridge of the Duldig Studio, Melbourne, and Arthur and Lurline Knee of the Tatura Irrigation and Wartime Camps Museum. They have always made us welcome. We thank them for their help and hospitality.

Staff at the Australian National Maritime Museum, Australian War Memorial, Geelong Grammar School, Ian Potter Museum of Art, National

ACKNOWLEDGEMENTS

Archives of Australia, National Film and Sound Archive, National Gallery of Australia, National Gallery of Victoria, National Library of Australia, National Portrait Gallery, State Library of Victoria, Sydney Jewish Museum, University of Melbourne Archives, and University of Sydney Library responded to our many requests with kindness and efficiency. We thank these institutions for their cooperation. Individual staff members to whom we are indebted are among those listed below.

For help of various kinds, our thanks to: Jaynie Anderson, Roger Averill, Peter Bajer, Paolo Baracchi, Chiara Barbieri, Jenny Bars, Paul Bartrop, Karran Beggs, Coral Bennett, Shannon Biederman, Jan Brazier, Sean Bridgeman, Jane Brown, Peter Browne, Laura Bunyan, Tertia Butcher, Laura Carmichael, Cleeve Charles, Bodie Clare, Janet Coffman, John and Janet Conroy, Max Corden, Alison Crossley, Ed Crossley, Michael Davis, Graeme Davison, Phillip Deery, Volker Dittrich, John Dobies, Claudia Downing, Albrecht Dümling, Steve Dyer, John Ebert, Sol and Diana Encel, Jane England, June Factor, Laurie Favelle, Ron Fraser, Helen Fry, Bill and Jan Gammage, Angela Gehrig, Salomea Genin, Nina Glasser, Andrew Griffin, Helga Griffin, Sasha Grishin, Poppy Groves, Bridget Guest, Catherine Hall, David Harrison, Michael Head, Susannah Helman, Daniel Herbst, Stephen Herbst, David Houston, Robyn Hovey, Renate Howe, Fiona Jeffery, Irene Kemper, Lee Kersten, Konrad Kwiet, Di Langmore, Geoff Laurenson, Judi Levine, Ben Lewin, Alison Lewis, Susan Lüdecke, Alexandra Ludewig, Pauline Lyle-Smith, Margie McClelland, Behan McCullagh, Sarah MacDougall, Stuart Macintyre, John McMahon, Andrew McNab, Andrew McNamara, John Martin, Steve Martin, Judy Menczel, Christoph Mentschl, Jane Miller, Jay Miller, Massimo Moretti, Rachel Naughton, Klaus Neumann, Brenda Niall, Nick Nicholson, Rhondda Orchard, June Orford, George Pados, Sheridan Palmer, Liz Parker, Bobby Pearce, Nicole Pearson, Walter Phillips, Rachel Pistol, Elena Plumb, Geoff Reed, Jessica Reid, Felicity Renowden, Leah Riches, Julia Rodwell, Kalli Rolfe, Suzanne Rutland, Resi Schwarzbauer, Inger Shiel, Gert Silver, Debbie Sleigh, Robyn Sloggett, Peter Stanley, Ann Stephen, Walter Struve, Peter Tanner, Alistair Thomson, Emil Toonen, Alex Torrens, Wendy Ugolini, Helen Usher,

Richard Vann, Christine Walker, Louis Waller, Frances Walsh, Georgina Ward, Kaye Watson, Karl Weber, Roy Wilcock, Murray Williams, Christine Winter, Katie Wood and Liz Zetzmann.

To anyone whose name we have overlooked, our apologies. We would be pleased to correct the record in any future edition of the book.

Thanks to our families for their support and patience. They have lived with the unanticipated presence of thousands of internees for a long time.

Our last words of appreciation are for Amirah Inglis. Although she did not live to see our project accomplished, her contribution has been immeasurably large. Vale, Amirah.

Ken Inglis
Seumas Spark
Jay Winter
October 2017

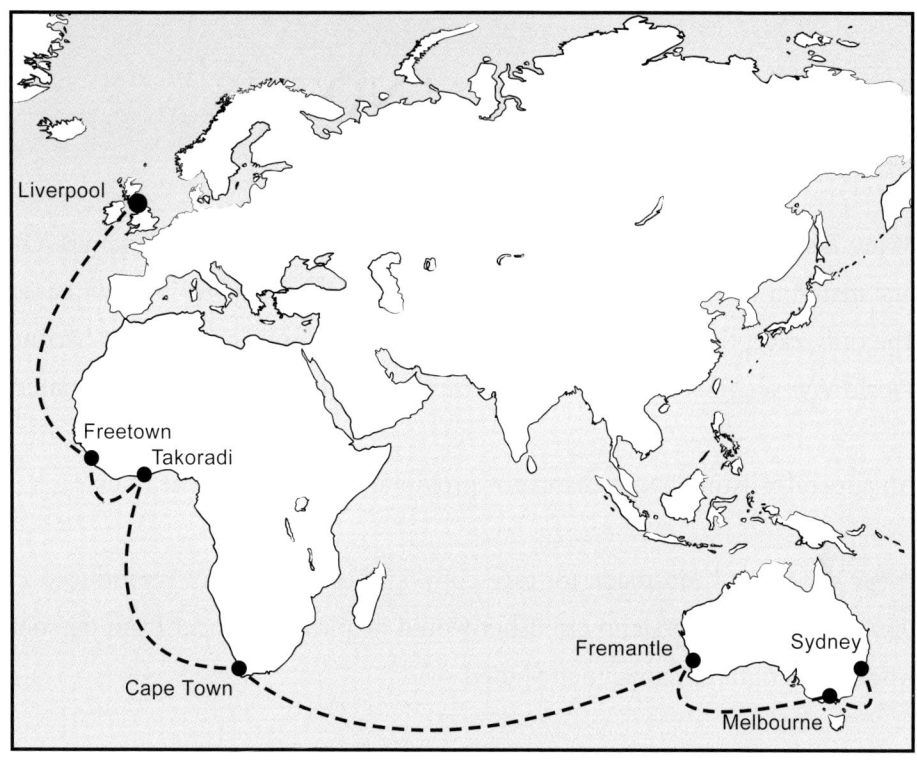

The voyage of the *Dunera*.

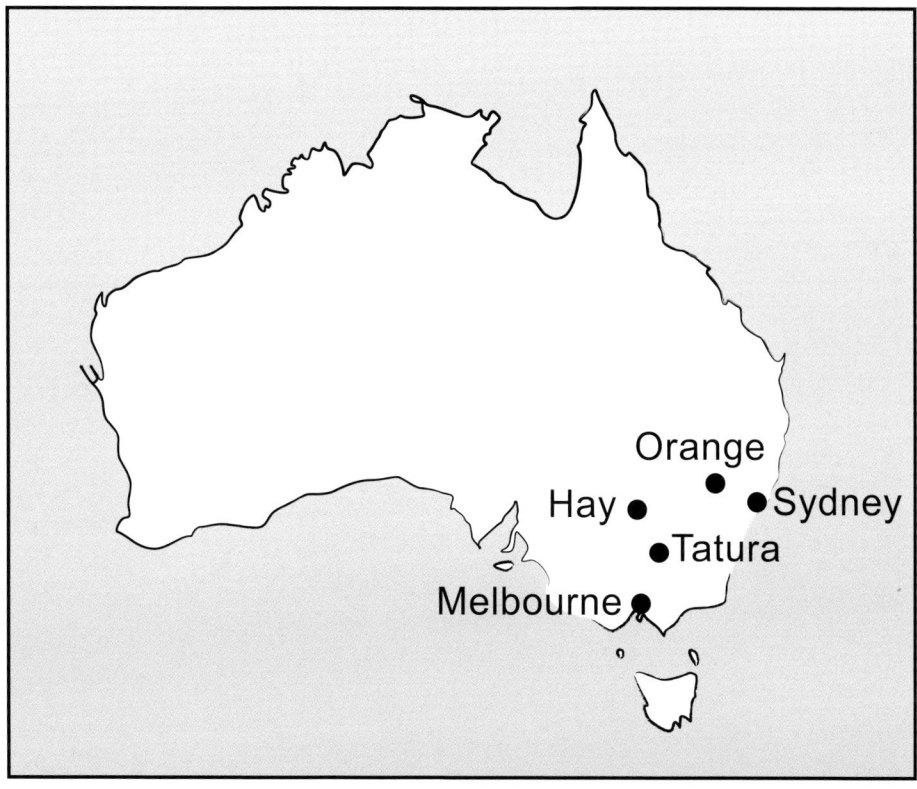

The locations of the Hay, Tatura and Orange internment camps in relation to Sydney and Melbourne.

AUTHORS' NOTES

Many *Dunera* and *Queen Mary* internees chose to change their names. On first mention we give the original name then the adopted name in parentheses. The only exception to this rule is if first mention comes in the post-Second World War sections of the book; in these cases we use only the adopted name.

An appendix listing name changes is provided at the back of the book.

Every effort has been made to trace copyright on the images reproduced in this book. The authors and publisher would be pleased to hear from persons whose copyright remains unattributed.

GENERAL INTRODUCTION

Refugees and Enemy Aliens in Wartime

The Hired Military Transport (HMT) *Dunera* sailed from Liverpool on 10 July 1940, carrying a population of around 2500 men and boys who were to be confined in camps in rural Australia. Among them were civilians of German, Polish, Czech or Austrian origin, who had sought refuge in Britain before and after the outbreak of war in 1939. Why were they on board this ship? What precipitated their arrest and deportation? In what historical context should we set this episode?

The history of refugees in Australia has been the subject of considerable scholarship and journalism over the past few decades. The story of the *Dunera* and its human cargo does not fit easily into this category. There is no better case than this episode to show that not all newcomers were refugees during the Second World War. If they were not refugees, then what were they? One answer is that they were prisoners, men who were 'captured', in the words of the official documentation, often by friendly policemen, and then detained as internees. This distinction mattered, since on the *Dunera* there were also German merchant seamen and Italian internees. Being civilian internees, they had neither the status of prisoners of war (POWs) nor that of refugees. On board the ship, their status was obscure, ambiguous, and vulnerable, a point driven home to them daily by rough treatment by their guards.

What was their crime? Until September 1939, most had been refugees. But after the outbreak of war that month, they became enemy aliens and a few were interned. In May 1940, by the stroke of his pen, the newly-installed Prime Minister Winston Churchill made them all internees, as well as enemy aliens. The logic behind this decision was that enemy aliens in Britain presented to the authorities the possibility of hiding Nazi agents in their midst. While invasion remained a real possibility, this risk, Churchill believed, could not be tolerated. Thus, several thousand males boarded ships destined for Canada or Australia. The *Dunera* transported men from age 16 to 66. They arrived at Fremantle on 27 August 1940, and at Melbourne on 3 September. The German merchant seamen and other German nationals and supporters of the Nazi regime, together with Italian internees, disembarked at Melbourne, as did about 125 of the 'enemy alien' internees of German, Austrian, or Czech origins, many of whom were Jewish. About 2000 of these men, almost all of whom were in no sense supporters of Nazi Germany or Fascist Italy, left the ship at Sydney on 6 September.

The internees who disembarked at Melbourne went to Tatura in the Goulburn valley in northern Victoria; those leaving ship at Sydney went west to Hay in the Riverina district of New South Wales. Later some were confined at Orange in the Central Tablelands of New South Wales. Whatever this story may have been, it was not a case of refugees seeking asylum. The story we tell in these two volumes reflects injustice, bureaucratic bumbling, and human error.

Today, these internees are commonly called the '*Dunera* boys'. Popular perception holds that all were Jewish, and that the majority were young. In fact, around 80 per cent were Jewish, at least according to Nazi racial laws, and most were grown men. There were labourers, scholars, artists, writers, con men, criminals, believers and unbelievers. What unites them is not their attitudes or their education, but rather the accident of fate. Almost all held, or had held, the nationality of a country with which Britain was at war.

Another misconception is that all Jews who arrived in Australia in the 1930s and 1940s were on the *Dunera*. Was Max Corden, the economist, on the *Dunera*? Was George Dreyfus, the composer? No. Both escaped Germany with their families and arrived in Australia in 1939. Separating their stories from those of the *Dunera* internees aids our understanding of the history of those who fled from the Nazis in the 1930s and of those who received them.

GENERAL INTRODUCTION

One reason for the continuing use of the term '*Dunera* boys' is the resonance of the title in television history. In 1985, Ben Lewin directed a 'telemovie' which established a narrative mixing facts and fiction in parts not easily discernible, even by those who had been on the *Dunera*. With the visual and textual material we have collected we can go beyond these generalisations about a diverse group of men and the lives they led, not only in wartime, but in the post-war decades.

Three weeks after the *Dunera* docked at Pyrmont wharf, more detainees – about 265 men, women and children – arrived in Sydney. They had sailed from Singapore on the *Queen Mary*. Our book tells their stories as well.

One feature of this narrative is the fashioning of a creative community both during the voyage to Australia and in the three internment camps these men inhabited. For those who came on the *Dunera* or the *Queen Mary*, Hay, Tatura, and Orange were confined spaces rather than prisons, in the sense that the internees virtually governed themselves. (Other detainees were not so fortunate: Italian and German POWs inhabited these camps and enjoyed little of the freedom of many civilian internees.) There were artistic and musical circles, study groups, religious communities and sports teams, all organised by the inmates. In what other detention centre of the Second World War did the inmates write a constitution or print their own currency? As Antonio Gramsci wrote in his prison notebooks, his intellectual horizons widened as his physical circumstances became more constrained. Perhaps this remarkable tendency for people to find a way to tolerate difficult circumstances applies to the men of the *Dunera*. As the Berliner Klaus Loewald observed, they fashioned 'little republics' in the Australian landscape.

Australian Jewish History

Another area of study to which our research contributes is that of Jews in twentieth-century Australia. It is not surprising that the story of the *Dunera* captured popular attention only in the late 1970s and 1980s, when the Holocaust arrived belatedly in popular consciousness in Australia and other parts of the world. Once the Holocaust became an iconic symbol of inhumanity and injustice, those who outlived the Nazis took on the status of victims and, perhaps more importantly, witnesses. They had something to tell us, something from which the young could learn about the dangers of racial prejudice and persecution. For some survivors, the Holocaust was the central event of their lives; for others, it was a framework with which to make sense of their personal trajectory.

Here too the new materials we have gathered help us to avoid stereotyping the *Dunera* internees. We need to bear in mind that while 80 per cent of these people were Jewish, a significant minority was not. And among those with Jewish ancestors or origins, there was a wide diversity of opinion in regard to the importance of their Jewishness to their families, and themselves. The Jewish internees escaped the Holocaust, a fact of which many became painfully aware as they sifted information about the fate of family members at the end of the Second World War. In this respect, they were fortunate. This is a story of survival after the humiliation of internment and transportation to Australia. It is also a story about the post-war integration of a varied population of German, Austrian, Polish and Czech-born Jews into the established Jewish community of Australia.

Winston Churchill came to regret, and even apologised for, the decision to intern indiscriminately those who had sought refuge in Britain. This regret became the basis for the payment of compensation, as early as 1941 for property 'lost' by internees during the voyage. Rarely do governments acknowledge their inglorious moments in this way, and for many of those who had sailed on the *Dunera*, this gesture did much to restore their faith in British justice.

GENERAL INTRODUCTION

Australia in the Second World War

Less than half of the population that sailed on the *Dunera* decided to stay in Australia, once that option became open to them. Several hundred men chose to serve in the Australian military forces as non-combatant soldiers: they wore the King's Australian uniform, slouch hat and all. Others found jobs in civilian life. Their part in the wartime history of Australia is another little-known chapter on which we throw light.

Australia in the Post-War Era

Perhaps the most compelling part of the history that we term '*Dunera* lives' is the resilience shown by so many men. There were failures as well as success stories, and our aim is to produce an accurate account of these unusual newcomers. Especially intriguing is what their stories tell us about the capacity of Australian society to provide space for them at a time of unprecedented demographic and economic growth. Those who stayed on in Australia not only married and raised families, as did most Australians of their time, but they found productive ways to contribute to the making and remaking of their adopted country.

In 1947 Arthur Calwell, Minister for Immigration, informed parliament that 913 men from the *Dunera* had remained in Australia.[1] Since then, this figure, or an approximation thereof, has been cited as definitive. Carol Bunyan has shown it to be too high. She has established that fewer than 700 former *Dunera* internees from Germany and Austria were living in Australia in 1950. This includes 16 men who had come to Australia a second time after having initially returned to Britain.

Sources

The writing of the history of the *Dunera* voyage may be dated from 1979, when Benzion Patkin published the first book-length study of the subject.[2] Four years later Cyril Pearl added to the public recognition of the *Dunera* story in his book entitled *The Dunera Scandal*.[3] A documentary resource book, compiled by Paul Bartrop and Gabrielle Eisen, was published in 1990.[4]

Since then memoirs have been published in journals and books by those who sailed on the *Dunera*, but they have not changed the narrative established by Patkin, Pearl, and Bartrop and Eisen.

Through a freedom of information request, we succeeded in gaining access to closed Home Office papers held in London at the National Archives of the United Kingdom. Cyril Pearl had been keen to look at these records, but was denied. He and others suspected that the papers were kept closed beyond the standard thirty-year embargo on public records because they contained damning information, perhaps about the actions of the British government. The truth is more mundane. There is nothing in the story of internment and release which we have to alter because of material in these records. Why the papers remain closed is unclear.

Administrative documents held at the National Archives of Australia (NAA) provided a point of departure for our research. The arrival of the *Dunera* internees in Australia generated two official records for each internee: these records, which belong to the MP1103/1 and MP1103/2 series, have been digitised and are available to all on the NAA website. Here we provide an example of both types of record. The MP1103/2 record (over leaf) is for the youngest internee on the *Dunera*, Gerhard Leopold Besch, who turned 16 on 24 June 1940. The MP1103/1 record (over leaf) is for the eldest internee, Heinrich Sachs, who was 66 in 1940. Besch was German-born, Sachs Austrian. In both cases the words Prisoner of War have been crossed out and replaced with a reference to internees. Thus, it is clear that these internees were an unusual group; not quite POWs. Both documents give place of birth, date of birth, trade or occupation, religion, and marital status. From these records we know that Besch took with him on the *Dunera* a gold ring and a chromium watch.

For each *Dunera* internee, these forms tell us of the length of internment in Australia and how it unfolded. Did he spend time in hospital? When did he enlist in the army? When was he released into Australian society or when did he return to Britain? The information given in the records can be misleading. The art historian Franz Philipp gave his occupation as 'farm labourer'. Some internees were Catholic and Protestant in name only, their Christian faith adopted to hide Jewish heritage from the Nazis. Still, these records reveal much about the *Dunera* internees, and we have drawn on them heavily.

We have used a host of other official documents and archival sources to trace the lives of those who came to Australia on the *Dunera* and the *Queen Mary*. Interviews with former internees and their families have been of particular importance.

What we term the 'memory boom' has added immeasurably to our documentation and how we interpret these sources. The Hay-Tatura Association, now the Dunera Association, was created in 1989. This organisation brings together men and women who are proud and curious about their history. They go on pilgrimages, and transmit to new generations stories that some did not believe would command the interest of their children. From 2011 to 2017, the Dunera Association was led by a '*Dunera* daughter', Rebecca Silk. The Dunera Association is one of many all over the world that aim to bring history and memory together. Remembrance happens when small groups of people come together in public to share thoughts and experiences about important facets of their lives and those of their families. The disappearance of the central characters in this story does not mean, therefore, that the story will fade away.

Of equal importance is the visual archive we have amassed from holdings throughout Australia and overseas. Many of these collections of drawings, paintings, photographs, etchings, and other items have never been made public, much less published. The startling variety of these images and visions made us conclude that these sources cannot be treated simply as documents or illustrations of our text. The visual record of these wartime internees requires its own description, elaboration, and interpretation. Some of these works of art are astonishing; others are moving; all are useful in presenting elements of the world in which these people were forced to live in wartime and the different environments in which they chose to live thereafter.

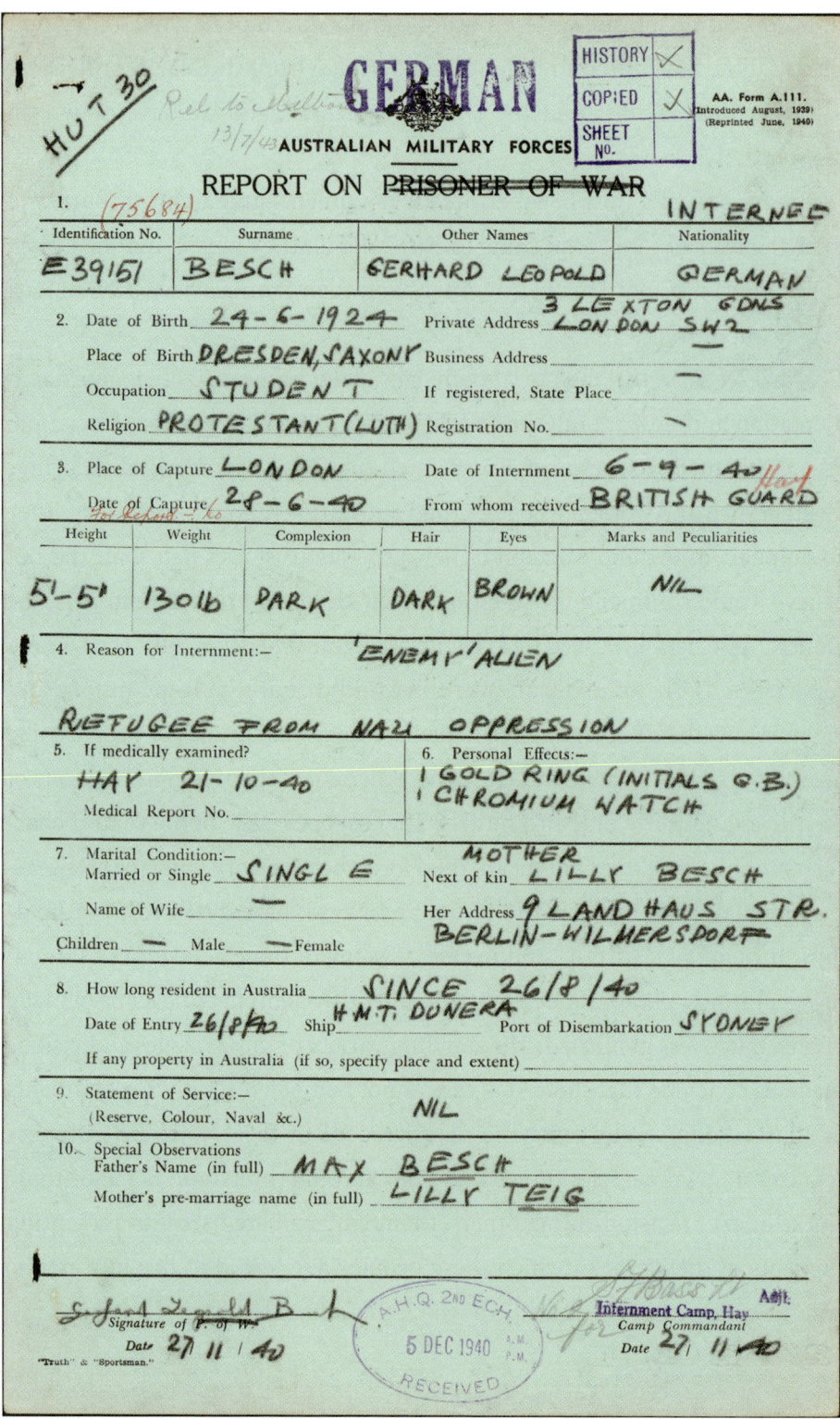

GENERAL INTRODUCTION

Source: NAA, MP1103/2, E39151 (left); NAA, MP1103/1, E40528 (above).

This is why we have chosen to tell the story in two volumes, with the first telling the story through the eyes and creative representations of those who lived through it. The images are a visual library of the survival and afterlives of a population of refugees turned internees turned citizens. Some were artists of distinction; others were not, but still found ways of expressing their individuality in verbal and non-verbal forms. The visual turn in historical study has liberated students of contemporary history from having to treat non-verbal, non-written documents as of marginal importance.

The second volume examines many kinds of written documentation to provide a sense of the variety of outcomes and achievements we acknowledge. Our choice of profiles in Volume 2 is, to a degree, arbitrary. We tell the stories of different men who made different lives, most in Australia, but some in Europe. There is no one *Dunera* or *Queen Mary* story. None of them knew their destinations when they boarded the *Dunera* or the *Queen Mary* in 1940. They did not choose their place of incarceration. They chose where to go and what to do after the yoke of internment and war was lifted from their shoulders. We can learn much from reflecting on these events and marvelling at the many ways these men and women, alongside so many others throughout the twentieth century and after, outlived war and the injustices it produces.

In our work on both volumes, we have been blessed to draw on the work of Carol Bunyan, who has compiled an authoritative database with information on the *Dunera* internees. Her work has enlarged our understanding of all facets of this subject. In time her statistical material will be available online, as will many of the visual images we have collected but not included in Volume 1.

Notes

1. *Commonwealth of Australia Parliamentary Debates*, 11 Geo. VI., vol. 190, 19 February – 25 March 1947, p. 433.
2. Benzion Patkin, *The Dunera Internees*, (Sydney: Cassell Australia, 1979).
3. Cyril Pearl, *The Dunera Scandal: Deported by Mistake*, (Sydney: Angus and Robertson, 1983).
4. Paul R. Bartrop with Gabrielle Eisen, *The Dunera Affair: A Documentary Resource Book*, (Melbourne: Schwartz and Wilkinson / Jewish Museum of Australia, 1990).

Section 1

THE BEGINNING OF THE END

INTRODUCTION

In interwar Germany and Austria, to paraphrase William Butler Yeats, the centre didn't hold. The hatreds unleashed by a lost war and a world depression made the fate of Jews and other opponents of the regime precarious at best. The Nazis brought the violence of the trenches into the streets of German cities. Following the assassination of a German diplomat by a Polish Jew in Paris, the Nazis organized a pogrom, in which synagogues and Jewish-owned shops and homes were set on fire or ransacked. This night – 9-10 November 1938 – is known as *Kristallnacht*, the night of broken glass.

These events were a heightened form of the maltreatment and persecution of Jews already under way throughout the Reich. When Austria was annexed to Germany in March 1938, fervently Nazi Viennese party members and ordinary citizens took pleasure in forcing Jews to clean the streets with brushes. Arrests, fines, and the destruction of Jewish property were all part of the Nazi affirmation of the new order.

Responding to this wave of violence, a variety of organisations, including the British Committee for the Jews of Germany and the Movement for the Care of Children from Germany (*Kindertransport*), pressed the British government to provide temporary travel visas to Britain for Jewish children under age 17 and evidently in danger in Nazi Germany. This privilege was extended to Czech children, whose country was absorbed into Germany in 1939. The violence of the times created conditions from which emerged both inhumanity and humanitarian care.

The *Kindertransport* brought some 7,500 Jewish children and 2,500 non-Jewish children to Britain before the outbreak of war. Priority was given to those whose parents were in concentration camps. Sponsors in Britain, prominent among whom were the Quakers, had to take responsibility for the material costs of the children's care, and to ensure that when the crisis was over, whenever that would be, these children would leave Britain and return home.

Many German, Austrian, and Czech families had left their homes for Britain before *Kristallnacht*. So had many solitary children or brothers and sisters who were sent abroad by prescient parents when they were able to do so. Other German families and individuals had moved to Britain for a host of reasons, including for work. Among them were Roman Catholics, Protestants, and Jews converted to Christianity, who were targeted by the Nazis under the Nuremberg Laws of 1935. The story of emigration from Germany to Britain in the interwar years is by no means only a Jewish story.

The disruption of family life in Germany at the end of the 1930s for anyone targeted by the regime was both terrifying and puzzling. Approximately 400,000 Jews had served in either the German or the Austro-Hungarian armies in the First World War, and many proudly wore their Iron Crosses as proof of their patriotism. Many hoped that once in power, the Nazis would be tamed. They were mistaken. Hitler's rabid anti-Semitism grew to become the core of the Nazi mission to rid Germany of the Jewish cancer that threatened, in his view, to destroy her. Non-Jewish socialists and communists, for whom, among others, the first concentration camp at Dachau was created in 1933, also walked a tightrope from the first days of the regime. Many Jews and non-Jewish groups refused to believe that their lives in Germany were over; fewer still understood that their lives were in peril. The name Auschwitz had no sinister connotation.

Threatened people tried desperately to keep alive the bonds of kin and friendship. Many of those who sent their children away when the Nazi regime took on a more radical racial outlook were part of the *Bildungsbürgertum*, the educated middle- and upper-middle classes. These were men and women who revered Kant, Goethe, and Bach; as did those from more modest families who also tried to shelter their children from the storm by finding a safe haven in Britain. Some did not see the reality of the disaster confronting them, others found the prospect of emigration too daunting, and others remained in Germany and Austria to care for family members unable or unwilling to leave. Family was a reason to leave the Reich and a reason to remain.

About a third of Germany's 500,000 Jewish population in 1933 lived in Berlin, a cosmopolitan city with strong socialist and independent Lutheran traditions. They had friends, allies, defenders. And yet the majority reluctantly came to the conclusion that they had to go. By July 1939, the Jewish population in Germany was about 200,000. Austria's Jews numbered 192,000 at the time of the *Anschluss*; a year later they had dwindled to 57,000.

This pre-war refugee wave, starting well before *Kristallnacht* and the *Kindertransport*, formed part of the population from which those who were to sail on the *Dunera* in 1940 came. None had the slightest idea that their refugee status in Britain was precarious. But the liberal humanitarianism which had reached out to help them before the war had little purchase after the outbreak of hostilities.

After 3 September 1939, these refugees, however young, turned into enemy aliens. No matter that they were despised by the Nazis, or that some had already taken up arms against fascism, or even that some were still children. The fear of foreigners, especially those born on enemy soil, fed a myth in Britain (and elsewhere) of a potential 'Fifth Column', a term invented during the Spanish civil war to indicate that Franco's forces would win, not because of the four columns advancing on Madrid, but through a silent, subversive force already there, prepared to undermine the Republic from within. Such thinking was masked by British civility and pride, but not for long. Once Nazi Germany declared war on Britain, Germans in Britain faced an uncertain future.

The Boemestrasse Synagogue, Frankfurt, 10 November 1938

There are times when we can see unmistakable signs of the end of one phase of history and the beginning of another. The Nazi persecution of Jews began in 1933, when they came to power, but it reached an irreversible stage five years later.

The systematic Nazi attack on Jewish institutions and people throughout Germany on 9-10 November 1938 is known as *Kristallnacht,* or the night of broken glass. It followed the assassination of a German diplomat in Paris by a Polish Jew.

The fires and acts of vandalism, matched by the arrests of Jews, were said to have emerged from the 'spontaneous' anger of the German people. Evidence that these events were choreographed by the Nazi party emerged later.

Crowds gathered in front of burning synagogues in many parts of Germany, watching anti-Semitism in action.

From then on, the hold Jewish people had on their future became so uncertain that thousands urgently sought a safe haven outside Germany and Austria.

The following images offer glimpses of the predicament faced by German and Austrian men and boys, many of whom came to see that they had no future in their native lands.

Source: Yad Vashem, item 24253. Copyright: Yad Vashem.

Jews cleaning the streets of Vienna, 13 March 1938

Public humiliation accompanied the destruction of Jewish property and institutions in Vienna after unification with Nazi Germany on 12 March 1938.

Members of the Hitler Youth forced some of Vienna's Jews to act like gutter dwellers, fit only to clean the city's streets. Passers-by including children joined in the spectacle.

Among the scrubbers elsewhere in Vienna was Erwin Lamm, aged 17. While taking a piece of fabric to one of his father's customers, he was stopped by German soldiers on the street and forced to his knees to clean the street. When the soldiers tired of this amusement, he made his way home.

Source: Yad Vashem, item 28520. Copyright: Yad Vashem.

Reinhold Eckfeld recalling the *Anschluss*, 1938

Reinhold Eckfeld was born in 1921 in Berlin to an assimilated family with Jewish ancestors. He was a school boy when Nazi Germany annexed Austria in 1938.

In 1940 he wrote about these events in an exercise book:

'Mass arrests. Nazis with arm bands cruising around on trucks and arresting Jews and Fatherland Front people [supporters of the ruling party] whom they could only persecute with their hatred during the previous period. Schools are closed for one week. On Sunday 13 March 1938 Hitler comes to Vienna and is received with frenetic cheering.'

'Pressed, pushed and pulled by Mother, I go to the District Office Döbling, on 29 April 1938, in nice weather, to register my leaving the Jewish faith and sign a paper which states that I have the intention to convert to the Roman Catholic religion.'

Source and copyright: Eckfeld archive.

THE BEGINNING OF THE END

Grade 1 class, Bickenbach primary school, Hesse, Germany, 1928

Normal life appeared to cover the deep fractures in German society exposed by the world economic crisis of the late 1920s and 1930s.

This photograph shows a class from a school in the town of Bickenbach. Ernst Wolf is third from the right, second row from the back. His future in Germany vanished when the Nazis came to power in 1933.

Source: Andrew and Anna Wolf.

Karl Loewenstein and his son Fritz in the North Sea, 1927

Father and son enjoy a German summer by the sea.

    Karl Loewenstein was a civil servant, proud of his war service in the German navy. Fully assimilated, the Loewenstein children attended Lutheran schools and received Lutheran religious instruction.

    Fritz Loewenstein (Fred Lowen) was sent to London to polish his English and to Lausanne for his French. His family was among the many who continued to believe even after 1933 that they could outlast the Nazi regime and continue to live a good, bourgeois life in Berlin.

Source: Monica Lee Lowen and Jocelyn Lowen.

THE BEGINNING OF THE END

Watercolours by Leonhard Adam

Born to a Jewish father and a Protestant mother in Berlin in 1891, Leonhard Adam was a polymath, whose range of interests embraced art, the law and ethnology. Completing his legal studies in 1916, he served in the German army, practised law and became a judge in the provincial court in Berlin. His research and publications focused on primitive law and ethnology. He was also a considerable artist.

The painting above top was done at Ragusa in Dalmatia in 1911, the one below at Büsum on the North Sea in 1923.

Source: Tatura Irrigation and Wartime Camps Museum. Copyright: Mary-Clare Adam and Tatura Irrigation and Wartime Camps Museum.

The Feuersteins in Dresden, 1935

Jews had assimilated so successfully in Germany that their dress and manners made them indistinguishable from their gentile neighbours, the *Bildungsbürgertum* or educated propertied classes.

THE BEGINNING OF THE END

Leon Feuerstein in German army uniform in the First World War

Patriotism was not enough. Leon Feuerstein was one of 100,000 German Jews who served in the First World War. His daughter Suse, who suffered from mental illness, was killed in 1941 in the Nazi euthanasia programme.

After *Kristallnacht*, his two sons Franz (Frank Firestone) and Gerhard (Jack Firestone) were sent to Buchenwald concentration camp. On their release, Franz traded his business expertise, useful to the Nazis, for a guarantee that he and Gerhard, known to his family as Gerd, would be allowed to leave Germany. In mid-1939 the brothers went to Holland and then Britain.

Leon and his wife Elise remained in Germany. On 26 April 1942, having already suffered violence at the hands of the Gestapo, and anticipating deportation to a death camp, they committed suicide by gassing themselves in their kitchen.

Source: Tom Firestone and Walter Firestone.

Jules Stocky, his two brothers and their grandmother, c.1930

The Stocky family were prosperous Roman Catholics, living in Düsseldorf. Jules, born in 1913, was a wanderer, who decided to leave Germany for England in 1936. He taught German and embarked on a business to import and export apple juice. Even after the First World War, many young Germans worked in Britain, and many young Britons sought their fortune in Germany.

Jules is the middle figure. His two brothers, Franz on his left and Helmuth on his right, were killed fighting for Germany in the Second World War.

Source: Stocky family.

Hans Rothe remembers *Kristallnacht*

Jews who lived through *Kristallnacht* would never forget it. Pillaging synagogues and setting them on fire was one dimension of the horror; even more insidious for some was the violation of Jewish homes, the assaults on individual men in the presence of their wives and children, and the arrests.

For many 10 November 1938 was the moment when terror broke down the boundaries between public and private life.

Hans Rothe, an Austrian cartoonist born in Vienna in 1905, captured that moment in this sketch done in internment at Hay, New South Wales, 1940.

Source: NLA, MS 5392, Records of Hay Internment Camp, 1940-1941.

Gerd Bernstein and family, Berlin, 14 December 1938

Gerd Bernstein (Bern Brent) raises a glass to toast his father, mother and grandmother. His portrait hangs on the wall. However precariously, the formalities of Jewish family life continued after *Kristallnacht*.

Gerd departed Berlin the next day, two days before his 16th birthday, on a *Kindertransport* to Britain.

Source: Bern Brent.

THE BEGINNING OF THE END

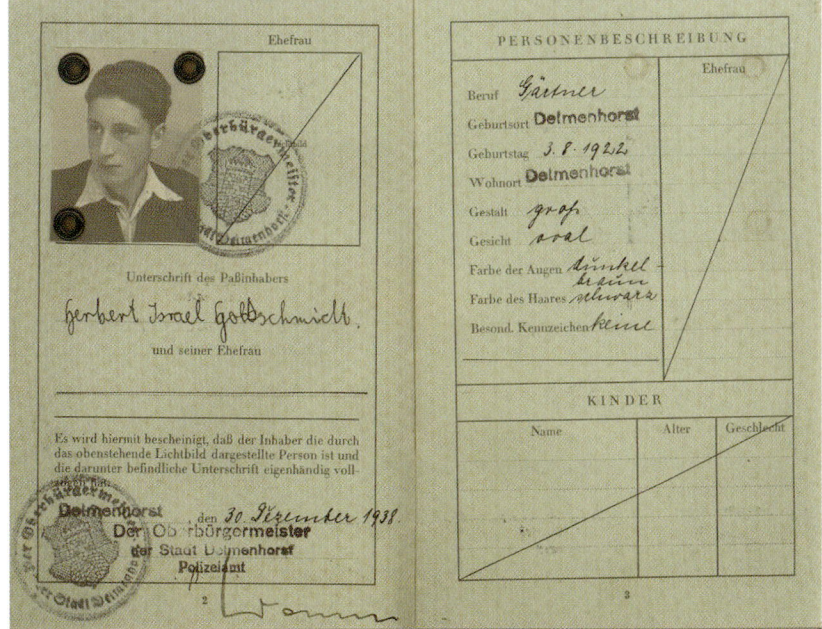

From Germany to Britain: Herbert Goldschmidt's journey

Before the outbreak of war, the Nazis stated that they wanted to facilitate the exit of Jews from Germany. Street collections were made by Berliners to buy what Nazis supporters termed 'one-way tickets to Jerusalem' for these unwanted people.

Source: Sydney Jewish Museum, M2011/041:004. Copyright: Sydney Jewish Museum.

Beglaubigte Abschrift aus dem Geburts-Register des Standesamts Delmenhorst.
Aa.

Herbert Goldschmidt führt nach der Verordnung vom 17. August 1938 zusätzlich den Vornamen "Israel".
Delmenhorst, den 23. Dezember 1938.
Der Standesbeamte.
Frese.

Geburtsurkunde

Nr. 377.

Delmenhorst, am 7. August 1922.

Vor dem unterzeichneten Standesbeamten erschien heute, der Persönlichkeit nach durch Eheschließungsbescheinigung anerkannt, der Kaufmann Moritz Goldschmidt wohnhaft in Delmenhorst, Bahnhofstraße 12 Religion und zeigte an, daß von der Wilhelmine Goldschmidt geborenen Sternberg seiner Ehefrau Religion wohnhaft bei ihm zu Delmenhorst im Wöchnerinnenheim der Wollkämmerei am dritten August des Jahres tausend neunhundert zwanzig und zwei Nachmittags um vier Uhr ein Knabe geboren worden sei und daß das Kind den Vornamen Herbert erhalten habe.

Vorgelesen, genehmigt und unterschrieben
Moritz Goldschmidt.

Der Standesbeamte
In Vertretung Frese.

Daß vorstehender Auszug mit dem Geburts-Haupt-Register des Standesamts zu Delmenhorst gleichlautend ist, wird hiermit bestätigt.

Delmenhorst, am 23. Dezember 1938.

Der Standesbeamte
Frese

educational purposes under the care of the Inter-Aid Committee for children.

THIS DOCUMENT REQUIRES NO VISA.

PERSONAL PARTICULARS.   2119

Name GOLDSCHMIDT. HERBERT.
Sex MALE. Date of Birth 3-8-22
Place DELMENHORST.
Full Names and Address of Parents
GOLDSCHMIDT MORITZ + WILHELMINE
GARTENBAUSCHULE.
AHLEM.

Bureaucratic reality was harsher, greyer, and more uncertain. When children applied for travel documents, delays and variable forms of payment, some illicit, were inevitable.

In 1938, Nazi authorities issued sixteen-year-old Herbert Goldschmidt with a new birth certificate. As a Jew he was forced to adopt the name 'Israel', becoming Herbert Israel Goldschmidt. Similarly, the letter 'J' on his travel pass assured close scrutiny when he began his journey from Germany.

In 1939, Herbert Goldschmidt succeeded in leaving Germany for Britain on a *Kindertransport*.

Source: Sydney Jewish Museum, M2011/041:003 (left); M2011/041:005 (above).
Copyright: Sydney Jewish Museum.

Heinz Lippmann training in metal work, ORT technical school, Berlin, c. 1938

Heinz Lippmann (Henry Lippmann) was the son of a Jewish carton manufacturer. The family lived in the prosperous Halensee district of Berlin. Heinz's high school was around the corner from the Königsallee intersection where the Jewish industrialist Walter Rathenau had been murdered by right-wing thugs in 1922, a year after Heinz's birth.

After the Nazi seizure of power, Heinz was forced to leave his state school. He continued his education in a private Jewish school and joined an Overseas Relief Training (ORT) programme to provide him with skills useful wherever he wound up. First in Russia in the 1880s, then throughout Europe and in North and South America, ORT schools gave young Jewish boys and girls a trade and a chance to resume their lives once free from persecution.

Lippmann is at right.

Source: Australian National Maritime Museum, ANMS0219[006]

Heinz Lippmann en route to England, 29 August 1939

Heinz Lippmann was lucky. He left Germany a few days before the invasion of Poland. He is second from left, pictured aboard the *Queen Emma* as she steams from the Hook of Holland to Harwich.

Half of the ORT students in Berlin, and some staff, escaped Germany. The rest were trapped when war was declared.

Lippmann continued his life as an ORT trainee in wartime London, Leeds and York.

Source: Australian National Maritime Museum, ANMS0219[004].

> Hilversum. 10 February 39.
> My dear boy, I was delighted to receive your card today and to know that everything has gone smoothly and you seem to have good accommodation. If there is anything you need don't hesitate to let me know; your Pepsi will be glad to do whatever he can to help.
> Concerning the possibility of getting you back here with me, I don't think that the Committee in London is the way to go. The best way is to approach the Dutch authorities, and I'll see what I can do from this end. Now I want to ask you to tell me everything connected with your trip out of Germany, my dear Erich, as well as everything that has happened since I left home. I would also like to give you one piece of advice my boy: try to be a good friend. If occasionally it goes against the grain, grit your teeth; if ever things get a bit too much force people to respect you and show yourself to be a man. Your Pepsi has lived through all this and is speaking from experience. Write as often as you can, also write home and to Tita. If you have not enough money, let me know and I will send you every week whatever I can do without. My dear child that's all I have to tell you today.
> Many kisses, Your Pepsi

Postcard to Erich Eckstein from his father in hiding in the Netherlands, 1939

Erich Eckstein (Eric Eckstein) was born in Düsseldorf in 1923. He tried unsuccessfully for an American visa, and left Germany on a *Kindertransport* in late 1938, his apprenticeship as a printer having ended after *Kristallnacht*.

Dated 10 February 1939, this card from his father Albert (also known as Alfred), urged Erich, by then in England, to try to join his father, who was in hiding in the Netherlands. Albert's touching advice to his son to force people to respect him captures the dignity as well as the vulnerability and loneliness of refugees in transit to safety and without the support of family and friends.

Source and copyright: David Eckstein.

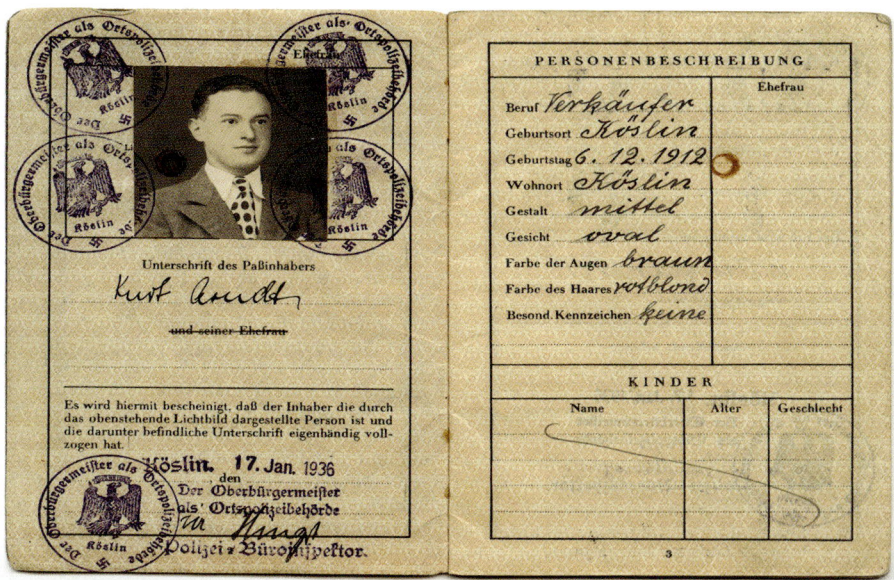

Kurt Arndt's passport

Arrested after *Kristallnacht*, Kurt Arndt was freed after six weeks in prison on condition that he leave Germany. He asked his girlfriend, Wally, to flee with him. She agreed, if first they married. After their wedding in Koslin on 22 December 1938, they left Hamburg on a Japanese liner bound for Shanghai.

Source: Janet Arndt.

SS *Fushimi Maru*

This is the Japanese transport ship on which Kurt and Wally Arndt fled Europe. It was sunk during the Second World War.

Source: Janet Arndt.

Party on the *Fushimi Maru*

Kurt and Wally Arndt are the couple facing each other at the front of the left table.

The ambience of a strange, floating world, detached from the violence building up both in Asia and Europe, suggests a vision from Conrad's *Lord Jim*.

In February 1939, the Arndts disembarked in Singapore, where Kurt had relatives.

Source: Janet Arndt.

Section 2

HAVENS?
BRITAIN AND SINGAPORE, 1939–1940

INTRODUCTION

In the first eight months of 1939, many of those who sought refuge in Britain from the Nazis were given a chance to learn a trade or continue their education. Jewish, Christian and secular institutions continued to treat those who had fled from Nazi Germany as their brothers and sisters in need. The British declaration of war on 3 September 1939 put an end to that chapter of voluntary philanthropy.

Air power had transformed anxieties about the nature of a new war. City dwellers in particular were aware they would be targets of the German *Luftwaffe*, the power of which many had seen in cinema newsreels of the Spanish civil war. The destruction of the Basque town of Guernica in 1937 left little doubt what the next war would bring. Before the war, the British government had prepared materials to provide up to a million coffins for civilian casualties. They were mistaken; the bombing would come later, but the fear of what was to come was palpable from the moment hostilities began.

This period of relative quiet from September 1939 to April 1940 is known as the Phoney War precisely because the imagined catastrophe of the massive aerial bombardment of London and other cities did not take place. In other parts of the British Empire and Dominions, British naval power and casual assumptions of racial superiority lulled populations into a belief that life could go on as 'normal'. In Singapore, waiters brought the gin slings in Raffles Hotel to elegant couples unaware that they were living on the edge of a precipice. British Foreign Secretary Lord Halifax urged British merchants to stay in Singapore and Malaya; he was under the widespread illusion that the defences of the island colony of Singapore were impregnable. Such assurances persuaded Europeans to flee from the war in Europe to shelter in the sanctuary of that city, where they joined other refugee families who had come there before 1939.

Just as in the First World War, enemy aliens became a touchstone for some British patriots who no longer tolerated neighbours among whom they had lived without trouble in peacetime. Yet despite the siege mentality of a nation at war, the British sense of decency and invulnerability opened doors and provided aid for many people who had nowhere else to go.

At the end of October 1939, formal procedures were approved by the British parliament to classify and monitor the 80,000 or so aliens in Britain who had German, Austrian or Czech nationality. It would have been absurd to treat them as if they were all Nazis, since many could document their abuse at the hands of Hitler's regime.

Tribunals were set up to divide this population into three categories. The 'A' category was reserved for those deemed sympathetic to or supporters of the Nazis, who were immediately detained. Aliens were placed in the 'B' category if the tribunals had some doubt about their sympathies. These people faced particular restrictions: they could not have cameras or bicycles; they had to report regularly to the police; they had limits on the distance they could travel from home. The label 'refugee from Nazi oppression' was applied to some enemy aliens in the 'B' category. The 'C' category was for those who posed no security risk: most in this group had fled Nazi tyranny and had been deemed refugees, though it also included some men who had lived in Britain for many years. 'C' category aliens faced no special restrictions other than those that applied to aliens generally. While Czechs were not treated as enemy aliens – their cases were reviewed by a separate tribunal – some were subject to the restrictions visited on Germans and Austrians.

As in all cases of hastily constructed bureaucracy, there were blatant injustices, inconsistencies and errors in the operation of these tribunals. Those called before them did better if they had good English and apparent wealth. Some magistrates showed astonishing ignorance of Nazi Germany. One Jewish man told the tribunal that the Gestapo had not arrested him; that was enough to deny him refugee status.

Still, this local, cobbled-together British security system, facing an influx in wartime of a cohort of enemy nationals much larger than had lived in Britain during the First World War, worked, and in a very British fashion. The few spies whom Germany did try to infiltrate into Britain were caught, and many of them turned, providing false information to their minders in Germany. On balance, the tribunals were fair-minded, annoying Britons who wanted enemy aliens in prison. While France had interned as many aliens as it could find as soon as the war began, in Britain internment was a weapon wielded lightly by a liberal nation at war.

What mattered most in the story of these displaced people in Britain in 1939–1940 was the support given to them by churches and other organisations, workmates and ordinary citizens who saw these refugees as miserable outcasts from a tyrannical regime that had forced a reluctant Britain to go to war again. In Britain civil society has long been more important than the state in regulating social behaviour; that would not change until the Nazis unleashed their forces in Norway, Denmark, the Low Countries and France in April-May 1940 and broke open the Phoney War. Then the treatment of German and Italian nationals in Britain and Singapore changed radically.

German refugees in England, c. 1939–1940

Hans Mannheim (Jack Mannheim) (bottom left) and Gerd Sostheim (Gary Sostheim) (top right in the bush) had lodgings together with Herbert Treidel at 19 Dunkeld Road, Dagenham, Essex.

Sostheim was born in 1923 in Dusseldorf. Mannheim was a year older, born in Gross Munzel near Hanover. Treidel was from Mayen in the Rhineland; he was also born in 1922. All three were Jewish students.

Mannheim was arrested after *Kristallnacht* and spent three weeks in Buchenwald concentration camp. He was released and went to England in February 1939 as part of the *Kindertransport* movement. Sostheim and Treidel were also *Kindertransport* passengers. The three young men had hoped for safe haven in the United States. Like many Jews trapped in Germany, they had applied for United States visas in 1938.

Source: Linda Mannheim.

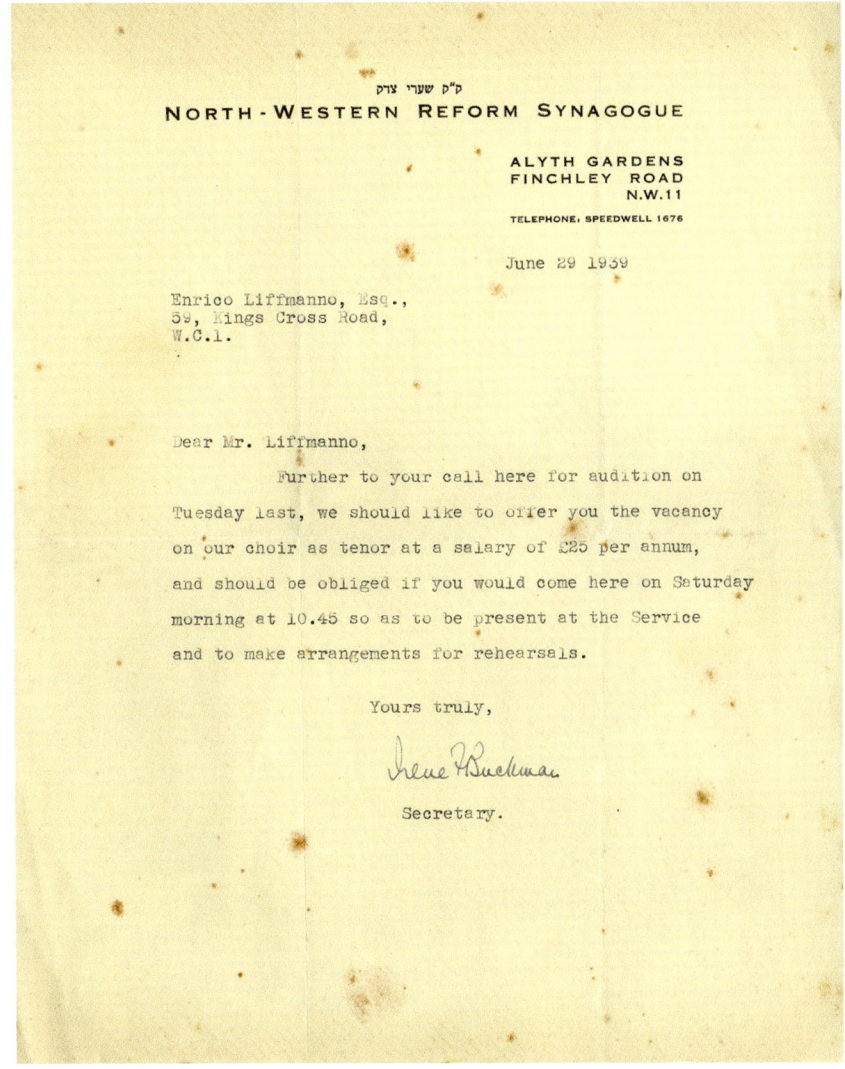

Letter to Erich Liffmann (Eric Liffman), offering him work as a tenor in the choir of a London Reform synagogue, 29 June 1939

Most refugees could not find work before the outbreak of war. Even if he had obtained a work permit, Erich Liffmann could not have managed for long on an annual salary of £25. The weekly wage of a manual worker was £3. Jewish congregations would have supplemented these meagre wages, but even so, the frustrations of enforced idleness and penury oppressed many refugees.

Did he hope to enhance his chances of getting a job by adopting a Caruso-like name?

Source: Kurt Liffman.

Heinz Schlösser and Fay Jackson in England, 1930s

Fay Jackson was born into a Jewish family in the Rhondda valley, Wales, in 1907. She joined the Labour Party and became a considerable linguist.

In Belgium she met Heinz Schlösser (Heinz Castles). He had fled Germany in 1933 in the wake of the murder of his father, a prominent trade unionist. Heinz was then 37. He had served in the German army in the First World War on several fronts including Gallipoli, and after the war had joined the *Reichsbanner*, the socialist veterans' organisation. He was raised a Catholic.

Fay and Heinz left Belgium for Britain in 1934. They were deterred from marrying, she said, because she had no wish to become a German citizen. In 1936, Heinz lost his German citizenship.

He had trouble finding a job in Britain, and the couple wound up running a youth hostel in Winchester.

In September 1939, a tribunal placed Heinz in category 'B', as being 'of dubious loyalty', which astonished him.

Source: Frank Castles and Stephen Castles.

Felix Bischofswerder and Fred Bischofswerder in London, c. 1936–1939

Felix Bischofswerder (Felix Werder) and Fred, his half-brother. Felix's mother died when he was a toddler, and his father, Boaz, re-married so the boy would grow up with a mother. Felix (at left), born in Berlin in 1922, was fond of Fred, who was seven years younger. Their father was a cantor at an Orthodox synagogue in Berlin. He and his wife and the two boys moved to London in 1933.

Some years later Felix and Fred changed their names, Felix choosing the second half of their father's surname and Fred the first half (Bischofs, altered to Bishop).

Source: Vera Werder.

 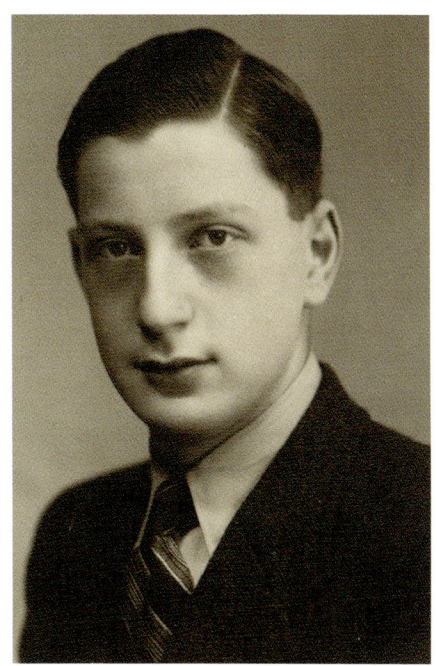

Gerd Buchdahl and Hans Buchdahl, c. 1937

Gerd Buchdahl (left) was born in 1914 to a Jewish family in Mainz. Hans was born five years later. Their father ran a furniture and bedding business. Both boys benefited from rigorous training in science and in the arts at a German *Realgymnasium*. After he left school, Gerd was offered a job in Berlin. That offer was withdrawn when the employer found out that Gerd was Jewish. This spurred Gerd to move to England, and he persuaded their parents that Hans needed to finish his education there too. They came to England in 1933. Hans received his BSc at Imperial College, London. Gerd qualified as a structural engineer in what is now Brixton Polytechnic, and received a permit to work as a civil engineer in 1938. The brothers continued to visit their family in Mainz until 1937.

On *Kristallnacht*, their father hid in a forest, but was later sent to Buchenwald. He was released, through a bribe given to the SS accountant who took over his business, and the parents left for England with all their furniture in June 1939. After the outbreak of war, their father was interned, but soon released, and the parents survived the war in London.

Source: Pamela Buchdahl.

A bridge in Hyde Park, London, 9 May 1940

Emil Wittenberg (Emil Witten) was an artist and architect born to a Jewish family in Vienna in 1910. There is no sign of war in this watercolour and pencil drawing, executed the day before Hitler's *Blitzkrieg* began. Wittenberg was interned on 27 June 1940.

Source and copyright: Martin Burman.

HAVENS?

Ssutu Jie and Karl Duldig, Singapore, 1939

Karl Duldig was born in Przemyśl in southern Poland in 1902. At age 12, he moved with his family to Vienna, where he studied sculpture. He was an athlete of national and international stature in football, tennis, and table tennis. In 1938 he married Slawa Horowitz, also a Polish Jew in exile and an artist. Their daughter Eva was born in 1938, shortly before the *Anschluss*. At that time Karl had sent sculptures for exhibition in Paris, where they remained hidden until 1961. The family had made its way from Austria, to Switzerland, and then to Singapore, where a niece had arranged a visa. Karl opened a sculpture studio there.

He is pictured with one of his students, Ssutu Jie, a sculptor well-known in his native China.

Karl Duldig (right) and Ssutu Jie, 3 St. Thomas Walk, Singapore, 1939, black and white photograph (Inv. No. 6043.03). Copyright: The Duldig Studio.

Karl Duldig's plaster cast of Aw Boon Haw, Singapore, c. 1940

Aw Boon Haw was among the wealthiest men in Singapore. He was known as the Tiger Balm king, after the ointment — promoted throughout Asia as a panacea — which was the source of much of his wealth. He was a newspaper proprietor and philanthropist. Carving his figure was a significant commission.

Workers smiling at completed plaster cast of Aw Boon Haw standing figure sculpture, c. 1940, black and white photograph (Inv. No. 6084). Copyright: The Duldig Studio.

New Year's Eve ball, Raffles Hotel, Singapore, 31 December 1939

It may have been a surprise, and possibly a respite, to find that while Jews were deemed to be *Untermenschen,* or a lower race, in Germany, as white people they were still part of the dominant race within the orbit of the British Empire. Celebrating the coming of the new year at Raffles Hotel in Singapore was the privilege of their race. They were living in a world about to be turned upside down.

Pictured on the previous page are members of the Seefeld family. Gerhard Seefeld (Gary Seefeld) is in the centre and Rosalie (Rosie), his second wife, in front of him in the striped coat. Helmut Seefeld, Gerhard's brother, is in the white dinner jacket at right. Helmut's wife Edith wears the hat. Helia and Max Sternberg, Rosie's sister and brother-in-law, are the couple at left.

How many of these European refugees, to be interned as enemy aliens within a few months, owed their lives to their arrest and deportation from Singapore?

Source: Loretta Forsey.

Section 3

ENEMY ALIENS IN BRITAIN, 1940

ADRIFT, ARRESTED, INTERNED, DEPORTED

INTRODUCTION

The Nazi military victories of April and May 1940 presented Britain and her new Prime Minister, Winston Churchill, with a prospect the country had not known before – of military defeat, national humiliation, and through an international diplomatic conference to be chaired by Mussolini, the forced recognition of Nazi hegemony on the Continent. With her armed forces trapped into a stretch of land and beaches near Dunkirk, the deal would give Britain the right to withdraw 300,000 British and French troops (without their guns) and tacit recognition from Germany of a new division of power in the world. Germany controlled Europe and Britain controlled her empire.

There was considerable support in Cabinet for taking the deal, but Winston Churchill would have no part of it. By refusing to recognise defeat, he effectively denied Germany her victory, which would remain incomplete as long as Britain was defiant.

This was Churchill's darkest and greatest moment. It was now he took a decision which he came to regret, but which disclosed how shaken he and his colleagues and advisers were by the worst disaster in British military history. The Royal Navy was intact, but could it defend the realm against invasion? The threat of a German landing in Britain impelled Churchill to accept the advice of the chiefs of the armed services to intern all Germans and Italians living in Britain, regardless of their security classification.

This meant that the 6,800 German-born, Austrian-born, or Czech-born people placed by Internment Tribunals in category B – the 'doubtfuls' – and more importantly, the 64,000 people who had been placed in category C as being of no threat, were subject to arrest and imprisonment, alongside the Germans in category A deemed to be sympathetic to the German or Italian cause, and certain other Italian men living in Britain. Since Italy had entered the war on 10 June 1940, 15,000 Italian nationals in Britain were in the same position as their German counterparts. 'Collar the lot' summarised

Churchill's bottom line on the subject, and though he may not have used the words himself, collared they were.

British xenophobia is little different from its counterparts elsewhere, and at this terrible moment it was all too easy for hot-tempered patriots to focus on symbolic targets rather than on the real enemies across the Channel. The shock of defeat in Norway and then in France and the Low Countries suggested that German forces had the support of locals or refugees who were really spies in disguise. The British press was outspoken about the predicament the country was in, and the possible risk of harbouring enemy agents posing as victims of the Nazi regime. Internment made sense in the spring of 1940. But Churchill's decision to remove what he and many others saw as a pool of foreigners among whom there *might* be Nazi agents went further still. He decided to arrange the detention of as many internees as possible in the Dominions.

The process of arrest and detention was carried out by the police, most of the time with tact and common sense. But even with the best intentions and many cups of tea, policemen could not soften the shock that many former inmates in German concentration camps felt when their safe haven in Britain turned into another prison. British authorities ensured that enemies of the Nazis who had suffered for their beliefs in Germany would suffer again simply because they had been born and raised in territory Hitler had turned into the Third Reich. Foreign-born Jews were treated with the same degree of intolerance in France, but then Britain never had a Dreyfus affair. Illiberalism was the ugly face of British defiance in the spring of 1940.

After spending time in police stations or collecting points scattered throughout Britain, German- or Italian-born internees were sent to internment camps. A ramshackle archipelago of camps had emerged to house them. Some camps were worse than others. Warth Mills, an old cotton mill in Lancashire, was one of the worst. That is where Italian detainees were sent. Many camps were located on the Isle of Man. Others were near Liverpool, at an uncompleted housing estate at Huyton, used for detainees in Britain in much the same way that French police used an empty housing estate at Drancy north of Paris.

On 1 July 1940, the SS *Arandora Star*, a luxury liner converted into a troop ship, set sail for Canada carrying internees from these camps. The next day the ship was torpedoed and sunk; over 800 of those on board lost their lives. As there was no embarkation list, confusion followed as to exactly who was dead and who was alive, though it was clear that most of the dead were Italians and some were German and Austrian refugees from Nazism. The average age of the men who died on that ship was near 50. On 3 July, another troop ship, the *Ettrick,* set sail for Canada with around 1000 internees on board; this time the ship had a destroyer escort and made the crossing.

One week later, a mixed group of about 2500 men and boys boarded the *Dunera*. Among them were 450 survivors of the sinking of the *Arandora Star*, including about 100 German merchant seamen, 200 Italian internees, German nationals who were known Nazi sympathisers, and political, racial or religious refugees who had been deemed suspect. The other 2050 were refugees primarily from Germany, Austria, and Czechoslovakia. Approximately 80 per cent were Jewish. Although a later usage would make them the '*Dunera* boys', most were men. The youngest on board had just turned 16; the oldest was 66; the median age was 29. The stories of these 2050 men and boys, alongside those of the internees on the *Queen Mary* who sailed from Singapore, and their vicissitudes in Australia and beyond, are the subject of the chapters that follow.

The first defeat: Winston Churchill addresses the crew of HMS *Hardy* after their return from Norway in April 1940

The Second World War took a dark turn for Britain with German victory in Norway in April and May 1940. Now the German fleet could roam throughout the North Atlantic, a freedom it never won in the First World War. Churchill, as First Lord of the Admiralty from the outbreak of war in September 1939, knew all too well the significance of this defeat.

Source and copyright: Imperial War Museum, London [IWM, HU 61306]

The British Expeditionary Force, France, 1940

Soldiers from the Essex Regiment study a map, 27 April 1940. Their location was Meurchin in northern France.

Source and copyright: Imperial War Museum, London [IWM, F 4121]

The second defeat: a hospital ship evacuating the wounded from Dunkirk, c. May–June 1940

In the spring and summer of 1940, the British army in France suffered the worst defeat in British military history. The total destruction of British forces was avoided only by the successful evacuation of approximately 300,000 British and French soldiers from the beaches of Dunkirk.

Source and copyright: Imperial War Museum, London [IWM, HU 73187]

Winston Churchill inspects a Tommy gun at Hartlepool, July 1940

Churchill's speeches were his most powerful weapons of war in the spring and summer of 1940. His address to Parliament on 4 June 1940 galvanised the nation and dismissed any notion that Britain would seek a negotiated peace with Germany, despite the defeats in Norway and France.

With Britain vulnerable, commentators in the press discussed openly the risk of spies among the nearly 80,000 German and Austrian residents of Britain. The commentators noted the presence of Nazi sympathisers in countries which had already fallen to the *Wehrmacht*. The British government's response to the perceived threat posed by these potential 'fifth columnists' was to intern and deport them.

Source and copyright: Imperial War Museum, London [IWM, H 2646A]

ENEMY ALIENS IN BRITAIN, 1940

***Wehrmacht* map showing planned invasion of Britain, 1940**

From mid-1940, control of the Channel ports gave Germany a platform from which to launch a multi-pronged invasion of Britain, codenamed Operation Sea Lion. The invasion never was, something Winston Churchill did not know when he ordered the internment of enemy aliens in Britain.

Source and copyright: Imperial War Museum, London [IWM, COL 238]

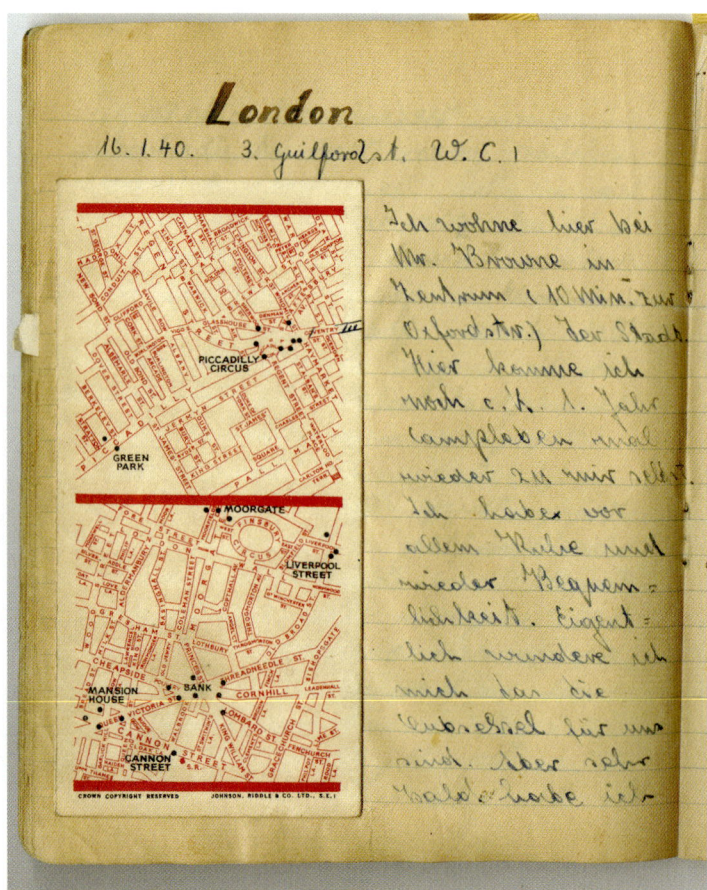

Hans Neuwahl's diary, London, 1940

Hans Neuwahl (Johnny Newall) was born in Schwerte in the Ruhr in 1921. He was Jewish and worked variously as a fitter, an electrician, and a farmer.

In London he was a tourist, marking his digs on a city map alongside tourist sites and tube stations.

Whereas the febrile London press saw him and other enemy aliens as potentially dangerous, he eagerly pursued the traditional tourist's search for the delights of London.

Source and copyright: Rosemary Newall, Karin Morrison and Susanne Platt.

Bunce Court, Otterden, Kent

From 1933 to 1940 Bunce Court was home to a small boarding school. Founded by Anna Essinger at Herrlingen, Germany, the school was non-denominational, co-educational, and much influenced by progressive ideas and practices in the United States. The school was an attractive option for German Jewish parents looking for a safe and congenial environment for the education of their children. Walter Kaufmann was a student at Bunce Court, as were at least three others he would meet on the *Dunera*. Two members of the school staff – Hans Schaye, a gardener born in 1921 who had come to Britain on a *Kindertransport*, and Hans Joseph Meyer, a handcrafts instructor born in 1913 – were also on the *Dunera*. Meyer, who had lived in Britain since 1934, volunteered for deportation as he did not wish to abandon his students. He was married and had a son.

Source: www.faversham.org, via Deborah Smith.

Internee in a cell

Fritz Schönbach (Fred Schonbach), a Viennese Jew born in 1920, depicts the moment when a Home Office official is about to enter a holding cell where an internee awaits interrogation. Schönbach was interned on 16 May 1940.

Fritz Schönbach, *No title*, c. 1940, pencil on paper. Jewish Museum of Australia collection 3067.11.2. Copyright: Schonbach family.

ENEMY ALIENS IN BRITAIN, 1940

'But I am a Czech, Pané Detectiv'

Fritz Schönbach's sketch shows the bemusement of a Czech man about to be interned. Being Czech, he could not understand why he was being interned as an enemy alien. He is addressing the detective using the Czech equivalent of 'sir'.

Many internees came not from Germany or Austria, but from other places in central and eastern Europe. They became German not by choice but because of German expansion under Hitler.

Fritz Schönbach, *But I am a Czech, Pane Detectiv*, c. 1940, pencil on paper. Jewish Museum of Australia collection 3067.17.2. Copyright: Schonbach family.

'Trying to make friends' and 'March through Bury'

Kempton Park race track, 20 miles north of London, served as one of many internment camps in 1940. The internees there (above) were more fortunate than those who were sent to the Warth Cotton Mill in Bury, Lancashire (right). Marching under arrest

through the town, the internees were subject to public scrutiny, sometimes humiliation. Warth mill was filthy. There were 20 basins and 20 latrines for 2000 POWs and internees. These sketches are by Fritz Schönbach.

Source and copyright: Schonbach family.

Fritz Schönbach, from arrest to internment, 1940

Schönbach presents a cartoon strip of the passage of an enemy alien from arrest to dejection.

Fritz Schönbach, *No title*, c. 1940, pencil on paper. Jewish Museum of Australia collection 3067.15.4. Copyright: Schonbach family.

ENEMY ALIENS IN BRITAIN, 1940

'Spy activities are successfully checked'

This sketch shows the processing of internees. One is inoculated, at left, another is photographed and given a number, at centre, and a third is fingerprinted, at centre right. On the right edge of the image, an internee is being X-rayed. The absurdity of the procedure as a protection against espionage is evident. The artist is unknown.

Unknown artist, *Spy activities are successfully checked*, pencil on paper. Jewish Museum of Australia collection 4415.

Ludwig Hirschfeld-Mack, self-portrait, Isle of Man, 1940

Ludwig Hirschfeld-Mack was born in Frankfurt in 1893. He was Protestant and married a Quaker in 1917. After serving in the First World War, he was among the earliest students trained in art at the Bauhaus, working with Lionel Feininger and Paul Klee.

His maternal grandmother was Jewish, which made him Jewish in the eyes of the Nazis. He left Germany in 1936, with one of his daughters but without his bed-ridden wife.

In Britain, he taught unemployed miners in south Wales how to make furniture. He also worked as an art master at the Dulwich preparatory school, which on the outbreak of war was moved from south London to Cranbrook in Kent. As a German, Hirschfeld-Mack was forbidden to live near the coast. He was interned on 12 May 1940 and sent to the Isle of Man. His anguish is evident.

Ludwig Hirschfeld-Mack (1893 1965), *Self Portrait, Isle of Man 1940*, watercolour. The University of Melbourne Art Collection. Gift of Mrs Olive Hirschfeld 1982, 1982.0145.063. Copyright: Chris Bell.

ENEMY ALIENS IN BRITAIN, 1940

Internees at Onchan, Isle of Man, 1940

Internees were kept in many places on the Isle of Man, some more agreeable than others. Fritz Schönbach's sense of humour is inscribed in both these sketches of internees at Onchan. The sketch above presents a scene that could have been transported directly from Berlin, where Café Bauer offered the best pastries and conviviality. It was easier to laugh at the strange turn of fate internees faced when they were housed on the Isle of Man than in more dismal camps. But no one lost sight of the fact that they were captives.

Source and copyright: Schonbach family.

SS *Arandora Star*, at Admiralty Torpedo Instruction School, 1940

This troop ship was sunk by a U-boat on 2 July 1940 with the loss of more than 800 lives, mainly Italian and German internees. Most of the German and Italian survivors were sent back to Liverpool to sail on the *Dunera* a week later.

Source: The National Archives, United Kingdom, ADM 189/142(1).

Uwe Radok diary entry, Tuesday 2 July 1940, aboard the *Arandora Star*

'Rainer and Jobst get up at 6 AM to get bread rations; he goes alone, I lie back down in my shorts and shirt. 12 minutes later a dull crack and breaking glass, sound of machines stops. Lights are not working. 'Alright, let's go, get out!' Smoke and gas in the hall, everyone is pushing upwards. Rainer is there as well without a life jacket. Try to find him one in the D-Deck, not possible without light.'

Uwe, Jobst, and Rainer Radok were brothers from Königsberg in East Prussia. Uwe was born in 1916, Jobst a year later, and Rainer in 1920. While their family was Protestant, Jewish ancestry denied them a future in Nazi Germany. All three came to Britain in the 1930s, and lived in Ormesby in Yorkshire. Jobst worked in export trades, Uwe worked as an engineer, and Rainer continued his studies in engineering. They were interned on 24 September 1939. As category A aliens, they were among the first to be detained. On the night of 30 June – 1 July 1940, they boarded the *Arandora Star*.

Their parents, sister Gundula, and brother Christoph, the eldest of the four boys, remained in Germany.

The seven members of the Radok family had been granted entry permits by the Australian government in August 1939, but the coming of war prevented their emigration.

Source and copyright: Radok family collection.

H. J. Radok 191/1008   10th July 1940

Sehr geehrter Herr Rotte, vor ein paar Tagen sandten wir Ihnen eine Postkarte mit der Mitteilung dass wir alle "safe" wären, die Ihnen wahrscheinlich etwas sonderbar vorgekommen ist. Zur Erklärung dazu möchte ich hinzufügen dass wir auf dem Wege nach Kanada waren und unterwegs zwei torpediert worden sind, aber glücklicherweise alle 3 heil davongekommen sind. Da wir nicht wissen, wo unsere Eltern sich aufhalten, müssen wir Sie bitten ihnen mitzuteilen dass es uns allen gut geht, und wir nur aus Ermangelung einer Adresse nicht an sie schreiben können. Dies in der Hoffnung, dass sie selbst wissen wo sie sind. Wir hoffen bei nächster Gelegenheit nochmals berichten zu werden und dann mit etwas mehr Ruhe. Da wir im Augenblick keinen festen Sitz haben, ist es sehr schlecht mit der Postverbindung, doch wenn sie an einen von uns schreiben, c/o. WAR OFFICE, der Brief sollte wohl irgendwann uns ankommen. Sobald wir wieder eine Adresse haben werden wir uns melden. In der Hoffnung, dass auch nur alles zu einem guten Ende kommt und mit besten Wünschen sind wir

Ihre ergebenen
John Radok
Uwe Radok
Rainer Radok

Uwe, Jobst and Rainer Radok letter to a family friend, 10 July 1940, the day they sailed on the *Dunera*

H.F. Radok 191/11008 10th July 1940

Honourable Mister Roth

A few days ago we sent you a postcard with the news that we are all safe. Most likely this is bound to appear unusual to you. In explanation, I would like to add that on the way to Canada we were torpedoed but luckily we all escaped the disaster.

Since we do not know where our parents are currently, we would be grateful if you could inform them that we are all doing well, and that we just are in need of their address; that is why we have not written to them. This is in the hope that you know where they are. We hope the next time to board a ship with more luck.

At the moment we do not have a firm address; it is difficult to communicate through the mail. But if you write to one of us c/o WAR OFFICE, the letter should arrive here some time in the future. As soon as we have a firm address, we will let you know.

In the hope that everything will end well and with our best wishes, we are your devoted

Jobst Radok

Uwe Radok

Rainer Radok

Source and copyright: Radok family collection.

> Dear Marguerite,
>
> I am leaving today. I was waiting for days for news from you and I am very disappointed that I have not got any. Why did you not send a telegram, why not a single word? I do not know ~~if I will write again. I have gone.~~ We have a promise from the Home Office that wives and dependents may follow; please do your best to meet me. Take all my personal belongings and my money with you. I find it only ridiculous that we shall now go to a country where they refused us admission before.
>
> It is perhaps interesting for you to know that the Unwer people had their chemist released after a few days from here. Off course they have done something for their people.
>
> With Love
> yours
> Georg
> (HAIM)

Georg Haim to Marguerite Haim, 10 July 1940

Georg Haim was born in Gmund in Austria in 1906 to a Jewish family. He and Marguerite married in Vienna in 1935. After two years in Palestine, they returned to Vienna for family reasons. They feared for their future in Austria and prepared to leave once more. In November 1937 Marguerite entered Britain on a domestic worker permit. Georg worked in France until 1938, when he joined Marguerite in Britain. They set up home in London.

He sent this note to his wife on the day he boarded the *Dunera*. He complains about not having received a letter from her, and then instructs her to bring all his belongings and money to Australia. He writes of a promise from the Home Office that she would be allowed to join him abroad. She was prepared to do so. The plan fell through.

Source and copyright: John Haim.

Section 4

AT SEA

ABOARD THE *DUNERA* AND THE *QUEEN MARY*

INTRODUCTION

There were two ships at sea in September 1940 carrying prisoners to internment camps in Australia. One was a troop transport, the *Dunera*; the other a grand ocean liner, the *Queen Mary*, on the way to conversion as a troop ship.

The passage of the 2050 or so interned men and boys who sailed on the *Dunera* bore no resemblance to the voyage of the *Queen Mary* from Singapore to Australia. The living conditions, overcrowding, and food on the *Dunera* were appalling, and so was the brutality of the ship's guards and the officers who commanded them. Probably many of the guards had little idea that there were German-born people who were not Nazis; to some of them, all the internees on board were their country's enemies, who deserved all the abuse they received.

After the first days at sea, the tedium of life in the semi-darkness of the lowest deck of the *Dunera* was relieved for a short period each morning by compulsory exercise sessions on an upper deck. Wearing only their underpants, internees half-walked, half-ran around the deck, pushed and prodded by guards, machine guns trained on them, while down below soldiers searched their clothes for items not already confiscated. In one well-remembered episode, the walkers were compelled to tread barefoot on fragments of glass from a beer bottle deliberately or accidentally broken on the deck.

The voyage rapidly became an outrage and a scandal. 'We slept in four layers', wrote Werner Pelz, a 19 year-old Berliner who had been working in England as a farm labourer. 'In hammocks, on the tables, the benches, the floor.'[1] Once the ship was on the open sea, many inmates were violently seasick. Faeces, urine and vomit flowed down to form a hideous pool. 'I was lucky', Sigmund Freud's student grandson, Anton Walter Freud, would recall, '… and found myself … able to be sick on everybody below me'.[2] When he could make it to the latrine he found, so he calculated, that with ten toilets serving 2050 bodies, each internee could use one, on average, for seven minutes every 24 hours. Karl Guttmann, a Viennese engineering draughtsman aged 21, who like most internees suffered from diarrhoea, counted the number of times he had to visit a latrine during one long night: twenty-two.[3] Toilet paper was rationed to two sheets per man per day. Night and day blurred as portholes were closed for all but a few minutes each day, making the ship, in Pelz's poetic phrase, 'the large dim womb that was to bear us into a new world.'[4]

Protests over maltreatment were treated by the commanding officer of the ship's guard, Lieutenant Colonel William Scott, with contempt. He warned the internees to stop 'running after' his officers with complaints, and while telling his troops to stop looting suitcases, assured them that as an old soldier he understood why 'the British Tommy looks upon a time like this as an opportunity to help himself to any unattended trifles.' He was 'only too aware', he said, 'that were we in the position of our guests, after being searched, we would be lucky if we had our belly buttons left.'[5]

Dismayed that British officers should condone and even incite theft and violence, their victims concluded that these men were the dregs of the service. 'From the shoulder flashes on their uniforms', observed Robert Kahn, an internee from Bavaria, 'we could see how as a military unit they had been cobbled together from members of various British regiments' using the *Dunera* as 'a convenient dumping ground for their own undesirables.'[6] The malefactors included men consigned to the *Dunera* after the evacuation at Dunkirk, a fiasco which perhaps had left them with an undiscriminating hatred of everything German.

The men and boys on the *Dunera* entered the grey domain of enemy aliens consigned to military imprisonment, in a ship like a borstal for delinquents and criminals. Their refugee status meant nothing once hostilities began. Official recognition – within months – of the wrong done to them alleviated but did not wholly extinguish the bitterness many internees bore about their treatment.

The *Queen Mary* was another world. Many of the 266 internees sailed with their families. To be sure, in both cases, the passengers were internees, under guard. But the *Dunera* was so overcrowded and run with such a heavy hand as to turn the vessel into what some called a hell-ship. On the *Queen Mary* there was some petty pilfering, but no brutality.

And when the men and boys on the *Dunera* finally figured out what they were never told – that their destination was not Canada, but rather the Cape of Good Hope, in the first instance – their African passage in equatorial heat came to resemble that of slave ships of earlier times. The traffic in slaves was long over, but the traffic in prisoners, in this case including civilian men deported from Britain, was well and truly alive. For those who had already served time in Hitler's prisons and concentration camps, this sea journey was the continuation of a pattern of injustice and persecution increasingly hard to endure. One internee, a 36 year old Austrian-born Jew named Jakob Weiss, committed suicide during the journey. Guards had torn up his papers about emigrating to Argentina, and on 21 August he jumped overboard. Four days later, Hans Pfeffen, a 52 year old Austrian, died of heart failure brought on by influenza. Another Austrian, Felix Friedemann, died on 4 September as the *Dunera* steamed from Melbourne to Sydney. He suffered complications after being punched in a scuffle with a fellow internee. He was 39. Pfeffen and Friedemann were buried at sea.

Injustice shared was injustice borne a little more easily. Friendships made on the *Dunera* helped many to survive. Orthodox Jews had their prayers to console them; others drew on whatever faith they had preserved, though in the late summer of 1940, the Allied cause was at a low ebb.

Like most prisoners in other places, they faced daily the challenge of boredom. Filling time was a major preoccupation. There were debates and lectures, foreshadowing things to come when the voyage was over. Men and boys proficient in English took classes for those less at home in the captors' language. As Felix Bischofswerder (Werder) recalled, the internees were invited to attend lectures given by 'anyone who knew anything'. 'Of course there were charlatans, intellectual buffoons, fossilized academics and cerebral ego-trippers.' He thought of Mr F, 'a somewhat aged authority on sexual practices in the back streets of Vienna', and Dr B, 'who let it be known that he would give a lecture and when asked on what topic, replied "What would you like to learn?"' Werder turned to other teachers, listening to learned lectures on topics as diverse as the philosophy of history, the influence of C. P. E. Bach on Beethoven, and Deutero-Isaiah. The lecturer on musical history was Peter Stadlen, an eminent pianist whose concerts some of the internees had attended in Vienna and Berlin. Werder doubted whether any university could match the performance of these lecturers, and the comparison came to other minds.[7] 'A sort of Ship's University', Hungarian-born Albert Karolyi called the lecture programme. 'I am starting on getting a lecture ready myself', he wrote early in the voyage. 'The story of the Vienna Boys Choir. (After all, I was a member of the choir between 1929 and 1931).'[8]

The style of the lecturers ranged from the anecdotal and personal to the formal. Dr Franz Borkenau, the Austrian intellectual who would not have been on board had the Home Office moved more swiftly to have him released in England, explored themes he had written about in his books *The Spanish Cockpit,* 1937, and *The Communist International,* 1938. He delivered lectures from his hammock as if it were a podium.[9]

In their enforced ignorance of what was going on in the world, internees relied heavily on Borkenau for understandings of the war, all the more so after a South African newspaper was smuggled to him in Cape Town, providing the first up-to-date news since the ship left Liverpool. Borkenau was also a leading participant in a debating group, known whimsically as the Staff Conference, which met to consider the state of the war. Dr Leonhard Adam's scholarly lectures on ethnology drew on his own soon-to-be published book *Primitive Art.* Gerd Buchdahl, Mainz-born graduate in engineering, taught philosophy using C. E. M. Joad's popular *Guide* to that subject, published in 1936.

Buchdahl joined Peter Herbst and Peter Laske in an even more ambitious project. On toilet paper, they wrote a 'camp constitution' in German as a guide to their taking control over their own affairs once placed in an internment camp. It is a remarkable affirmation of their right to self-government once the voyage of the *Dunera* had come to an end.

Many of the lectures were designed to help prepare internees for life after internment, and to that end had upbeat titles, general and particular: 'Future plans and possibilities', 'How to drive a car', which had as teaching aid a crude cockpit made out of fruit boxes from the ship's pantry, and surprisingly, 'Australia economic, agricultural, geographical'. It was unclear who knew enough about Australia to provide a profile of it for others.

During the 57 days on board the *Dunera*, men learned or practised skills. There are many sharp and insightful sketches internees made of fellow travellers. A pencilled profile served to remind both artist and subject that whatever they had lost, their individuality and their integrity had not been taken from them.

Some employed sardonic humour. Caricatures of the epidemic of petty theft on board appeared alongside a sketch of 'The Wondering [not wandering] Jew', puzzled by the turn of fate that brought the artist to this pass. One placed Hitler in the water ahead of the ship. This was probably a reference to the risk of sinking by submarine, the fate of the *Arandora Star*. Survivors from that ship were added to the internee population to sail on the *Dunera*, which left Liverpool a week later. The danger of submarine attack was never far from their minds.

The sheer length of the voyage of the *Dunera* made it a test of psychological and physical endurance in a way the passage of the *Queen Mary* never was. Australia was the only destination possible for the *Queen Mary*, which sailed on 18 September and arrived in Sydney a week later. But none of the passengers on either ship knew where their odyssey would take them.

The dark side of the story of the *Dunera* emerged publicly less than a year after its arrival in Australia. In late 1940, British officials opened an enquiry into complaints about what had happened on board. The investigation itself displayed some of the incompetence which had contributed to the abuses. In November 1940, Military Intelligence thought it had identified the person responsible for the mistreatment of internees aboard the *Dunera* – an Englishman named Gannef. Further enquiries were set in motion to establish his exact identity. Across a document in the National Archives of Australia someone has written in red pen: 'Gannef is the Yiddish for thief'.[10] This note was added in April 1941. Had Military Intelligence spent five months looking for Gannef? Graham Greene or John Le Carré could not have invented a better instance of the internal contradiction within the phrase 'military intelligence'.

In May 1941 a court-martial recorded the abuse of internees on the *Dunera*, and severely reprimanded the senior officer on the ship, Lieutenant Colonel Scott. Regimental Sergeant Major C. A. Bowles admitted to two charges of theft. He was reduced to the ranks, gaoled for a year and dishonourably discharged from the army.[11] A fund of £35,000 was set aside formally to compensate for property 'lost' by those on the *Dunera*. To be sure, this degree of official recognition of the injustice done to these men was hardly commensurate with what they had experienced. But by May 1941, everybody concerned – from Churchill down – recognised the story of indiscriminate civilian internment and deportation of German- and Italian-born refugees as a regrettable consequence of official panic in the darkest days of the war.

The voyages of both the *Dunera* and the *Queen Mary* were errors of state which should never have taken place. Once set in motion, internment and deportation turned into a gratuitous exercise of brutality. The passengers on the *Dunera* were among people persecuted both by the Nazis and by the governments of countries to which they fled for protection and survival. They had no rights and no nation; rather they were outlaws in the nation in which they were born, and thus did not have the right to have rights. They were in possession only of what the Italian philosopher Agamben terms 'bare life'.[12] It was with that attribute alone that they landed in Australia to face further incarceration, not for what any of them had done, but for being enemy aliens in Britain or in a British colony at a desperate moment in the war. Never a threat to the defence of the realm, these refugees first benefited from the liberal tradition of British humanitarian aid for refugees and then suffered from the illiberal tradition of British maltreatment of enemy aliens evident in both world wars.

Notes

1. Werner Pelz, *Distant Strains of Triumph*, (London: Victor Gollancz, 1964), p. 76.
2. Helen Fry, *Freuds' War*, (Stroud: The History Press, 2009), p. 113.
3. Paul R. Bartrop with Gabrielle Eisen, *The Dunera Affair: A Documentary Resource Book* (Melbourne: Schwartz and Wilkinson / Jewish Museum of Australia, 1990), p. 175.
4. Pelz, *Distant Strains of Triumph*, p. 76.
5. Cyril Pearl, *The Dunera Scandal: Deported by Mistake*, (Sydney: Angus and Robertson, 1983), pp. 32–3.
6. Robert L. Kahn, *Chapters from my Past*, pp. 103-04. Manuscript in possession of authors.
7. Benzion Patkin, *The Dunera Internees*, (Sydney: Cassell Australia, 1979), pp. 59–60.
8. Bartrop with Eisen, *The Dunera Affair*, p. 191.
9. Sue Everett, *Not Welcome: A Dunera Boy's Escape from Nazi Oppression to Eventual Freedom in Australia*, (Melbourne: Hybrid Publishers, 2010), p. 61.
10. NAA, MP729/6, 63/401/141, Complaints Internees Dunera, 1940–1.
11. Pearl, *The Dunera Scandal*, p. 139.
12. Giorgio Agamben, *Homo Sacer: Sovereign Power and Bare Life*, trans. Daniel Heller-Roazen, (Stanford: Stanford University Press, 1998).

The *Dunera*

The MS (Motor Ship) *Dunera*, launched in 1937, was built as a troopship for the British India Steam Navigation Company to specifications set by the British government. She was named after a village in India. During the war her prefix was HMT, for Hired Military Transport. She carried Australians and New Zealanders to Egypt in 1940 before docking at Liverpool to pick up her cargo of 2546 'enemy aliens', among whom were German merchant seamen and 2239 civilian internees, including 200 Italians. She sailed on 10 July 1940.

The watercolour was the work of an unknown internee.

Photograph source and copyright: Australian National Maritime Museum, ANMS0413[060]. Watercolour source and copyright: Unknown artist, *British India S.N.C.O.'s S.S. Dunera*, watercolour on paper. Jewish Museum of Australia collection, 4134.

'*Dunera* Reception'

This watercolour drawing by Fritz Schönbach depicts the moment at which the bewildered internees are subjected to search and confiscation. The guards treated the internees with cruelty.

    Many internees carried documents and letters which told of the lives they had left behind. To lose these traces of loved ones and happy memories was crushing, and that was probably the point. These were, after all, prisoners, suspected of being spies or potential enemies.

Dunera Reception, July 10 1940, watercolour and pencil on paper. Source: Archive of Australian Judaica, Rare Books and Special Collections, the University of Sydney Library. Copyright: Schonbach family.

AT SEA: ABOARD THE *DUNERA* AND THE *QUEEN MARY*

'You damn'd Hitler spy!'

Robert Hofmann was born in 1889 in Vienna to a Protestant family with Jewish ancestors. He worked as an artist. After the *Anschluss,* he made his way to London, where he was interned on 2 July 1940. He boarded the *Dunera* eight days later.

His caricature expresses the absurdity of the charge that brought these men to the *Dunera*. That Nazis would operate under the cover of Orthodox Jews stretches the imagination beyond belief. The use of a Jewish stereotype to highlight the poor treatment of Jews on the *Dunera* is both striking and puzzling.

It is likely that the internee is Dr Ernst Ehrentreu, chief rabbi in Munich before the war and the senior Jewish religious figure among the *Dunera* internees. When he complained about conditions on the ship, an officer told him 'that he would hang him at the mast, swing him by his beard round the mast, [and] throw him overboard'.

Robert Hofmann, *You damn'd Hitler spy!*, c. 1940, pencil on card. Source and copyright: Jewish Museum of Australia collection, 7026.

Quotation from JMA, 4471.2, Appendix to the Dunera Statement.

At sea, 17 July 1940

Emil Wittenberg captured the fate of the *Dunera* internees enduring the heat of July, with no idea where they were headed.

Source and copyright: Martin Burman.

AT SEA: ABOARD THE *DUNERA* AND THE *QUEEN MARY*

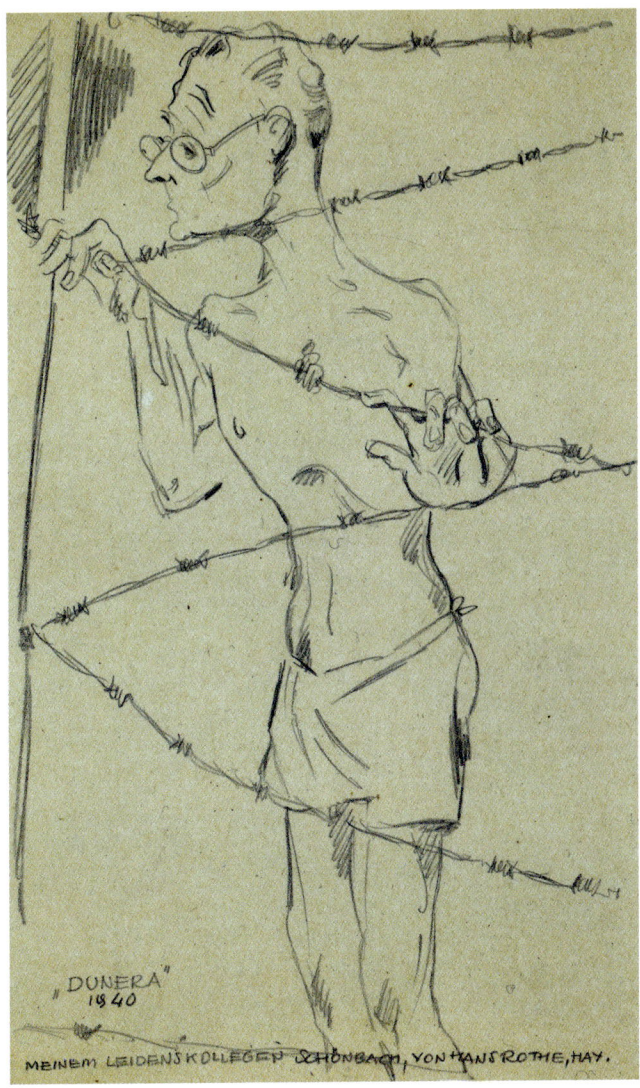

Internee on the *Dunera*

The physical vulnerability of internees confined on the *Dunera* is depicted in this sketch by Hans Rothe.

Source: Schonbach family.

Internees 'exercising' on the *Dunera*, 1940

These sketches by Fritz Schönbach capture moments of the arbitrary cruelty of the guards' treatment of the internees on the *Dunera*.

Source and copyright (above): Schonbach family.

Source (below): Archive of Australian Judaica, Rare Books and Special Collections, the University of Sydney Library. *Dunera Exercise*, August 1940, pencil on paper. Copyright: Schonbach family.

AT SEA: ABOARD THE *DUNERA* AND THE *QUEEN MARY*

African ports

The *Dunera* stopped at Freetown, Takoradi and Cape Town to take on fresh water and supplies. By the time the ship reached Cape Town (below), its inmates knew for certain that Canada was not their destination. They were headed further east. The sketches are by Fritz Schönbach.

Source and copyright (above): Fritz Schönbach, *No title*, c. 1940, pencil on paper. Jewish Museum of Australia collection, 3637.3.3.

Source (below): Fritz Schönbach, *No title*, c. 1940, pencil on paper. Jewish Museum of Australia collection, 3637.4.2. Copyright: Schonbach family.

'The Wondering Jew'

This sketch, artist unknown, spoofs the theft of Jews' clothes on the *Dunera,* but does so in an unusual manner. The Jew is caricatured and so is his German accent, 'asking ' the man who is facing him to 'giff me back's zi jacket'. But the man wearing the jacket hardly looks like a British guard. The 'wondering' Jew is an object more of ridicule than of sympathy.

Reproduced with permission of Co.As.It. – Italian Historical Society, Melbourne.

'Conditions on troopship'

The indignity of having personal possessions seized and treated like rubbish marked the voyage on the *Dunera* for many passengers, Emil Wittenberg among them.

Source and copyright: Martin Burman.

Hammocks

Overcrowding on the *Dunera* created this geometry of bodies arrayed wherever possible; only a lucky few found a hammock to sleep in. Emil Wittenberg documented this enduring image of misery, but not the accompanying stench.

Source and copyright: Martin Burman.

AT SEA: ABOARD THE *DUNERA* AND THE *QUEEN MARY*

Aboard the *Dunera*

Fritz Schönbach's image of men stripped down to cope with the sweltering conditions on board the *Dunera* is marked by a striking, almost Christ-like, figure with his hands raised in the centre.

Hans Rothe's sketch of a man on his side, attempting to sleep in a hammock he fills entirely, shows the same awkward vulnerability and discomfort of below-deck life.

Source and copyright: Schonbach family (top). Source: Schonbach family (bottom).

ISSUE OF MEAGER RATIONS

OUR ONLY PLEASURE: SALT WATER SHOWERS

DECK 'LEADER' MEETING

'COIFFEUR POUR MESSIEURS' (UNDER GUARD)

Günter Kirschner

Lassitude: Fritz Loewenstein sketches aboard the *Dunera*

A number of artists captured the slow rhythms of daily life and lassitude on the ship. Among them was Fritz Loewenstein, who had sought refuge in Belgium, and had escaped the fighting at Dunkirk. He was picked up by one of the flotilla of British ships, large and small, which rescued British troops trapped at Dunkirk. Internment followed.

Source and copyright: Monica Lee Lowen and Jocelyn Lowen.

AT SEA: ABOARD THE *DUNERA* AND THE *QUEEN MARY*

'SOCIAL LIFE' - THE FO'C'SLE LATRINE

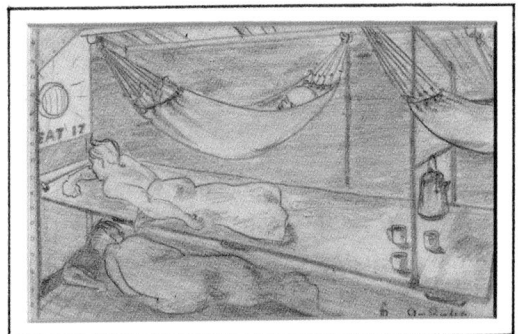

OVERCROWDED! 3000 ON A TROOPSHIP FOR 1400

SKETCHES MADE ON BOARD THE 'DUNERA' BELOW DECK & BEHIND BARBED WIRE
LEFT LIVERPOOL 10.7.40. VIA FREETOWN, TAKURADI, CAPETOWN, ARRIVED SYDNEY 6.9.40

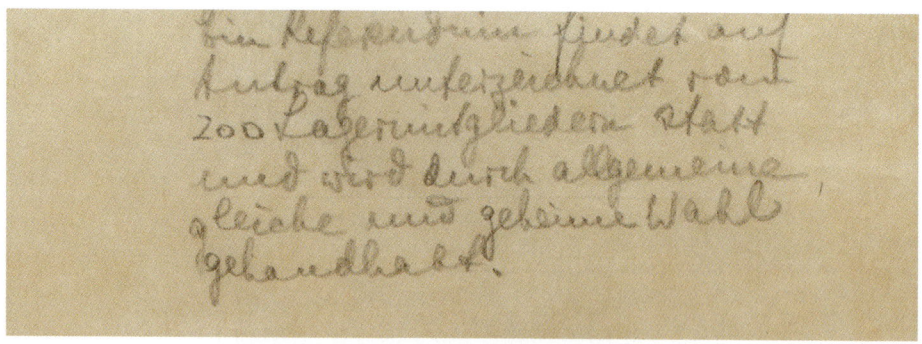

Camp constitution: in German and English (pp. 86-98)

In August 1940, on board the *Dunera*, Gerd Buchdahl, Peter Herbst and Peter Laske composed in German a constitution to serve internees wherever they were to be incarcerated. The text was written on toilet paper, a precious roll of which they had confiscated. The translation was by Gerd Buchdahl, at an unspecified later date.

Camp Constitution, Gerd Buchdahl, Peter Herbst and Peter Lasky, 1940, on board HMT *Dunera*, Jewish Museum of Australia collection, 3161.1. *Camp Constitution* [English translation], Gerd Buchdahl, 1991, United Kingdom, Jewish Museum of Australia collection, 3161.3.

AT SEA: ABOARD THE *DUNERA* AND THE *QUEEN MARY*

```
                    PROPOSED CAMP CONSTITUTION
```

Written on a toilet roll and drawn up whilst being transported on HMS Dunera during August 1940, prior to arrival at Sydney and Hay. (Joint Authors: Gerd Buchdahl, Peter Herbst and Peter Lasky. Punctuation etc. as in original.) Transl. from the German original by Gerd Buchdahl.

```
                   PROPOSAL FOR A CAMP CONSTITUTION
```

The camp inhabitants agree on the following rules:

I. Each hut elects a representative for a minimum period of 14 days. He will be re-elected automatically for a similar period, provided he has not lost the confidence of his voters. A deputy, elected in a similar way, deputises for him during his absence.

II. The representatives form a council which meets at least once a week, as well as on the request of a quarter of its members. The council elects a chairman who may not accept any other office. The latter nominates a secretary outside of the council. The council possesses legislative function which it exercises via majority vote. The representativesa are obliged to pass on all informations, decisions and orders to their huts.

The council meets in public except in special circumstances. The representatives must pass on written proposals, signed by at least five

Peter Herbst, a student of philosophy, was born in 1919 in Heidelberg. On his mother's urging he left Germany for Britain in 1933. He was educated at Haileybury College and had gained admission to Cambridge, but could not afford to accept the offer. Peter Laske was the youngest of the authors of the constitution, born in Berlin in 1920. He worked as a chartered accountant before being interned and deported on the *Dunera*.

of their voters, to the council chairman who will read them to the council after "Questions Time". Majorities can request their representative to represent their ideas at the council, but they may not, because of refusal, force him to a premature resignation. Representatives may not hold any office in the business organisation. (See infra)

III. Representatives of six neighbouring huts elect each a group-representative who requires confirmation by the council which can also dismiss him. These [group representatives] form a committee, to which the council nominates [bestimmt] the camp manager [Lagerleiter; camp leader] and his deputy, respectively, as chairman. They have seats and [deleted: but no] votes in the council. The committee of seven, formed in this way, confers with the department managers of the business organisation in order to hand on directives in line with the intentions of the council. They formulate or deal with all plans, proposals and projects that are concerned with the various problems, including the orders of the military.

They sign on the basis of authorised representatives of the council for the latter. Their rights are limited. They have no legislative power, and their decisions require ratification through the council.

In particular, the group representatives are the link between the council and the business managers [deleted: and the camp spokesman].

Contact with the military authorities will be maintained by the camp manager or his deputy, respectively, who however have no right to make binding undertakings or accept proposals. The camp manager will be in continuous contact with the group representatives under the council.

The constitution incorporates checks and balances on executive power, including a ruling council and a court of arbitration, on which at least one constitutional expert would sit. The constitution provided for all aspects of a self-governing state, except the right to organise police and a defence force.

3

The council may nominate subcommittees whose chairmen are hutrepresentatives. These subcommittees should include at least one expert who will if necessary be brought in from outside the council.

Standing orders will be formulated by a subcommittee after the first meeting of the council, and after acceptance is to form a part of this constitution.

IV. Camp members are to be assured of freedom of speech and writing, and similarly of meetings, as well as freedom of forced labour or work which is being demanded as an alternative to unjust limitations and impositions. On the other hand, camp members must obey the decrees of the council, despite individual differences of opinion. They must comply with appeals to the court of arbitration and must keep clean their living accommodation and surroundings. [Note: Section IV is in square brackets.]

V. Business organisations such as kitchen, "store", canteen, bank, post-office, labour corps, Qudbe [?] office, orderly service, laundry, educational institutions and occupations are supervised by the Committee of Seven. At the top of each section stands an expert whose qualifications make him suited for the job. These heads of sections are nominated by a sub-committee which accepts applications after public advertisement and decides without prejudice. The heads of sections select their personnel in accordance with the same principle and submit their lists to the council for confirmation. It is intended that the works managers as well as their personnel retain their offices permanently

"Question Time" dem Konzil vorliest. Majoritäten können ihre Vertreter ersuchen, ihre Meinung im Konzil zu vertreten, aber können ihn wegen Weigerung nicht zu einem verfrühten Rücktritt zwingen. Vertreter dürfen im Betriebswesen kein Amt bekleiden (siehe infra).

III. Vertreter von 6 benachbarten Hütten wählen je einen Gruppen-obmann, der der Bestätigung des Konzils bedarf, das ihn auch absetzen kann. Diese bilden ein Komitee, in welchem das Konzil den Lagerleiter als Vorsitzenden bestimmt. Sie haben Sitze und Stimmen im Konzil.

Das so gebildete Siebener-Komitee konferiert mit dem Abteilungsleitern des Betriebswesens um ihnen im Sinne des Konzils Direktiven zu geben. Sie formulieren oder bearbeiten alle Pläne, Vorschläge und Referate, die sich mit den verschiedenen Problemen befassen inclusive den Befehlen des Militärs.
Sie zeichnen auf Grund von Konzils Bevollmächtigung für letztere.
Ihre Rechte sind beschränkt. Sie haben keine legislative Macht und ihre Beschlüsse bedürfen der Ratifizierung durch das Konzil.
Vor allem sind die Gruppen-obleute das Verbindungsglied zwischen Konzil & Betriebsleitern

4

although they can be made redundant by the council. In this case they may appeal to the court of arbitration whose decision is final. The personnel is reponsible to its chief of section who in turn is responsible to the council, and may be requested at any time to report to it concerning the activity of its section.

The Orderly Service exists in order to facilitate a smooth running of the camp business, and to carry out new regulations and decrees of the council. Orderlies may not take action against anyone forcibly without written authorisation of the court of arbitration and are not permitted to use force except in self-defence or in the course of the execution of an order of the court of arbitration.

VI. Finance- and business control will be exercised by an auditor and his personnel who must inspect all sections of the business. He will be nominated by the council after public advertisement, and he chooses his assistants in the manner similar to that of the section managers. He will supply regular reports to the council concerning the financial and other matters, and if necessary, publish these. At the request of the council or the court of arbitration he will institute checks and investigations. All books, references and other documents of the various sections must at all times be available to the accountant and his assistants, and they must be handed all informations and explanations. He can demand a hearing at the council.

VII.

The court of arbitration consists of three judges [arbitrators], (what

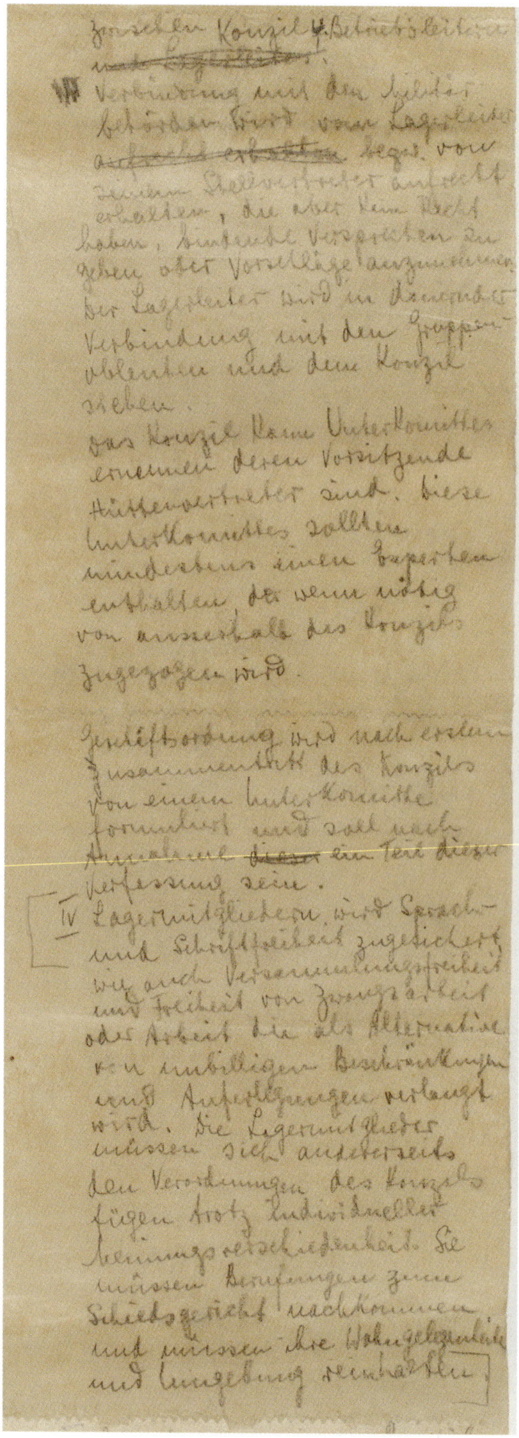

zwischen Konzil u. Betriebsleitung
~~und Lagerleiter~~.
III Verbindung mit den Militär-
behörden wird vom Lagerleiter
~~aufrecht erhalten~~ bezw. vom
seinem Stellvertreter aufrecht
erhalten, die aber kein Recht
haben, verbindliche Versprechen zu
geben oder Vorschläge anzunehmen.
Der Lagerleiter wird in dauernder
Verbindung mit den Gruppen-
obleuten und dem Konzil
stehen.
Das Konzil kann Unterkomittees
ernennen deren Vorsitzende
Hüttenvertreter sind. Diese
Unterkomittees sollten
mindestens einen Experten
enthalten, der wenn nötig
von ausserhalb des Konzils
zugezogen wird.

Geschäftsordnung wird nach erstem
Zusammentritt des Konzils
von einem Unterkomitte
formuliert und soll nach
Annahme ~~diese~~ ein Teil dieser
Verfassung sein.
IV Lagermitgliedern wird Sprach-
und Schriftfreiheit zugesichert
wie auch Versammlungsfreiheit
und Freiheit von Zwangsarbeit
oder Arbeit die als Alternative
von unbilligen Beschränkungen
und Auferlegungen verlangt
wird. Die Lagermitglieder
müssen sich andererseits
den Verordnungen des Konzils
fügen trotz individueller
Meinungsverschiedenheit. Sie
müssen Berufungen zum
Schiedsgericht nachkommen
und müssen ihre Wohngelegenheit
und Umgebung reinhalten.

5

follows has been placed in square brackes in the original text) [of whom one should be a constitutional expert. These will be elected by means of universal, equal and secret ballot from a single list, which will be put together by the council and which contains the names of at least ten willing candidates. The candidate who receives the most votes will be the president of the court of arbitration. The judges can be removed individually by means of a referendum. They nominate a secretary who like themselves is empowered to pass orders and summonses. The council nominates a list of qualified solicitors, from which it respectively chooses one as advocate of the council. Those summoned have the right of legal defence, and can choose an advocate from the list.

The court of arbitration has hence the tasks to act to some extent as a final authority in constitutional questions; secondly, to arbitrate in personal disputes, and thirdly, to hear and to judge concerning public accusations. The court meets in public and can consult jurors.]

VIII. The shape of the trade- and professional organisation will develop either in corporate or private manner in line with future camp conditions.

IX. Public moneys from all sources, as for instance canteens, will be administered by the bank following the stipulation of the council.

X. A copy of this constitution, like all subsequent legislative measures, must be accessible daily to all camp members at times to be determined.

V Betriebswesen wie zum Beispiel Küche, 'Store', Kantine, Haupt-post, Labour Corps, India Office, Orderly Service, Wäscherei, Erziehungswesen und Berufe wird vom Siebener-Komitée überwacht. An der Spitze einer jeden Abteilung steht ein Experte, dessen Qualifikationen ihn für das Amt ergeben. Diese Abteilungsleiter werden von einem Unterkomitée ernannt, welches nach öffentlicher Ausschreibung Anträge entgegen-nimmt und dan vorurteilslos entscheidet. Die Abteilungs-leiter wählen ihr Personal nach demselben Prinzip und unterbreiten ihre Listen dem Konzil zur Bestätigung. Es ist beabsichtigt, dass die Betriebsleiter Söhne der Personell ihre Kinder davon innehalten, doch können sie vom Konzil entlassen werden. In diesem Fall können sie sich an das Schiedsgericht berufen, dessen Entscheidung endgültig ist. Das Personell ist seinem Abteilungsleiter verantwortlich, der wiederum dem Konzil verantwortlich ist und jederzeit aufgefordert werden kann, über die Aktivität seiner Abteilung zu berichten.

Der Orderly Dienst besteht, um eine glatte Abwicklung des Lagerbetriebes zu ermöglichen und um Bestimmungen und Verordnungen des Konzils durchzuführen. Orderlies dürfen ~~nicht walten auch~~ gegen niemand gewaltsam einschreiten.

6

This constitution will be accepted by means of a majority decision of the hutrepresentatives, and altered by means of a two-thirds majority of the council or by referendum. A referendum takes place on application signed by 200 camp members, and will be handled by means of universal, equal and secret ballot.

AT SEA: ABOARD THE *DUNERA* AND THE *QUEEN MARY*

Untitled, by Klaus Friedeberger

In November 1940 in Hay, Klaus Friedeberger, an 18-year old printer born in Berlin, revisited in memory his time on the *Dunera*. The dislocated life he was forced to lead is symbolised in the jumbled elements of his time on board. In this sketch the ship dissolves into elements of cloud, water, and a surrealist's porthole.

Klaus Friedeberger, *not titled (Voyage)* 1940, drawing in watercolour, gouache and black pencil, image 14.8 x 18.6 cm, sheet 21 x 23.6 cm. National Gallery of Australia, Canberra, purchased 1998. Copyright: Klaus Friedeberger.

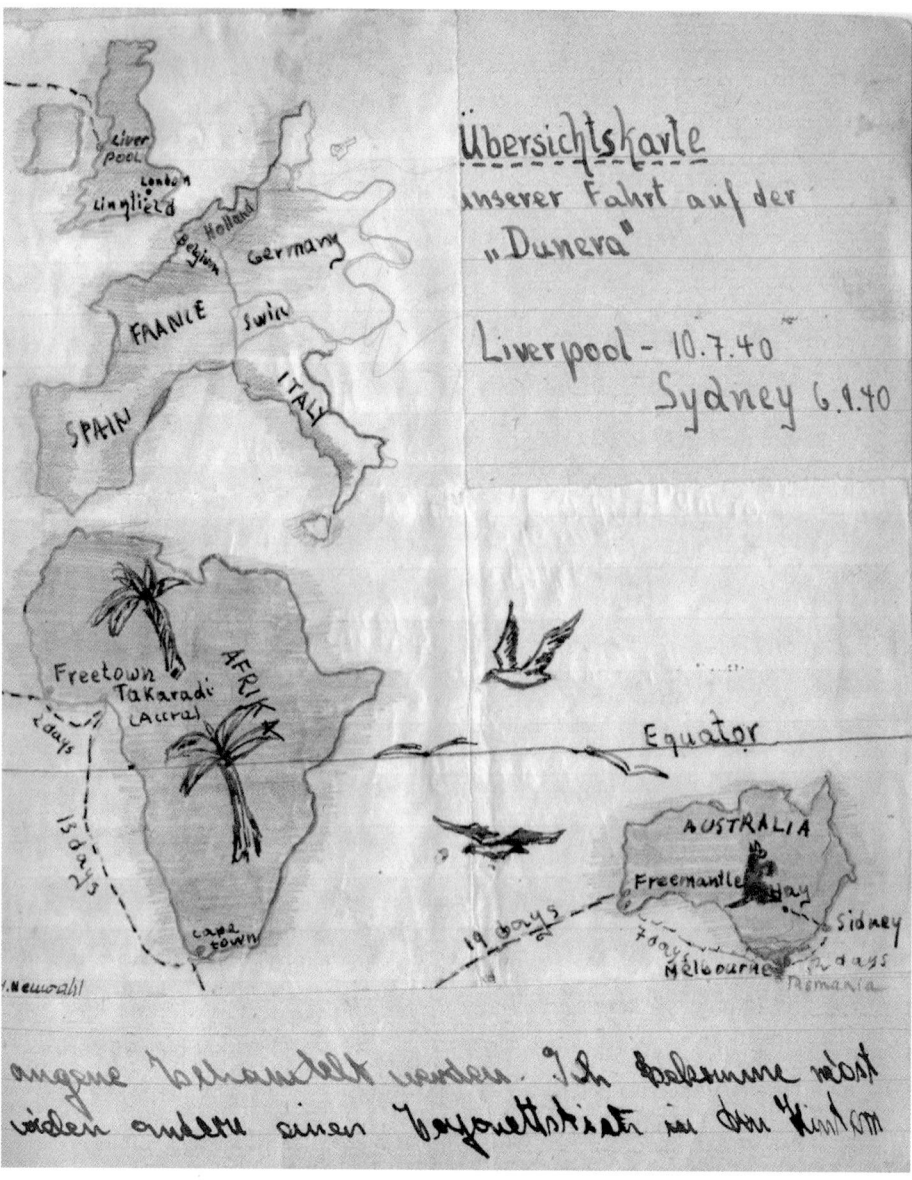

Hans Neuwahl, map of the *Dunera*'s journey

This sketch, from the diary of Hans Neuwahl, shows how one internee made his own voyage a journey of discovery. Neuwahl's resort to his diary helped pass the long days and nights on the *Dunera*.

Source and copyright: Rosemary Newall, Karin Morrison and Susanne Platt.

Reinhold and Waldemar Eckfeld, c. 1939–1940

Reinhold Eckfeld (left, photograph taken 1940 in Londonderry, Northern Ireland) was born in September 1921 in Vienna. He was six years younger than his brother Waldemar (right, photograph c. 1939), a medical student. Reinhold's account of the German takeover of Austria in 1938 is in section 1. Though still a school boy, he was arrested after *Kristallnacht*.

Both brothers escaped to Northern Ireland, where they were arrested, interned, and deported on the *Dunera*.

Waldemar had a nervous breakdown on the *Dunera*. When the ship docked in Melbourne, en route to its final destination in Sydney, he donned a British sergeant-major's uniform and tried to escape, unsuccessfully. Guards beat him so severely that his brother did not recognise him. On arrival in Sydney, Waldemar was admitted to a mental institution, where he remained for the next nineteen months.

Source: Eckfeld archive.

Fritz Schönbach, a comic look back at the voyage of the *Dunera*, Hay, 1941

Two clerks are approached by a traveller, with a stamp on his suitcase 'See sunny Hay'. One clerk says to the other: 'He says he wants to travel by liner – not by mistake'.

This drawing by Fritz Schönbach at Hay in 1941 looks back with sardonic humour on the unlikely voyage of the *Dunera*.

Source: Archive of Australian Judaica, Rare Books and Special Collections, the University of Sydney Library. *He says he wants to travel by liner – not by mistake*, Hay, 1941, watercolour and pencil on paper. Copyright: Schonbach family.

AT SEA: ABOARD THE *DUNERA* AND THE *QUEEN MARY*

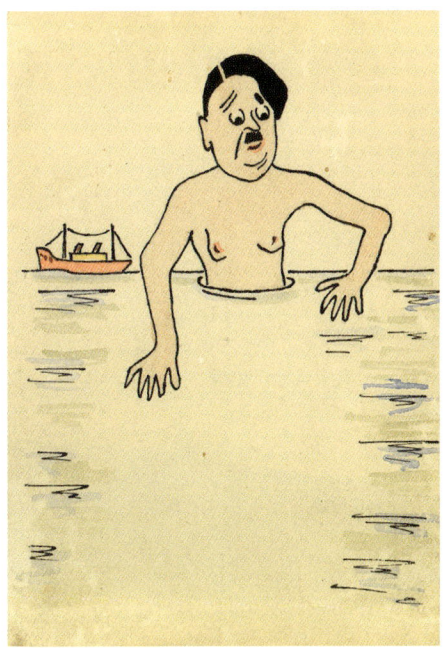

Hitler swimming, bitten by a crab

Emil Wittenberg's reverie of his revenge against the Führer, the *Dunera* in the background. The underwater scene is visible only when the image is placed against a light.

Source and copyright: Martin Burman.

The *Queen Mary*

The *Queen Mary* was in 1940 the biggest luxury liner afloat. It was refashioned as a troop ship during the war. Even allowing for its new purpose, internees from Singapore were in far more comfortable surroundings than the men on the *Dunera*.

The Singapore internees were mostly married men and women with families. By and large they were well treated by their guards.

Source: Janet Arndt.

AT SEA: ABOARD THE *DUNERA* AND THE *QUEEN MARY*

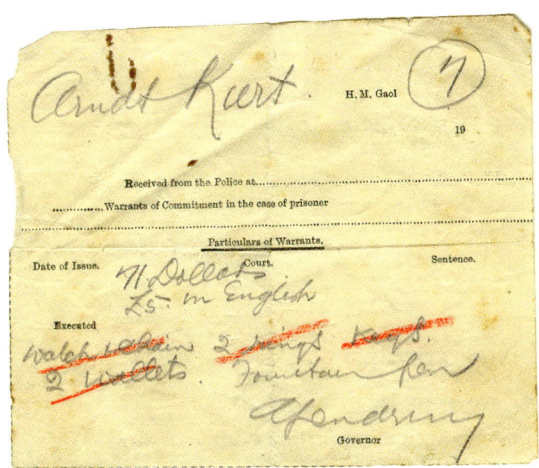

Wally and Kurt Arndt, items seized on board the *Queen Mary*, September 1940, and never returned

Possessions taken from internees tended to disappear even on the *Queen Mary*, but the systematic destruction of personal papers on the *Dunera* was a form of cruelty, especially to young and lonely men, unknown on the *Queen Mary*.

Kurt Arndt was arrested in Koslin, Pomerania, after Kristallnacht. As we have already noted, after his release he married Wally, a lodger in the Arndt household, and they immediately boarded a Japanese ship bound for Shanghai. They disembarked in Singapore, where Kurt had relatives, and were later interned there.

Source: Janet Arndt.

Music and lyrics, 'Nights of Singapore'

These sheets of music are from the collection of Kurt and Wally Arndt. 'Why had I to leave you so very soon', reads one lyric from 'Nights of Singapore'.

Source: Janet Arndt.

AT SEA: ABOARD THE *DUNERA* AND THE *QUEEN MARY*

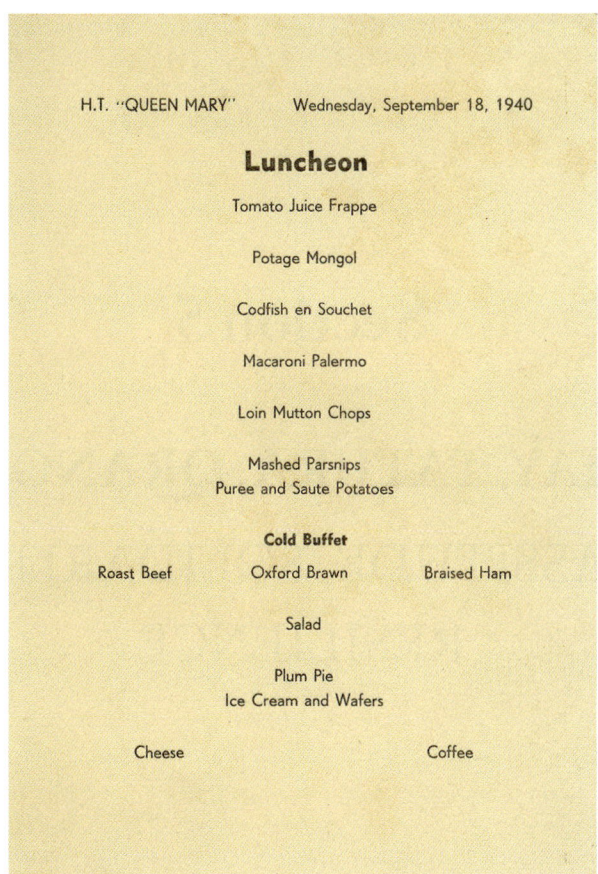

***Queen Mary* luncheon menu, 18 September 1940**

Nothing could differentiate more the history of the *Dunera* from that of the *Queen Mary* than this menu for 18 September 1940, by which time the *Dunera* internees were already in Hay and Tatura.

Many who sailed from Singapore to Sydney on the *Queen Mary* remembered festive meals such as this one.

The *Queen Mary* docked in Sydney on 25 September 1940.

Source: Janet Arndt.

Section 5

HAY, TATURA, ORANGE
LASSITUDE, SOLIDARITY, RESILIENCE

INTRODUCTION

There were pathways of cultural resistance to imprisonment in many of the camps holding inmates of various kinds. Often these efforts unfolded under extreme duress. In Ravensbrück concentration camp in 1944, French ethnologist Germaine Tillion hid in a cardboard box during the day, and having escaped her work detail, was able to compose an operetta, *Verfügbar aux Enfers*, roughly translated as 'The camp worker in hell'. Every evening she shared elements of the operetta and added dark humour and song suggested by her fellow prisoners. In Theresienstadt, Hitler's 'showcase camp', Jewish children performed Czech composer Hans Krása's *Brundibár*, an opera for children he had written just before the war; he continued to write music until he was deported and murdered in Auschwitz. Children's drawings from Theresienstadt and other camps form a heartrending archive of the imagination of the young who vanished in the Holocaust.

In prisoner of war (POW) camps, the fight against inactivity and lassitude frequently took the form of individual or collective cultural projects. Some were intended to preserve 'morale', however defined; many were intended to fill the seemingly endless expanses of time prisoners faced. A game of football or a sing-song were easy enough to get going; so were concert parties in the evenings. At these events, prisoners could almost imagine normal life; what it once was and one day might be again.

By the time the internees on the *Dunera* reached their inland camps, hunger and maltreatment were things of the past. Their main enemies were boredom and bitterness. The internees were held at three Australian internment camps – at Hay in western New South Wales, Orange on the Central Tablelands of New South Wales, and Tatura in northern Victoria – and in each place a kind of enforced cultural life took root.[1] This was true even of Hay, where the physical circumstances were most arduous.

At this point it is important to note an irony. While none of the internee population chose incarceration, imprisonment saved many from a worse fate. The 265 or so men, women and children arrested in Singapore and deported on the *Queen Mary* were spared Japanese occupation. The men arrested in England and deported on the *Dunera* were not under the Blitz in the autumn and winter 1940; none was in combat. Some did later serve in the armed forces, but most of the *Dunera* population never fired a weapon, and never had a weapon fired at them.

The internees occupied a variety of political positions across a spectrum from communism to Nazism. The numbers are hard to calculate. There were at least 60 committed socialists and communists, and possibly more, though the Commonwealth Investigation Branch's estimate of 120 communists is probably an exaggeration.[2] Many communists were attracted by the Party's trade union credentials rather than its Marxist or Stalinist ideology. One such man was Ludwig Baruch, who had been heavily involved in trade unionism in Bradford, where he had lived since 1925. He was a Jewish tailor's cutter originally from Hamburg.

Alongside socialists and communists were Nazi sympathisers, but not many. Hundreds of other internees had no more political commitment than Australians at large. For the camp authorities at Hay, Orange and Tatura, the political persuasion of internees was a concern only when verbal and physical disagreements led to disturbances, as happened occasionally. Otherwise a man's politics were less important than his loyalty: was he for or against the Allies?

Australian politics also exercised the internees. The election in October 1941 of John Curtin's government was well received at Tatura, for many internees perceived the Labor Party to be more sympathetic to their predicament than the United Australia Party. In opposition, senior Labor politicians, including Curtin, Herbert Evatt and Ben Chifley, had raised concerns with government ministers about the incarceration of the *Dunera* and *Queen Mary* internees.

Internment left scars on many internees. Paul Schatzki drew a 'Nightmare' filled with memories of the *Dunera*. Ludwig Hirschfeld-Mack's visual reverie, which has become known as 'Desolation', though he left it untitled, captures another sombre mood, that of a man gazing at the stars, living behind barbed wire, powerless in the face of fate. Robert Hofmann's sardonic sketch 'God punishes us' is a dark and ambiguous meditation on the difficulties faced by the Orthodox Jews among the internees.

In many cases, internees struck a positive note. In portraiture, sketches and paintings, the internees depicted the strength of individuals, the habits of fellow internees, daily life in the camps, and the land beyond the barbed wire. Flowers, birds, trees and hills served as subjects for those who worked in black and white or in colour.

Internees played in and attended concerts, gave and listened to lectures, and wrote poetry, some in German, others in English. Protestants and Catholics prayed alongside robust Jewish *minyanim*. Bible study and explorations of the Talmud flourished. *The Boomerang*, one of a number of camp publications, included articles on a range of subjects to entertain and inform internees: some of the writing in this camp newspaper was of startling quality. Irreverent and breezy revues evoking the night life of Berlin and Vienna may have diminished the loneliness and disorientation of men far from home, however they configured that term.

What makes these internees' projects unusual is their cultural coherence, marked by the love of learning of the *Bildungsbürgertum*, or the educated German and Austrian middle classes. As in other, more terrifying, camps in Europe and Asia, learning was profoundly important to internees in Hay, Orange and Tatura. Participation helped create a collective, a brotherhood beyond that already formed on the *Dunera*. Together they organised what Klaus Loewald called 'little republics', autonomous islands of sanity in a world gone mad.

There are similarities between the cultural resistance of these German and Austrian internees in Australia in the Second World War, and that of civilians from Allied countries in the First World War who were stuck in Berlin and interned at the city's Ruhleben racetrack. There eminent scholars taught and younger men studied languages and science in ways that anticipated the *Collegium Taturense*, the camp university established by internees at Tatura. American citizens of Japanese origin interned in prison camps in the Second World War in the United States also developed children's schools and classes for adults.

In creating a self-governing college at Tatura, the *Dunera* and *Queen Mary* internees added unknowingly to a rich tradition of study and scholarship among prisoners in the Pacific theatre. British POW Frank Bell even organised examinations for his secret students at 'Kuching University', located within a Japanese prison camp in Borneo. Elsewhere, POWs worked towards degrees through the International Red Cross. There was an educational programme at Changi prison in Singapore. One scholar entitles her study of these projects 'The Barbed-wire University'.[3] The *Collegium Taturense* was part of that world.

The civilian internees in New South Wales and Victoria were not under the physical or psychological pressure of many POWs; they were not starved and did not fear arbitrary beatings or death. Yet there is abundant visual evidence of their ingenuity, intelligence, talent and energy, and their determination to keep their minds active. Their arrival and stay in Australian internment camps was the product of rank injustice; what they managed to do together was to support each other and to draw from their skills, their self-respect, and their learning a sense that the wrongs they had endured did not define them. Their vision was greater than that of the authorities who had interned them.

✳✳✳

On arrival in Australia, most internees from Britain went directly to Hay, where they were held in camps 7 and 8. By mid-1941 they had been sent to camps in Tatura, where the climate was more temperate. For medical care and other reasons, about 400 internees went from Hay to Tatura via a camp in Orange.[4]

The four parts of this section trace these trajectories. The first focuses on Hay. The second deals with Tatura in the period September 1940 to mid-1941, when the camps at Tatura housed some *Dunera* internees and all the *Queen Mary* internees. The third shows aspects of life in the camp at Orange. The fourth returns to Tatura and tells the story of internment from mid-1941 on.

In this section there is more on Hay and on the later months of internment at Tatura, in sections 1 and 4, than on the early months at Tatura and on internment at Orange, in sections 2 and 3. This distribution of images enables the reader to follow the path of most *Dunera* and *Queen Mary* internees in their years of Australian confinement.

Notes

1. Some *Dunera* internees were held in camps at Loveday in the Riverland of South Australia. Most of these men were on their way back to Britain and remained at Loveday for a short time only. The *Dunera* population at Loveday was always transient.
2. NAA, MP508/1, 255/744/344, Refugee Deportees from England, 1941-2.
3. Midge Gillies, *The Barbed-Wire University: The Real Lives of Prisoners of War in the Second World War* (London: Aurum, 2011). See also: http://www.dailymail.co.uk/news/article-2004037/British-prisoners-studied-degrees-trained-doctors-WW2-captivity.html#ixzz4XeA6h5SF
4. 51 internees were interned only at Hay or at Hay and Orange. Menasche Bodner died at Hay. 50 other internees returned to Britain before the men from the *Dunera* were brought together at Tatura in mid-1941.

SECTION 5A

INTERNMENT: HAY, 1940–1941

SECTION 5A.1
THE PHYSICAL ENVIRONMENT

THE PHYSICAL ENVIRONMENT

Hay railway station, c. 1940

For most of the *Dunera* internees, Hay railway station marked the end of their passage from British arrest to Australian incarceration. Their disorientation was intensified by the harshness of the landscape; most were city dwellers.

Hay Railway Station, Hay, Australia. Jewish Museum of Australia collection, 3138.2

Dust storms, Hay

Fred Harrison, a Hay resident, took these photographs in the late 1940s. Dust storms, remote from the experience of the *Dunera* internees, covered everything and everyone in their paths. A dust storm greeted internees on their arrival in Hay.

Source and copyright: David Harrison.

THE PHYSICAL ENVIRONMENT

Hay, Australia

A hand-drawn and painted image of Australia bounded by barbed wire. The only site marked on the continent is Hay.

Robert Loewenstein, born in 1921 in Laufenselden, South Hesse, Germany, gave this card to Werner Hirschfeld in May 1941. Hirschfeld was born in 1922 in Küstrin, Prussia. Küstrin is now Kostrzyn Odra in western Poland.

The *Dunera* internees were held in camps 7 and 8. Camp 7 housed liberal Jews, Zionists and Orthodox Jews who chose to observe Jewish dietary laws. It was also home to men and boys who had been refugees at the Kitchener internment camp in Britain, and the ORT boys from Berlin who had studied and lived together in Leeds. Assimilated and non-observant Jews were lodged in both camps. Catholics, Protestants, and internees professing no religion, principally communists and social democrats, were also found in both camps, though more of them lived in camp 8 than 7. In the jocular shorthand of the Australian guards, camp 7 was 'kosher' and camp 8 'communist'. The labels are misleading, for hundreds in camp 7 were not orthodox Jews, and communists were a small minority in camp 8.

Werner Hirschfeld collection, Sydney Jewish Museum, M2015/018:010.

Sandstorm, 1940

Ludwig Hirschfeld-Mack conjures a Hay 'sand storm' filled with menace. Dust storms, as they were known locally, carried with them bits of grit and sand which stung the skin.

Ludwig Hirschfeld-Mack, *Sandstorm* 1940, drawing in watercolour over black pencil; additions in varnish. Image 20.5 x 21.7 cm, sheet 20.5 x 21.7 cm.

National Gallery of Australia, Canberra. Gift of Chris Bell 2015. Copyright: Chris Bell.

THE PHYSICAL ENVIRONMENT

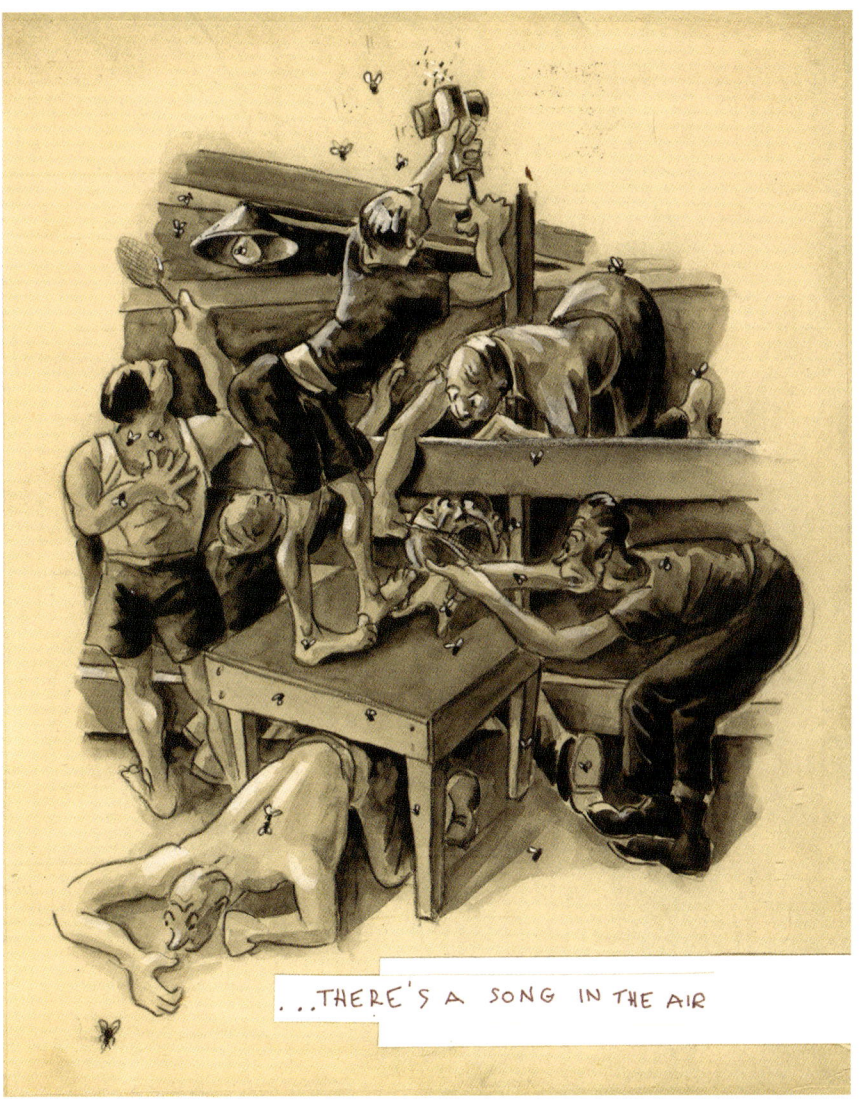

There's a song in the air

Fritz Schönbach's sketch shows flies of all kinds creating a maddening cacophony. The frenzy induced by these pests describes a battle the internees lost in the hostile climate. The title refers to 'The Donkey Serenade', a song popular since the late nineteenth century.

There's a song in the air, undated. Black and white gouache on paper.

From the Archive of Australian Judaica, Rare Books and Special Collections, the University of Sydney Library. Copyright: Schonbach family.

On the edge of the world

Two internees stroll along a barbed wire fence, beyond which a watch tower and a dead eucalypt define the forbidden world of freedom. The drawing was probably done at Hay. The artist is unknown.

<small>*On the edge of the world*, c. 1940–1942, pencil on paper. Jewish Museum of Australia collection, 7030.</small>

THE PHYSICAL ENVIRONMENT

Sic Transit Gloria Mundi

Emil Wittenberg's sketches of internment as infinite lassitude drew in new directions Breughel's motif of sleeping peasants in a field. There is also an echo of Max Beckmann's paintings of the death of Rosa Luxemburg and the revolutionaries of 1919, whose splayed feet signal defeat and execution. The parrot perched on the wire above the internee is an Australian touch. The Latin title *Sic Transit Gloria Mundi* – so passes the glory of the world – tells of the internees at low ebb.

Source and copyright: Martin Burman.

'A Sign of Civilisation' and 'Barbed Wire'

Barbed wire became a symbol of the internees' plight. Wittenberg returned to this motif repeatedly. The top image Wittenberg called 'A Sign of Civilisation'. He gave the bottom image a more prosaic title: 'Barbed Wire'.

Source and copyright: Martin Burman.

THE PHYSICAL ENVIRONMENT

Beyond internment

In the top image, the road leads out of a camp toward something resembling life. To get there, Wittenberg shows the need to break the Lilliputian bonds and nails securing each of his stained fingers to the ground (bottom). E40941 was Wittenberg's internee number.

Source and copyright: Martin Burman.

In a different time and place

Fritz Schönbach takes a sardonic look at the plight of internees. His caption for this image reads: 'To think that I used to have fifty 'phone-calls a day'.

Source and copyright: Schonbach family.

THE PHYSICAL ENVIRONMENT

Cigarette tin

The front of a cigarette tin, engraved at Hay, shows an Australian scene; the back a European townscape. The Australian floral images are folded into messages of thanks and good wishes; the European scene is a tourist's image of old Europe, replete with battlements and wooden-beamed houses. The identity of the artist, initials A. W., is unknown.

Source: Sydney Jewish Museum, M2015/009:034.

SECTION 5A.2
WAITING FOR FREEDOM

'Camp-Parliament'

In camp 7 a meeting on 18 September discussed the constitution written on a roll of toilet paper while the *Dunera* was heaving through the Indian Ocean. The authors of that document – Gerd Buchdahl, Peter Herbst and Peter Laske – were believers in liberal democracy as they had experienced it in England, and trusted that a British dominion would give them more humane and civilised treatment than they had been getting at the hands and boots of the guards on the *Dunera*. In writing the constitution they had assumed that there would be a compound of huts such as internees had occupied in English camps.

Each hut would elect a representative to a council which would meet in public at least once a week, and which would possess legislative powers, exercised by majority vote. Its members would forward written ideas for camp policy which the council chairman would read out at every meeting after 'question time'. Every six neighbouring huts would also elect a committee – a kind of cabinet – which under the chairmanship of a camp manager nominated by the council would supervise the work of the kitchen, canteen, bank, post office, laundry and orderly service. The committee's decisions would require ratification through the council. A three-man court of arbitration, elected by universal and secret ballot, would act as final authority in constitutional matters, arbitrate in personal disputes, and judge public accusations. The constitution would have to be accepted by a majority of hut representatives, and could be altered by a two-thirds majority of the council or by referendum.

Andreas Eppenstein, a 25-year-old Jewish statistician from Breslau (to Poles Wroclaw) and a graduate of the London School of Economics, was elected leader of camp 7. As his deputy the camp elected an older man, Dr Hans Frankenstein, a 40-year-old physician from Allenstein in East Prussia who was spokesman for a group of about 250 refugees from the Kitchener camp. Eppenstein now chaired the debate on the constitution, leading the discussion line by line through both the Buchdahl-Herbst-Laske text and a contending proposal. The structure adopted was not very different from the one described on the ship's toilet paper.

On Eppenstein's initiative, the elections to camp 7's parliament, as it came to be called, were completed before the end of September. The inmates of camp 8 had voted for a structure so similar as to suggest that the separation of the two camps was not yet total until it was formally effected on 26 September.

In both camps the machinery of self-government was soon working well enough to satisfy most of its users, and to have successive Australian army officers, assigned to Hay as camp commandants, content to let the internees conduct their own affairs. Klaus Loewald, an internee born in Berlin in 1920, wrote of camp 7 that it 'assumed the character of a small working republic.'

In the image on the previous page, Fritz Schönbach captured the vigorous character of democracy among the internees in Hay. Simply having a voice in their own affairs mattered to those deprived of freedom.

Source and copyright: Schonbach family.

Quotation from K. G. Loewald, 'A Dunera Internee at Hay, 1940–41', *Historical Studies* 17: 69, 516.

Camp currency

Like prisoners in other times and places and conditions, internees at Hay and Tatura used their wits to devise rudimentary systems of exchange to act as substitutes for money. They were not allowed to hold British or Australian currency except with permission of the military authorities and then only in small amounts. In the early months of incarceration, enterprising individuals made vouchers intended to be used for the purchase of modest items – shaving gear, canned fruit, cigarettes – at camp canteens. Early in 1941 one group at Hay – the Roebucks, who occupied hut 26 in

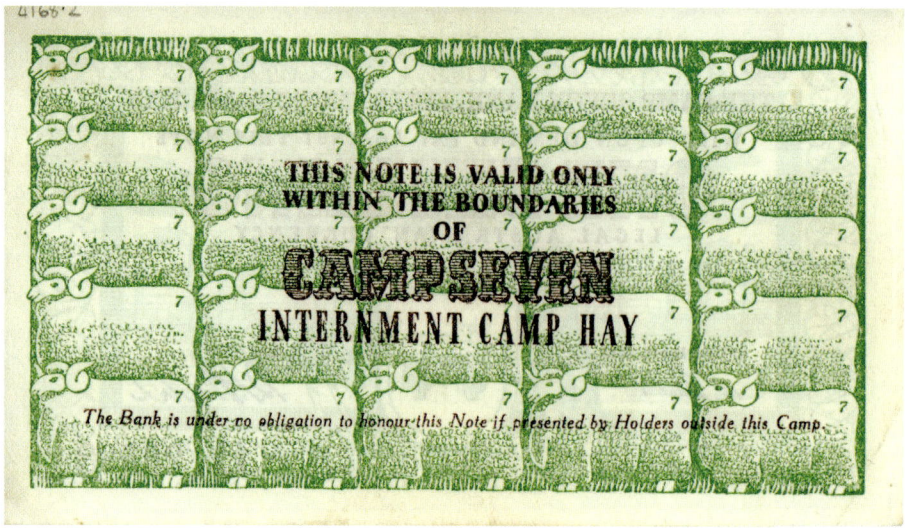

camp 7 – created an elaborate monetary arrangement involving the use of what they proudly called 'our camp money'. The experiment did not last long, but it was remembered as evidence of the internees' will to civilise the environment into which fate had cast them.

This hut accommodated a formidable array of artistic, professional and intellectual talent, presided over by camp 7's elected spokesman Andreas Eppenstein. Among them were the artist Erwin Fabian, the aspiring philosopher Kurt Baier, and the young banker Richard Stahl. Possibly the most accomplished occupant was George Teltscher, a 37-year-old Viennese of Jewish origins and Lutheran persuasion. In the course of an adventurous life he had embraced communism, fought for the Spanish

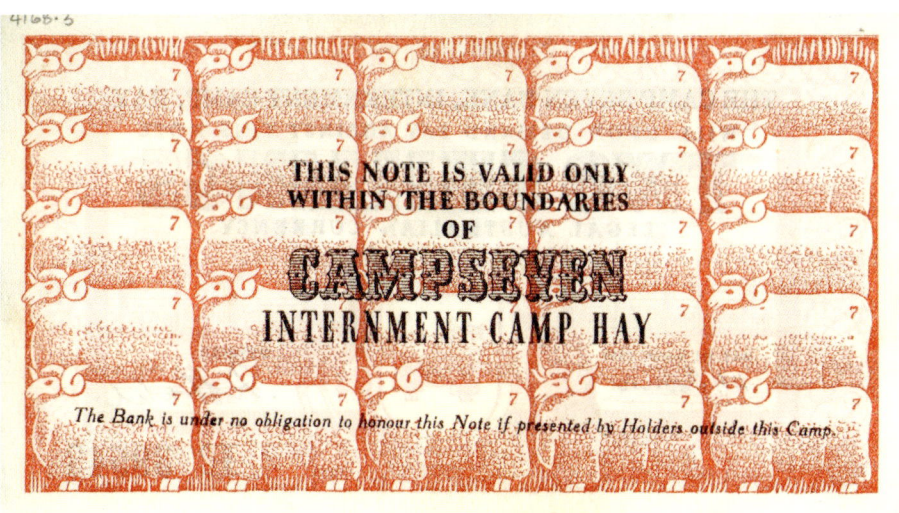

republic, studied in Weimar at the Bauhaus, where he lived by the movement's gospel that art and craft are one, and designed a coin for Austria's banking system. One way and another Teltscher was remarkably well equipped to design a camp currency. The commandant of camp 7 gave his approval for the project. A local printing firm, publisher of the bi-weekly newspaper *The Riverine Grazier*, welcomed the prospect of collaboration across the otherwise separate worlds of town and prison. At a price within the reach of internees who had accounts with the Hay branch of the Commonwealth Bank, the printer supplied 'banknotes' of three denominations: blue for sixpence legal Australian currency, green for one shilling, red for two shillings.

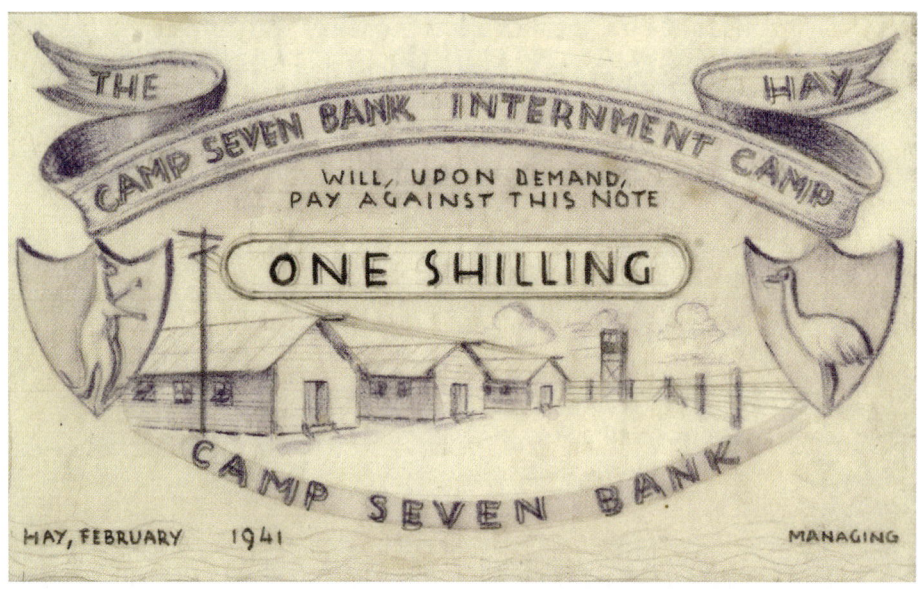

Teltscher's design was rich in meanings overt and hidden. On the front of each note an emu and a kangaroo support a coat of arms bearing the image of a merino ram into whose fleece is woven the name of Eppenstein. They are about the same size as actual Australian banknotes, though of much smaller denominations as befitted their modest purpose, proclaimed on the reverse as being 'valid only within the boundaries of Camp Seven Internment Camp Hay'. The reverse side is occupied by a phalanx of merino rams, five rows of five, each with the numeral 7 embedded in its rump.

Three thousand notes of each denomination were delivered to camp 7 in the last days of March 1941, to be greeted with admiration by all parties involved in their making. 'The design and artistry are attractive and splendidly executed,' wrote the manager of the Commonwealth Bank's Hay branch to his counterpart in camp 7, keeper of the camp bank, 'and very creditable to Mr Teltscher.' He sent a set of notes to head office in Sydney, 'where, I know, they will create a good deal of interest.'

In Sydney the notes created interest and alarm. Careful scrutiny – perhaps more careful than anyone at Hay had undertaken until then – revealed that within the rim of curled barbed wire depicted on the obverse side of every note run the words WE ARE HERE BECAUSE WE ARE HERE BECAUSE WE ARE HERE BECAUSE WE ARE HERE. This old soldiers' lament, sung to the tune of Auld Lang Syne, was so familiar to the internees and so apposite to their plight that they called it the Hay-Tatura hymn.

WAITING FOR FREEDOM

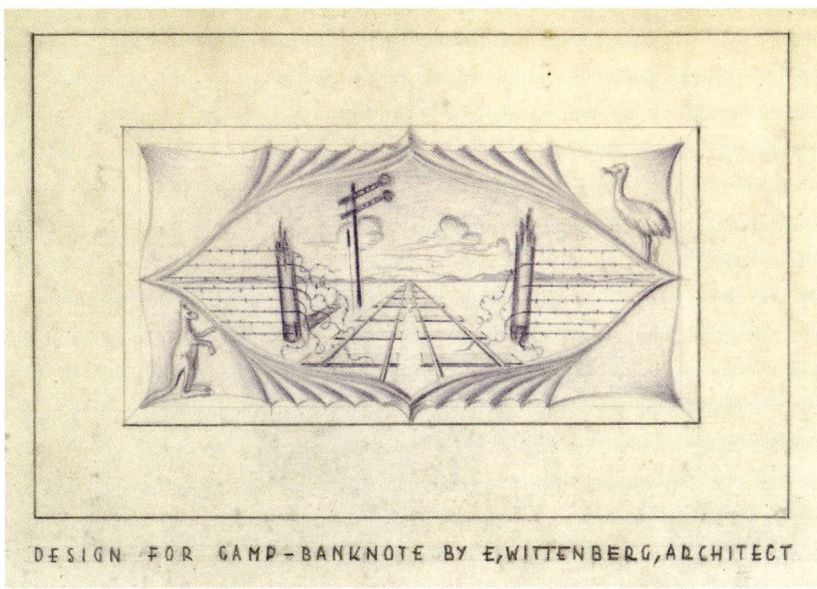

DESIGN FOR CAMP-BANKNOTE BY E. WITTENBERG, ARCHITECT

Cautious officials could see that such a bleak statement of the internees' plight should not be allowed to emanate from a document for which the Australian government bore ultimate responsibility. Moreover, when they looked up the relevant statute they discovered that the purported banknotes were illegal. An order was issued for the collection and destruction of the notes. Some prescient internees spirited theirs away.

Connoisseurs of currency can read a rich history in Teltscher's handiwork. Their price at auction has soared over the years. In 2006 a shilling note fetched $12,500. 'These wonderful banknotes', writes Nick Anning, 'offer an insight into the pride, artistic talent and optimistic spirit of the internees'.

Teltscher won the right to design the currency by entering a competition. Another entrant was Emil Wittenberg of hut 13, camp 7. His proposed designs appear on this page and the previous page. One of the scenes is familiar (see page 123).

Images on pages 129-31. George Teltscher, *Sixpence, one shilling and two shilling notes,* 1941. Jewish Museum of Australia collection, 4168.1, 4168.2, 4168.3. Copyright: Sara Adams.

Images on pages 132-33. Source and copyright: Martin Burman.

References

Correspondence Concerning Camp Currency, 1941-42, Jewish Museum of Australia collection, 4129.1-11

M.H.R. Bulluss, *The Hay Internment Camp Notes: A Catalogue of Confirmed Surviving Specimens,* (Sydney: The Metropolitan Coin Club of Sydney, 1994).

Nick Anning cited in James Cockington, 'In World War II, Refugees in Australia had their own Currency', *Sydney Morning Herald,* 2 March 2016.

'Not too overbad. Isn't it?'

Hans Rothe's 1941 cartoon shows Australian soldiers at the top of a watchtower at Hay. The town has been converted into a flooded plain. One internee, submerged, raises his hand from the water to demand release.

Hans Rothe, *Not Too Overbad. Isn't It?*, 1941, ink on paper. Jewish Museum of Australia collection, 3346.

WAITING FOR FREEDOM

'The Galah from Hay'

This series of four drawings (this page and over leaf) by Fritz Schönbach places the internees' longing for freedom on the wings of the galah. The woman who gives the galah a home in a cage is knocked over by the force of the bird's cry for release.

Source and copyright: Schonbach family.

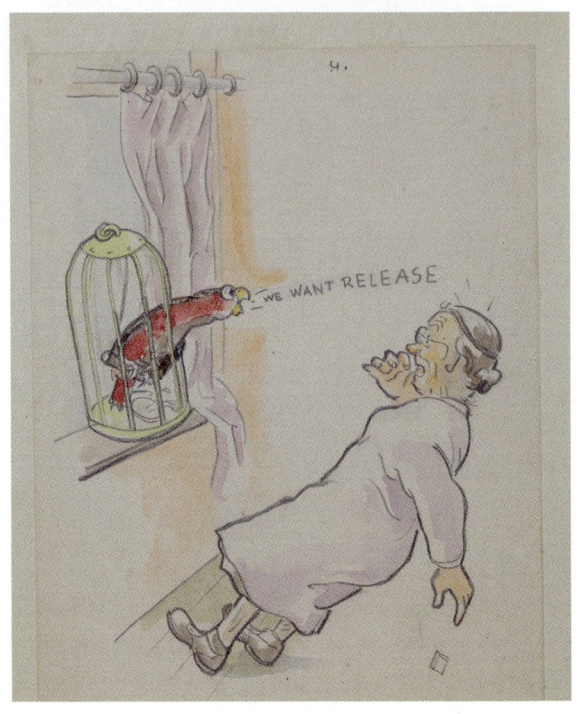

WAITING FOR FREEDOM

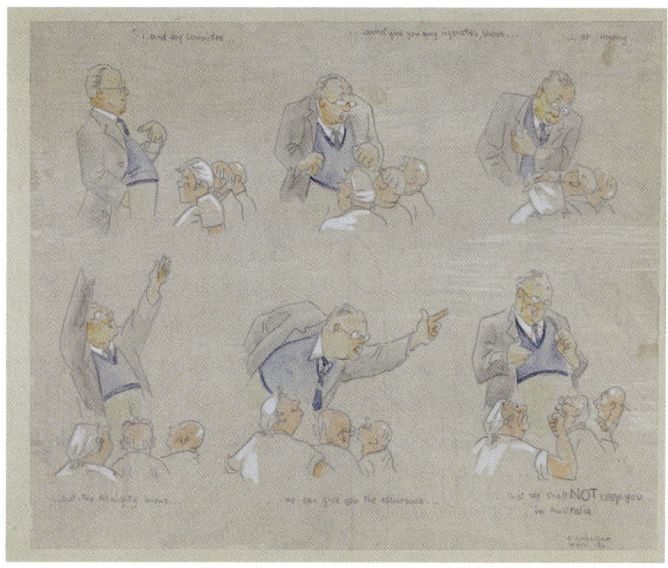

Walter Brand's visit to Hay

Fritz Schönbach captured the visit to Hay of Walter Levi Brand, secretary of the Australian Jewish Welfare Society. A London-born immigrant to Australia in 1920, Brand was officious and condescending to the internees, warning them that, while he sympathised with their plight, they were not welcome in Australia.

Brand was among those Jews who saw these potential refugees as troublemakers threatening the gains made by existing Jewish communities in Australia. His remarks embittered a number of internees.

Source and copyright: Schonbach family.

'God punishes us'

Robert Hofmann's caricature of four Jews pondering their fate is entitled 'A propos Meschumadim'. This term refers to reprobate Jews; those who have abandoned their brothers and their faith.

The man on the left, clearly puzzled, says: '"God punishes us", said Brand, but this is not possible here among us when we don't even have Matzah'.

The caption is ambiguous, and may mean simply how can we be punished any more than is already the case?

Robert Hofmann, *A Propos Meschumadim*, 1941, pencil on paper.

Jewish Museum of Australia collection, 7024.

Margaret Holmes

Margaret Holmes (1886–1981), general secretary of the Australian Student Christian Movement, was a founder in 1938–39 of the Victorian International Refugee Emergency Committee. From that base she did more than anybody to help *Dunera* internees find their way into Australia. She was active in supplying them with books, musical instruments, sheet music, and other resources for study which enabled them to take university courses. In 1945 she became Australian secretary for World Student Relief. Internees and others remembered her as an outstanding representative of interdominational activism, a Melburnian tradition.

This photograph was taken in 1951.

Source: Renate Howe.

Julian Layton

Major Julian Layton was the British Home Office's emissary, sent to sort out problems associated with compensation, repatriation and other issues affecting internees. He expected to stay a year; in the event he stayed until almost the end of the war. As his rank was honorary, he wore civilian clothes, always dapperly.

This photograph was published in Sydney newspaper *The Sun* on 25 March 1941, the day after Layton's arrival in Australia.

The Sun, Sydney, 25 March 1941, p. 5. Source: National Library of Australia.

They said: 'All your cases will be investigated'

Fritz Schönbach's sketch, complete with punning label, depicts an internee sitting on his bunk. Head on hand, elbow on knee, this is the classic pose of melancholy. The label on the internee's valise, or suitcase, reads: 'Travel by liner'. Schönbach often turned to droll humour, bringing a light touch to serious matters.

They said: 'All your cases will be investigated' Hay, 1940, pencil on paper.

From the Archive of Australian Judaica, Rare Books and Special Collections, the University of Sydney Library.

Copyright: Schonbach family.

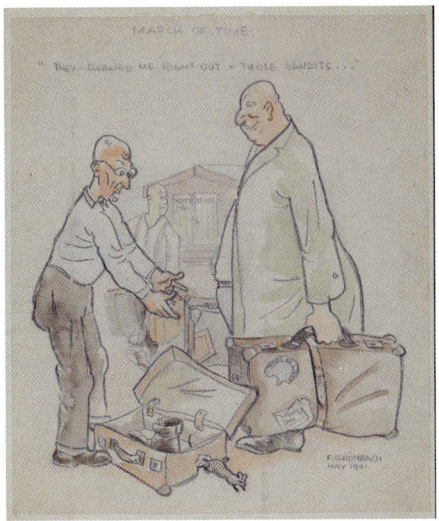

'March of time' (1)

Fritz Schönbach produced several series of images which he labelled the 'march of time'. He used these images to highlight the absurd ways in which the internees' situation changed.

In the top image, one internee asks a second to sympathise with him for having had personal effects stolen from him during the *Dunera* voyage. In the image below, the internee bemoans his fate: compensation is now on offer, yet he had no personal items stolen.

Source and copyright: Schonbach family.

'Hay-camp Nachtstimmung' and 'Worries'

Layton's visit to Hay in April 1941 inspired hope in some and anxiety in others. Those already disoriented by internment had no idea what the future would bring. Not surprisingly, these thoughts disturbed the nights of some internees. Nachtstimmung translates as 'night atmosphere'.

Fritz Schönbach's images were often biting, and rarely meant only as light visual entertainment. At times he returned to caricatures and added to them, as in these drawings.

Source and copyright: Schonbach family.

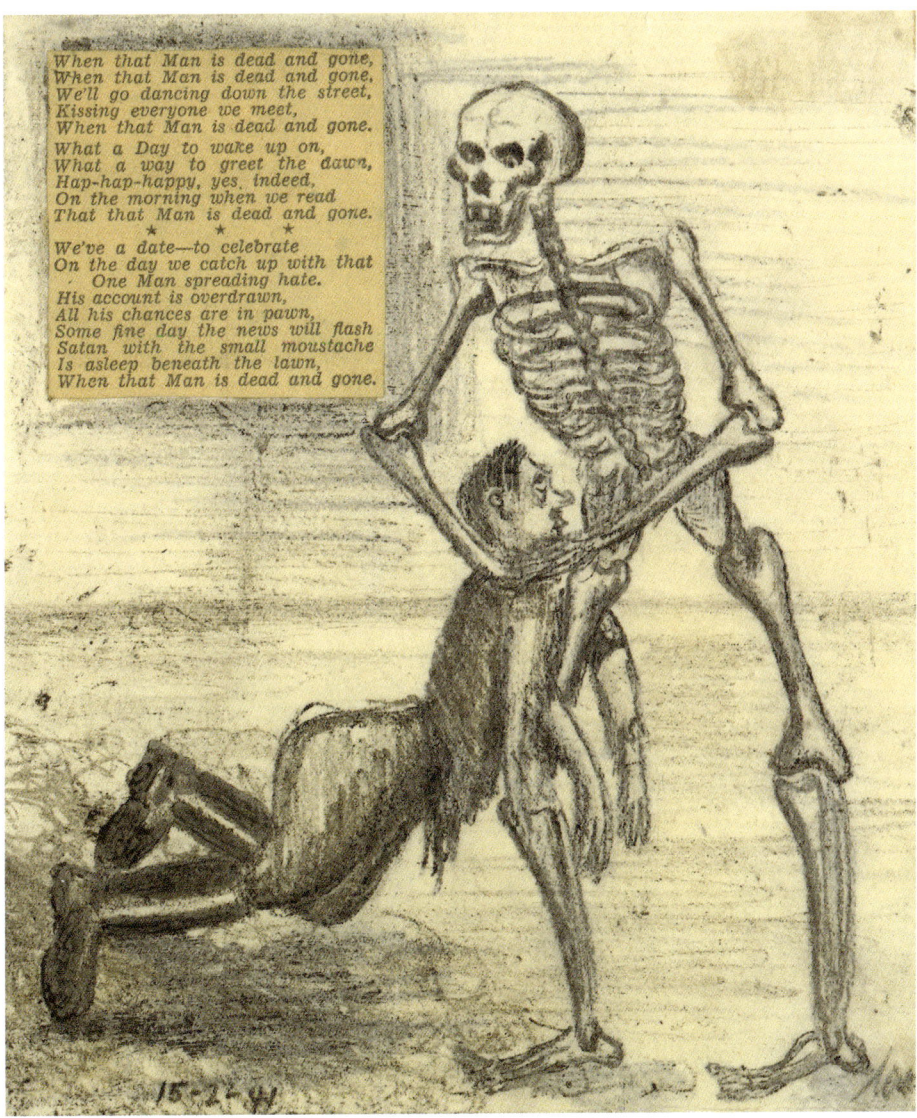

The future?

Emil Wittenberg turned the savagery of the Nazis against them in this sketch of a skeleton strangling Hitler.

Source and copyright: Martin Burman.

SECTION 5A.3
ADAPTATION

ADAPTATION

Scenes of camp life

The prospects of release and compensation were not the only matters that exercised internees. From the time they arrived at Hay, efforts were made to build and shape a polity. Reminiscent of George Grosz's teeming drawings of Berlin and Berliners, Fritz Schönbach's sketch is both less savage and more humorous.

In the foreground, men read, play football, or enjoy a game of cards. In the middle ground naked figures use the camp showers. Gardeners tend their sunflowers under the gaze of a parrot on the right, while gymnasts exercise on the left. In the background, beyond the barbed wire, guards march and a horse-drawn wagon goes about its business.

Fritz Schönbach, *Scenes of camp life*, 1940–1942, pencil on paper. Jewish Museum of Australia collection, 7036.

Food at Hay (1)

Fritz Loewenstein's evocation of breakfast at Hay gives no hint of complaint about camp cuisine. The internees enjoyed the food they were given. Among the internee cooks were chefs who had worked in posh hotels in Europe – one at the Savoy in London – and who were able to transform army rations into the tastes of home; schnitzel, frankfurts, strudel and other German and Austrian specialties. Sachertorte and chocolate cake were sold at camp canteens.

Several months after the internees' arrival at Hay, arrangements were made for Orthodox Jewish internees, including rabbis, to visit local abattoirs and oversee the preparation of kosher meat.

Fred Lowen, *No title*, 1941, pencil on paper. Jewish Museum of Australia collection, 3114.

ADAPTATION

Food at Hay (2)

Alfred Landauer, an artist and musician born in Vienna in 1910, painted this watercolour in 1940 or 1941. The man cooking at the end of the table is Karl (also Carl) Hans Nathan Strauss, later known as Charles Strauss, born in 1901 to a Jewish family in Mülhausen, Germany, now Mulhouse, France.

Among the men waiting eagerly for Strauss to dish up is Herbert (Max) Bruch, a Jewish motor mechanic born in Insterburg, East Prussia, in 1920. He is in the centre foreground, to the left of the man smoking a pipe.

Source: Bruch family.

Inside a hut (1)

Although internees enjoyed vastly more space in Hay than on the *Dunera*, their conditions were cramped and privacy was hard to find. The sketches are by Emil Wittenberg. The second image he entitled 'Home, Sweet Home'.

Source and copyright: Martin Burman.

ADAPTATION

Inside a hut (2)

Theodor Engel, born in Vienna, was one of the older internees. An engineer, he was 54 when he sailed on the *Dunera*. Engel was a keen artist, who used different styles and media to depict the *Dunera* experience. He created an extensive and diverse visual record of internment.

Sydney Jewish Museum, M2015/009:014.

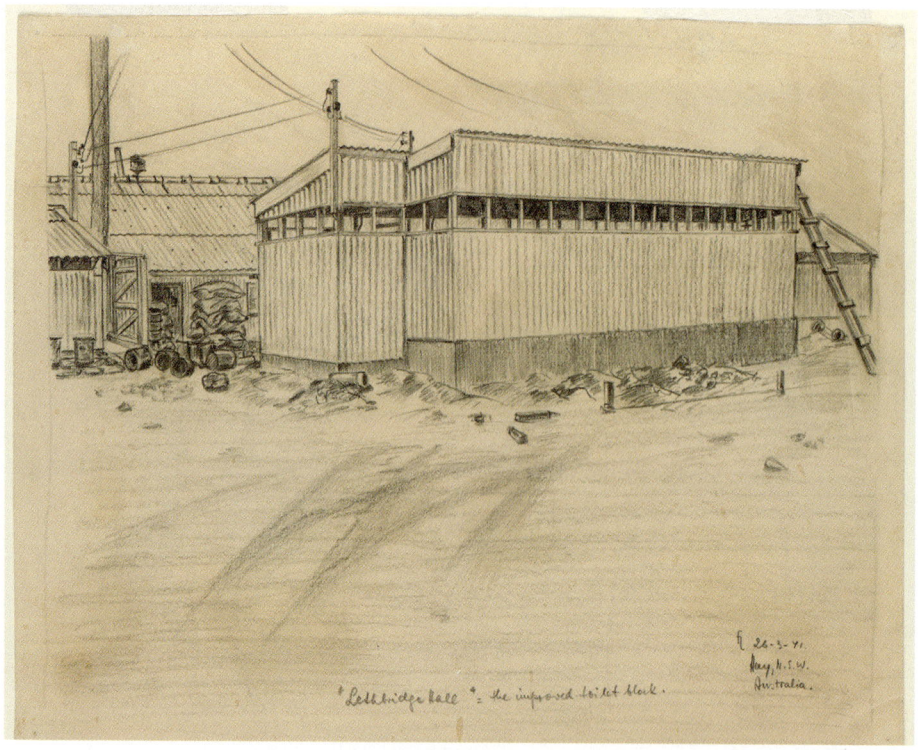

'Lethbridge Hall', Hay

Fritz Loewenstein's view of the collective privy, Hay, March 1941. Sanitary arrangements in the camps were well organised but spartan. Internees called this amenity Lethbridge Hall, in honour of a visiting medical officer who was widely believed to underestimate their discomfort.

Fred Lowen, *'Lethbridge Hall' – The improved toilet block*, 26 March 1941. H91.350/4, Pictures Collection, State Library of Victoria. Copyright: Monica Lee Lowen and Jocelyn Lowen.

ADAPTATION

'Hay Camp Hospital'

Theodor Engel's sketch of the camp hospital in Hay is peaceful. A seated gentleman, probably an internee, reads his newspaper, while someone further along sweeps the path. Engel spent weeks in the hospital as a patient in late 1940.

Theodor Engel, *Hay camp hospital*, 1940, pencil on paper. Jewish Museum of Australia collection, 3918.

'Man reading', Hay 1941

Erwin Fabian, a Berlin-born artist, presents the internee-reader. Reading was an essential element in camp culture. For the young, it was part of their informal education. For the older internees, it was a window on worlds past and present.

Both camps 7 and 8 had libraries, each with collections of more than 1200 books. An escape into fiction or non-fiction was a way to fill the tedium of captivity.

Erwin Fabian, *Man reading* 1941, brush and ink wash over pencil, 37.5 x 27.8 cm (image) 44.2 x 28.2 cm (sheet). National Gallery of Victoria, Melbourne. Presented through The Art Foundation of Victoria by Mr Erwin Fabian, Member, 1997 (1997.56). Copyright: Erwin Fabian.

ADAPTATION

Sport at Hay (1)

To occupy their enforced leisure, internees resorted to a wide variety of competitive activities. Indoors, dining tables served between meals for table tennis and playing cards, while chess enthusiasts sat hunched for hours over their boards. Those who played in the regular table tennis tournaments faced stiff competition: Alfred Liebster from Vienna was a professional table tennis player and one of the best in the world.

Among outdoor activities, football (soccer) was the most popular sport, followed by European handball. The contests pitted against each other teams from clusters of huts and attracted followings hardly less ardent than the European originals from which some of them took their names, such as Arsenal or Juventus. They had, of course, never heard of Australian Rules football.

The diary kept by Gunter (Mike) Sondheim, born in Dusseldorf in 1916, provides vivid evidence of the importance of sport in camp life. About 200 internees watched a table tennis tournament he organised in camp 7 in late November 1940.

Many internees would remember the months in camp as the fittest time of their lives.

This drawing, by Fritz Loewenstein, is entitled 'Hay – watch tower and sports field'.

Fred Lowen, *Hay – watch tower and sports field*, 17 April 1941. H91.350/5, Pictures Collection, State Library of Victoria. Copyright: Monica Lee Lowen and Jocelyn Lowen.

Sport at Hay (2)

This card, printed from a Ludwig Hirschfeld-Mack woodcut, was presented to Dr Alfred Wiener, an industrial chemist born in Jaslo in Poland in 1906. He served as a spokesman for internees in camp 8, and was an honorary member of the camp's champion football team, 1940–1941.

The image at right belonged to Werner Hirschfeld, a keen sportsman. It was given to him by Kurt Lindenberg.

Above: *Card given to Dr Alfred Wiener*, 1941. Jewish Museum of Australia collection, 4120.1.

Right: Werner Hirschfeld collection, Sydney Jewish Museum, M2015/018:005.

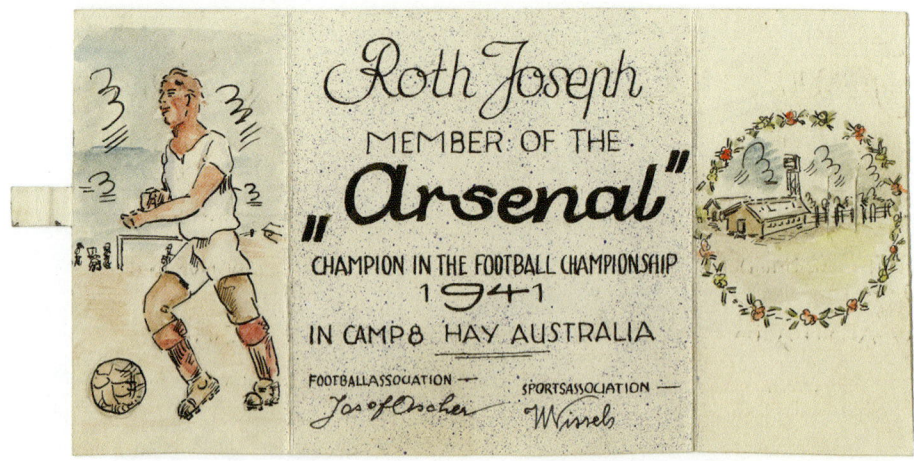

Sport at Hay (3)

This card was presented to Joseph Roth, member of the 'Arsenal' football team which won the football championship in camp 8, Hay, 1941.

The formal signatures of the secretary of the camp's Football Association and its Sports Association parody the sports press in Britain and Germany. So does the laurel wreath on the right made of barbed wire.

The German form of quotation marks around Arsenal, and the inversion of the footballer's name, suggest that the transition from German to English grammar and syntax was incomplete.

Membership card of Joseph Roth, 1941. Jewish Museum of Australia collection, 3302.

> HAND BALL   TEAMS
>
> KANGAROOS   FIRST XI
>
> PETER SIRKIN   HUT 23
>
> MARTIN SCHENTHAL ALFRED LEWINSKY
>
> KURT WEISS · K.H. SCHÄDLICH · HEINZ DANZIGER
> HUT 21   CAPTAIN
>
> A. STERN · RUDI METH · SIGI GROSBARD · C.A. ROTHENBERG · HEINZ SIMON
> HUT 25   HUT 21
>
> WILLI HERR · ERNST MONDSCHEIN · FRITZ LEVY · ROLF KOENIGSBERGER · AXEL KOWALIK
>   HUT 25   HUT 21
>
> JOHNNY GROSBARD ·   HEILNER ·   ERNIE MICHAELIS
> CAPTAIN   HUT 21
>
> ERICH DELFINER   · KURT ABRAHAMSON
>
> MANFRED LINDNER   HUT 21
>
> KANGAROOS   SECOND XI

Sport at Hay (4)

Alfred Lewinsky from Berlin, known to friends in camp 7 as 'Alfred the Great', was a member of the Kangaroos first XI European handball team. Internees looked to the new world as well as the old in naming their sporting teams.

Birthday card to Alfred Lewinsky, 1941. Jewish Museum of Australia collection,, 3463.

'Murrumbidgee River'

In hot weather, internees at Hay could be escorted to swim in the Murrumbidgee River. Emil Wittenberg drew the scene in February 1941. Guards watch the internees from a distance.

Source and copyright: Martin Burman.

ADAPTATION

Swimming in the Murrumbidgee

Ludwig Hirschfeld-Mack's woodcut gives an almost abstract feel for the palpable relief of men swimming in the summer heat.

Ludwig Hirschfeld-Mack, *Hay (Bathers on the Murrumbidgee River, N.S.W.)*, 1940–41, woodcut, printed in dark brown ink, from one block, printed image 13 x 18 cm, sheet 20.6 x 26.1 cm.

National Gallery of Australia, Canberra. Gift of Olive Hirschfeld 1979. Copyright: Chris Bell.

'Camp Fashion Welfare Outfit', Hay, 1941

This bearded figure with a pot belly and a cane used a pith helmet to protect his head from Hay's fierce sun. Another man, possibly a guard, strides purposefully in the opposite direction. Mockery of the foibles of inmates was a common response of prisoners of all kinds in both world wars. The identity of the artist, initials S. H., is unknown.

Camp fashion, welfare outfit, 1941, pencil on paper. Jewish Museum of Australia collection, 3609.

Advertisement for the Pacific Hairdresser, camp 8, Hay

Leonhard Posner, from Dresden, was 30 years old when interned and deported on the *Dunera*. His wife and child remained in Britain.

A hairdresser by trade, Posner worked as the camp 8 barber. This poster, drawing on the conventions of Madison Avenue, did more than impart information: it sought to attract custom.

The Pacific hairdresser shop poster, 1941. Jewish Museum of Australia collection, 3404.

'Still thinking of his girl'

Fritz Schönbach captures the loneliness of isolated men, longing for their loved ones on the other side of the world. All the men seated are in pairs, finding some kind of solace in male companionship. But what of the single man in the centre of the drawing, striding alone, without an outlet for his frustration?

Source and copyright: Schonbach family.

SECTION 5A.4
LEARNING AND LIVING

Heinz Lippmann's book

At Hay, Heinz Lippmann, 19, continued his studies. On the front of his exercise book he offered his own wry commentary on his 'subject' and 'class'. Art, music, and learning helped internees adapt to their having been exiled to a strange new world.

Source: Australian National Maritime Museum, ANMS0220[002].

> XIII. SCHOOLS: Numerous courses have been commenced by interned professors. Text books are provided as much as possible by the authorities. Recently an order for £150 was sent for the camp schools at Hay.
>
> The school at No. 7 German camp has 101 subjects comprising 181 classes and is followed by 560 pupils. There are classes in languages, natural science, technology, agriculture, arts and religion.
>
> German Camp No. 8 has 75 professors teaching 110 subjects to 380 pupils and 400 listeners. Subjects comprise, English French, Italian, Spanish, Latin, Greek, Hebrew, Esperanto, Music, Arts, Geography, Mathematics, Physics, Chemistry, Biology, Medicine, Psychology, Botony, Zoology, Agriculture, Minerology, Economical Political and Commercial Science and Civics.

Continuing education

Dr Georges Morel, delegate of the International Committee of the Red Cross in Australia, inspected the Hay camps in March 1941. He described a vivid educational world, with fully 75 'professors' teaching 110 subjects to 380 internees in camp 8 alone. Camp 7 had 181 classes attended by 560 pupils.

Source: National Archives of Australia, A2908, P22, Part 4, Internees from UK to Australia, Dunera, 1940–1. Copyright: National Archives of Australia.

UNIVERSITY	NAME	COURSE	YEAR
OXFORD	Rapp G.	Mod.Lang.	second
	Schmidt C.M.J.	Chemistry	third
CAMBRIDGE	Danziger H.	Medecine	fifth
	Danziger P.	Medecine	sixth
	Freudenstein E.G.	Chemistry	first
	Koenig H.P.	Medecine	sixth
LONDON	Abrahamson K.	Economics	second
	Altmann P.	Elec.Eng.	fourth
	Arnstein H.	Engineering	first
	Blumenthal H.	Philosophy	first
	Buchdahl H.	Physics	for Ph.D.
	Cineder B.	Chemistry	first
	Eisenklam P.	Engineering	first
	Darnbacher F.	Architecture	first
	Feuchtwanger O.	History	first
	Freuthal G.	Engineering	first
	Guttmann R.	Engineering	second
	Grodzinsky H.	Economics	first
	Hager G.A.	Elec.Eng.	second
	Hoffmann H.	English	for M.A.
	Koenigsberger H.P.	Law	first
	Loeb H.W.	Science	first
	Loehr M.L.	Engineering	first
	Loewensberg P.	Economics	first
	Michaelis W.G.	Chemistry	first
	Mayer P.	Economics	second
	Nowottny H.	Classics	for Ph.D.
	Preisinger F.	Engineering	first
	Reichmann K.	Engineering	second
	Ruhstadt K.	Engineering	first
	Schaedlich K.	Mod.Lang.	third
	Steckelmacher W.	Engineering	first
	Strauss R.	Metallurgy	first
	Weber I.	Law	fifth
	Weinberg S.	Engineering	third
MANCHESTER	Schwarz F.	Chemical Eng.	second
LEEDS	Baumgarten G.	Engineering	first
	Billitzer A.W.	Chemistry	third
DURHAM	Forell G.	Divinity	first
	Mautner F.	Physics	first
NOTTINGHAM	Goldschmidt E.	Textiles	first
	Merzbach H.M.	Textiles	first
BELFAST	Ewald A.H.	Chemistry	first
BRISTOL	Levistein B.	History	for M.A.
LOUGHBOROUGH	Kessler H.P.	Autom.Eng.	fourth
ROY.COLL.PHYS. AND SURG. (Scottish Branch)	Dr.C.Weiss	Medecine	qualifying exam.

List of internees whose university studies were interrupted by internment

Among the internee population at Hay were 46 students who had matriculated at British universities, 29 at London, 17 at Oxford, Cambridge and other universities.

Source: National Archives of Australia, MP508/1, 255/714/64, Dunera Internees at Hay, Memo by Sir Frederick Jordan, 1939–41. Copyright: National Archives of Australia.

LEARNING AND LIVING

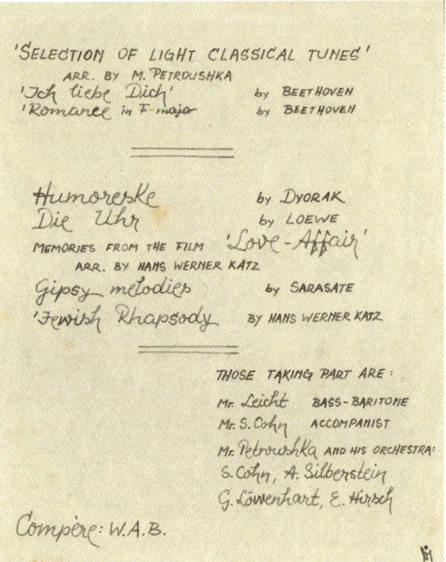

Programme for music concert, Hay, December 1940

Majer Pietruschka, a Hungarian, was born in Opatow in Poland in 1901. A talented musician, he organised an orchestra which gave concerts in camp 7. The audience at this performance was treated to a wide selection of music, from Beethoven and Dvořák to gypsy melodies and a Jewish rhapsody. The concert was staged by the camp's Recreation Department. The watercolour on the programme cover is by Paul Glass, an artist born in Vienna.

National Library of Australia, MS5392/4, Records of Hay internment camp, 1940–1941 (Rabbi Falk collection). Copyright: Valerie Reynolds.

 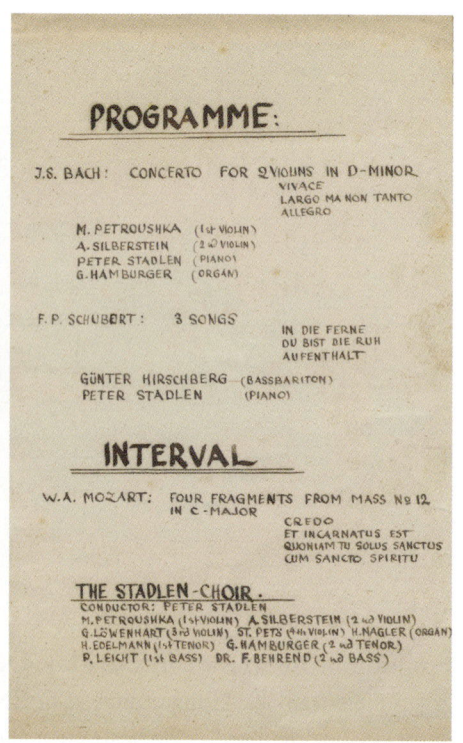

Programme for music concert, Hay, February 1941

The eminent Viennese pianist Peter Stadlen and 'the Stadlen choir' perform a concert of Bach's double violin concerto, Schubert *Lieder*, and sections of Mozart's *Requiem*. This camp 7 concert was staged by the Musical Department. The watercolour of Venice is by Paul Glass.

Sydney Jewish Museum, M2015/009:015a-b.

LEARNING AND LIVING

Poster, Peter Stadlen piano recital

Bertold Meier was a German-born poster artist, who used his skill to create a poster advertising a Stadlen concert, including works by Schubert, Beethoven, Chopin and Stravinsky.

Music was one way in which Berlin and Vienna were brought to the bush.

Piano recital poster, 1941. Jewish Museum of Australia collection, 3152.

Setting the stage

This picture, possibly of a stage set from a camp production, was drawn by the surrealist artist Hein Heckroth for Emil Wittenberg. Wittenberg designed the stages for many performances in Hay and Tatura. Heckroth's sketch includes a Harlequin from the *Commedia dell'arte* tradition (left), and an abstract female figure, boots and all (right).

Source and copyright: Martin Burman.

LEARNING AND LIVING

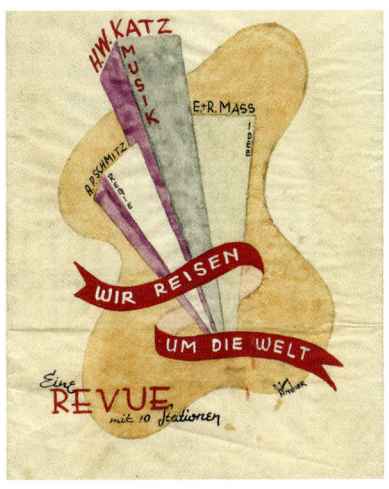

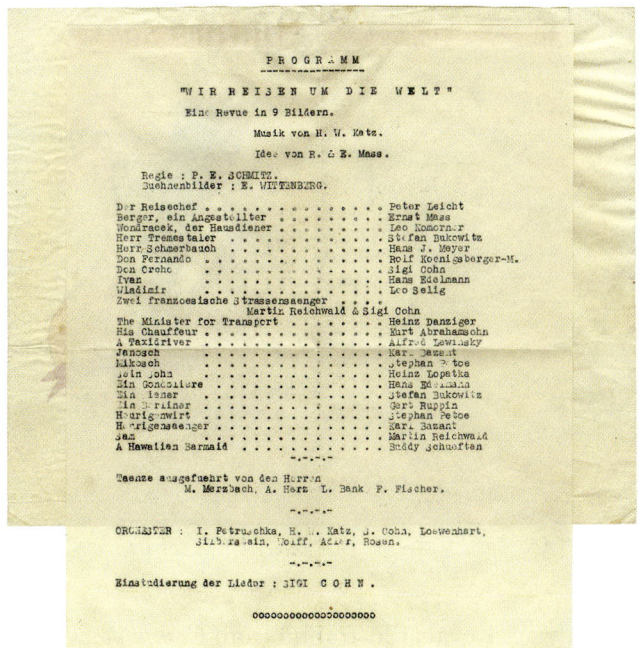

Programme and cast list for the revue *Wir reisen um die Welt*, Hay, 1941

Internees in camp 7 at Hay staged a revue entitled 'We Travel Around the World', based on an idea of the Viennese brothers Robert and Ernst Mass. The director was Peter Schmitz, a former ballet dancer from Berlin, and Hans-Werner Katz, a Danzig-born composer, wrote the score. The stage sets were designed by Emil Wittenberg. The revue was staged in English in May 1941.

P. Schnitz, *Wir reisen um die Welt*, 1941. Jewish Museum of Australia collection, 3458.

'Always Happy – Always Loyal', illustration from *Camp News*

Animal visitors to the zoo (also known as internment camp) are impressed with the decorous, satisfied, and smiling demeanor of the species behind bars.

This illustration, artist unknown, appeared in *Camp News*, first published in camp 8 in December 1940. The articles were in German.

Internees in camp 7 could boast of an earlier publication. The first edition of *The Forum*, an English-language newspaper, appeared on 25 November 1940.

National Library of Australia, MS5392/4, Records of Hay internment camp, 1940–1941 (Rabbi Falk collection). Copyright: Nina Glasser.

LEARNING AND LIVING

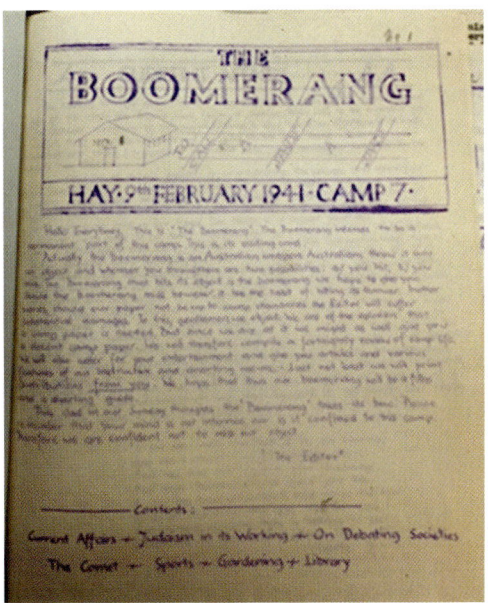

The Boomerang, camp 7, Hay, February 1941

'Please remember', the editors of the first number of *The Boomerang*, a new camp newspaper, wrote in February 1941, 'that your mind is not interned, nor is it confined to this camp'. The editors capture the spirit of defiance which drove efforts to organise cultural life in Hay and Tatura. The newspaper offered enlightenment on a range of subjects from current affairs to Jewish matters to sports and gardening. *The Boomerang* usually appeared weekly. It was published both in Hay and in Tatura, and ran to at least June 1942 and fifty editions. One issue included letters from internees in Canada to their brothers in Australia.

The Boomerang, 1941. Jewish Museum of Australia collection, 4173.

Invitation to a reading of Kipling and short stories, Hay, May 1941

Alfred Lewinsky, the reader, was a 23-year old Berlin-born handbag-maker and designer. He was a Londoner who had escaped Germany with his mother. His fluency in English gave him a skill which internees would have to master, both in camp and in their uncertain post-internment lives.

Kipling's verse and children's stories were best-sellers world wide.

Invitation to a poetry reading by A. Lewinsky, 1941. Jewish Museum of Australia collection, 3437.

LEARNING AND LIVING

Hans Lindau, botany of Australia

Written on 2500 individual sheets of toilet paper, Hans Lindau's exploration of the botany of Australia is both a labour of love and an instance of the kind of affirmation of the life of the mind created by the internees.

One of the older internees, Lindau was born in Berlin in 1895, and had left Germany for England well before the Nazis came to power. After the war he taught geography at a school on the Mornington Peninsula in Victoria and planted his beloved eucalypts in front of the school.

This photograph was taken in the mid-1960s.

Source and copyright: National Library of Australia, MS10098. Papers of Hans Lindau, 1940–1943.

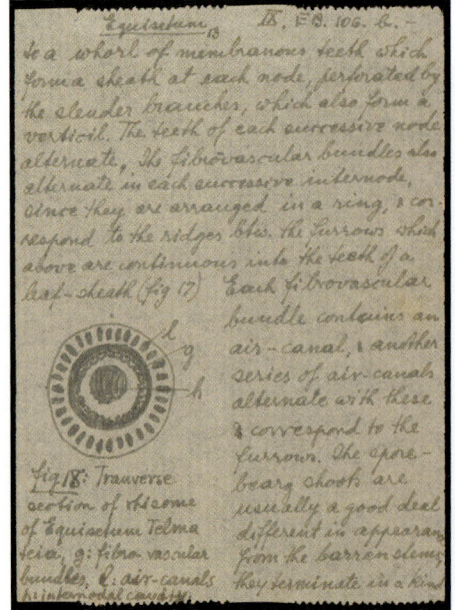 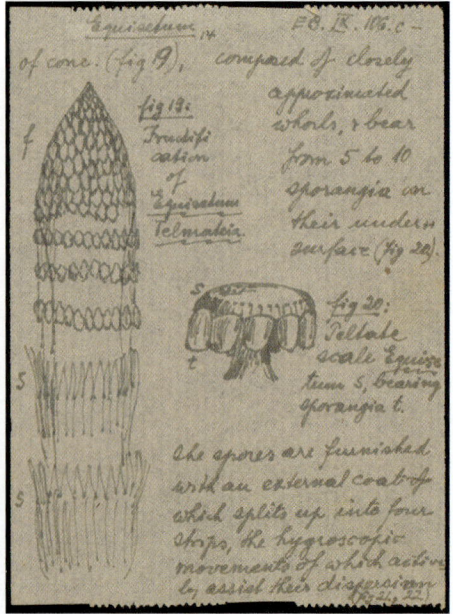

Botany

The care and acute intelligence of the botanist enabled Hans Lindau to study Australian plants in rigorous and original ways.

Lindau's miniatures included studies of the structure of spores (right) and comments on the pharmacological uses of certain plants.

The fountain pen and ink Lindau used to create his botanical study were provided by Quakers.

Source and copyright: National Library of Australia, MS10098, Papers of Hans Lindau, 1940–1943.

LEARNING AND LIVING

Worship at Hay

There were about 400 Christians, of varying commitment, among the *Dunera* internees. Of this number, about 160 Protestants are named on the lists of the Reverend Franklin Alcorn, a Church of Christ minister and army chaplain. He conducted interdenominational services and was much respected by his congregations in camps 7 and 8. He supplied them with reading material, friendship and spiritual comfort. Before Alcorn's appointment in early 1941, services were conducted by local Protestant ministers, or by the internees themselves.

The sketch is by Alfred Landauer, a member of Alcorn's camp 8 congregation.

For the 130 or so Catholics, initially Mass was said by the local priest, and in camp 8 by Father Walter Koenig, a Jesuit. Later, Koenig worked with a Catholic army chaplain to provide for the religious needs of Catholic internees. Born in 1881 in Herford, Germany, Koenig was one of the oldest internees.

For the majority of *Dunera* internees at Hay who identified as Jewish, the authorities did what they could to provide amenities for worship. The commandant allowed internees in camp 7 to convert an unused hut into a place of worship, with separate sections reserved for Jews and Christians. Liberal Jews were more likely than Orthodox to see the hut as a synagogue.

Orthodox Jews at Hay observed strict dietary laws and studied Torah and Talmud, much of it committed to memory by learned members of their group. Hut 3, camp 7, was one centre of Orthodox Judaism at Hay. Rabbis Hans Blumenthal, Ernst Ehrentreu, and Oscar Feuchtwanger were among its occupants. The one rabbi in camp 8 was David Moritz, born in 1875 in Gimbsheim, Germany.

Sydney Jewish Museum, M2015/009:023.

Holy Communion, Hay

A farewell notice of morning service and communion, led for the last time by the Reverend Alcorn. Seats were set aside for non-communicants.

Sydney Jewish Museum, M2015/009:032.

> Strange things do happen in the world to-day,
> And one, indeed, is our way to Hay.
> Cast out by Nazi rule for good,
> We set on England our wandering foot;
> The freedom found there is but short,
> For nations soon to war resort.
> Across the seven seas we strive
> Souls, bodies broken – just alive.
> Then in the depth of our distress
> You, Sir, are first to give us bless.
> And our faces become bright,
> Forget the dark and see the light,
> And even life in here so grey
> We easier bear without dismay.
> And now there comes the day you part –
> Too quick for many a sorrow heart;
> But our friendship will remain:
> No, not "Good bye", – "See you again"!
>
> Hay, Easter 1941.
>
> *Eric Lipmann*

Poem for Reverend Alcorn

The Viennese brothers Erich (Eric) and Bruno Lipmann, born in 1917 and 1918 respectively, were raised in a secular household. Their Jewish father and Catholic mother had abandoned religion in order to marry. On arrival in Australia Bruno and Erich gave their religion as Protestant. Most likely they were Protestants in name only, their 'faith' determined by the need to declare a religion for officials registering the internees.

This poem, written by Eric, could be seen as evidence that his attachment to Protestantism was nominal. It reads as a tribute to a friend rather than as an affirmation of Christian faith.

Sydney Jewish Museum, M2015/009:006.

SECTION 5A.5
THE LANDSCAPE OF INTERNMENT

THE LANDSCAPE OF INTERNMENT

Rain at Hay (1), 1941

This painting by Theodor Engel of camp 8 at Hay is unusual in depicting the landscape as waterlogged. In winter the rains came, but most internees recalled the dryness of their environment.

Source: National Library of Australia, MS5392, Records of Hay internment camp, 1940-1941 (Rabbi Falk collection)

Rain at Hay (2), 1941

The sight of water also caught the eye of George Teltscher, a Bauhaus-trained artist. He painted this picture in early May 1941.

Source: Stocky family. Copyright: Sara Adams.

THE LANDSCAPE OF INTERNMENT

'Hay camp, with sentry-box', 1941

Some internee artists had difficulty adjusting their European eyes and palettes to the Australian landscape. Others, including Erwin Fabian, captured with ease the different hues of land and sky.

Erwin Fabian, *Hay Camp, with sentry-box* 1941 , gouache, 34.1 x 52.0 cm (image) 36.5 x 52.0 cm (sheet). National Gallery of Victoria, Melbourne, purchased 1997 (1997.55). Copyright: Erwin Fabian.

Hay skies

George Teltscher depicted both the big sky of inland Australia and the space internees had once they left their huts.

Teltscher, like Fabian, was able to adapt his style to capture something uniquely Australian. This picture was painted in April 1941.

Source: Stocky family. Copyright: Sara Adams.

THE LANDSCAPE OF INTERNMENT

'Australia', Hay, 1941

Hein Heckroth presents a vision of Australia as a chess board on which naked figures exist in isolation. A man at centre leans on a pawn, above a dog with a hat, rather than a horse. A naked woman looks in a mirror on the left. None of these figures sees each other or the future.

Heckroth, born in Giessen in 1901, started his career with the German National Ballet. He fled Germany, and worked as a stage designer for *Don Giovanni,* the first opera staged at Glyndebourne in 1936.

By then most German surrealists were labelled by the Nazis as degenerate artists, whose works were to be destroyed. This supposedly insulting title was a sign of honour for those who bore it.

The red of this surrealist scene anticipates Heckroth's greatest film success. He received an Academy Award for the best art design (colour) in film for the 1948 picture 'The Red Shoes'.

Hein Heckroth, *Australia* 1941, oil on board, 47 x 59 cm.

National Gallery of Australia, Canberra. Purchased with the assistance of James Agapitos OAM and Ray Wilson OAM 2007. Copyright: Christian Routh and Jonathon Jodi Routh.

Red kangaroo

Local flora and fauna were frequently portrayed in internees' drawings, such as this one by Emil Wittenberg. To depict a kangaroo in full flight was subtly to describe the frustrations of imprisonment.

Source and copyright: Martin Burman.

THE LANDSCAPE OF INTERNMENT

'Schwejk feeding his Australian parrots'

An Austrian Jew like Fritz Schönbach would have read at school Jaroslav Hašek's *The Good Soldier Schwejk*. Covering his head with a handkerchief, this Schwejk shows all the unmilitary awkwardness of the original.

Fritz Schönbach, *Schwejk feeding his Australian parrots*, 1941, pencil on paper. Jewish Museum of Australia collection, 3148.20.2.

Australian birds

This page from the diary of Hans Neuwahl shows that he could not quite get the hang of the spelling of 'Coikaburra'. These two kookaburras sit on barbed wire, a common visual reference and motif among camp artists.

This sketch was Neuwahl's version of the picture printed on the front of internees' exercise books (page 164).

Source and copyright: Rosemary Newall, Karin Morrison and Susanne Platt.

THE LANDSCAPE OF INTERNMENT

Tortoises

George Teltscher used red and blue-grey tones to paint tortoises on the Murrumbidgee River.

Source: Stocky family. Copyright: Sara Adams.

New year's card, Hay, 1940–1941

A kangaroo offers presents to an inmate on the other side of the barbed wire. Here is one anonymous take on Australian generosity, with the kangaroo's pouch serving as a substitute for Father Christmas's sack of season's greetings and gifts.

Presents also passed the other way. To mark Christmas 1940, the internees made toys to give to local children whose families were poor. As the local newspaper reported: 'The toys were made chiefly of scraps of materials, paper, cardboard, rags, and odds and ends of wood. Some of them bore signs of having been executed with no small degree of skill and patience, despite the lack of tools and suitable materials.'

New Year postcard, 1941. Jewish Museum of Australia collection, 3448.

Quotation from *The Riverine Grazier*, 31 December 1940, p. 2.

SECTION 5A.6
FAREWELL TO HAY

'March of time' (2)

Fritz Schönbach offers a sartorial panorama of the passage of internees from elegant civilian attire, to dishevelled dress on the *Dunera*, to the torn clothes of an internee, to fig leaf and slouch hat. The heroic figure wearing the slouch hat holds a rifle. Did Schönbach, in 1941, foresee the possibility of internees joining the Australian army?

Source and copyright: Schonbach family.

FAREWELL TO HAY

Farewell card

Internees leaving Hay camp often departed with a copy of this woodcut print by Ludwig Hirschfeld-Mack, complete with signatures and good wishes. Versions are found in many collections of *Dunera* material.

'IXL' was an advertiser's pun for a jam familiar to Australian households and evidently well known to internees. In the circumstances of 1940–1941, to use such coded language was a sign of being part of a community. Here the jam tin is used as a flower pot.

Ludwig Hirschfeld-Mack (1893–1965), *Hay camp 1940–41*. 1940, woodcut on paper.

The University of Melbourne Art Collection. Gift of Mr Reinhold Eckfeld 2006. 2006.0104.

Copyright: Chris Bell.

Our thanks to Kurt Morgenroth for pointing out the IXL association.

SECTION 5B

INTERNMENT: TATURA, 1940–1941

SECTION 5B.1
DUNERA INTERNEES AT TATURA, 1940–1941

DUNERA INTERNEES AT TATURA, 1940–1941

Tatura, c. 1940

The *Dunera* docked at Port Melbourne on 3 September 1940. German merchant seamen and Italian internees disembarked, as did all other survivors of the *Arandora Star*. A further 95 men disembarked because the camps at Hay could not accommodate everyone aboard the *Dunera*. All these men were taken directly to Tatura, where they were interned.

The selection of the 95 may have been based on the alien classification they were assigned in Britain. Alternatively, selection may have been random.

Source: Kurt Liffman.

Camp 3, Tatura

There were four internment camps at Tatura in which internees from Australia and overseas were housed. Camp 3 is pictured here. The photographer is unknown.

The photograph is from the collection of Bern Brent, who as Gerd Bernstein was among the *Dunera* internees who left the ship at Melbourne on 3 September 1940. They were taken initially to camp 2 at Tatura. By the end of the month he and other non-Fascist internees had been moved to camp 3, away from those whose sympathies lay with Hitler's and Mussolini's regimes. In August 1941, Bernstein was moved to camp 4.

Tracing the movement of internees at Tatura can be difficult. In many cases we do not know who was held in which camp at what time.

Source: Bern Brent.

DUNERA INTERNEES AT TATURA, 1940–1941

Camp scene, 9 December 1940

There is nothing to suggest confinement in this watercolour by Leonhard Adam of a summer camp scene at Tatura in late 1940. Adam's paintings tell of more than rank injustice.

Leonhard Adam, *Group of men, Tatura camp*, 1940, watercolour, 19.6 x 28.4 cm, Australian War Memorial ART28627. Copyright: Mary-Clare Adam.

'Sonnenaufgang', 16 March 1941

Adam's sunrise captures the pastel shades of the sky set against the blue-green trees. As usual in Adam's paintings, we see no barbed wire. We do see fence poles, but the barrier is suggested rather than shown.

Leonhard Adam, *Sonnenaufgang (Sunrise), Tatura camp*, 1941, watercolour, 19.5 x 28.5 cm, Australian War Memorial ART28626. Copyright: Mary-Clare Adam.

DUNERA INTERNEES AT TATURA, 1940–1941

Leonhard Adam, self-portrait, January 1941

The penetrating blue eyes and carefully combed hair of Leonhard Adam made him a distinctive figure in Tatura. Fifty years old in 1941, he was an accomplished scholar and amateur artist, with a set jaw and a determined look.

The signature of the artist at bottom right includes the Latin phrase 'Ipse feci' or 'I myself did this'. Was this reference the playfulness of an educated man, or the pride of a self-taught artist, a man like the German painter Dürer who looked at himself and the world without flinching?

Source: Tatura Irrigation and Wartime Camps Museum. Copyright: Mary-Clare Adam.

Arandora Star memorial

Robert Felix Emil Braun, a German Lutheran, was born in Nancy, France, in 1902. His internee forms list his occupation as 'Master of Art'.

This picture shows the sculpture he created to the memory of those who died when a German U-boat torpedoed and sank the *Arandora Star* on 2 July 1940. Braun was one of the men who was rescued from that disaster and put aboard the *Dunera* a week later. They left the ship when it docked at Port Melbourne.

The sculpture, erected in camp 3 in July 1941, was demolished in 1947 or 1948.

'Tatura 1941', *Collegium Taturense Anniversary 1940–1941* booklet, Sir Thomas Karran Maltby collection, University of Melbourne Archives, 1961.0018.00001, p. 17. Copyright: Maltby family.

SECTION 5B.2
QUEEN MARY INTERNEES AT TATURA, 1940–1941

Mothers and children at Tatura, December 1940

The *Queen Mary*, carrying internees from Singapore, docked at Sydney on 25 September. The internees made the long trip, by ferry, train and truck, to Tatura, where they entered camp 3. They lived in separate compounds. One held married couples, children, and single women, the other single men aged 16 and over.

Loretta Seefeld (hand raised in the centre) is shown with a group of mothers and children. Loretta's mother Doris had died in Singapore in 1934, shortly after giving birth to Loretta's sister, also Doris. Doris and Loretta had an older brother, Freddy. The three children had lived with their paternal grandparents Dr Arthur and Sophie Seefeld in Hamburg from 1935 to early 1939. They fled the Nazis in February 1939 for Singapore leaving Freddy, for educational reasons, in London with an aunt and uncle. Gerhard Seefeld, the children's father, had remarried in 1938. His second wife Rosie gave birth to Gerald in 1938 and Valerie in March 1940.

Three generations of Seefelds were deported from Singapore on the *Queen Mary*: Gerhard and Rosie; children Loretta, Doris, Gerald and Valerie; Gerhard's parents Arthur and Sophie Seefeld; and Gerhard's brother and sister-in-law, Helmut and Edith Seefeld. Edith's mother, Sophie Meier, was also on board.

Gerald is the small child immediately to Loretta's left. Doris is next to Gerald. Rosie is the woman in the back row framed by the tree in the background. She has dark hair and is holding a baby. The woman next to Rosie holds baby Valerie.

Gerhard and Rosie had two more children. Alec was born in September 1941 and Derek in October 1942. Both were born in the Tatura region: their parents remained interned until January 1943.

Source: Loretta Forsey.

QUEEN MARY INTERNEES AT TATURA, 1940–1941

The 'apple parade', Tatura, 1940

The photograph shows smiling children at Tatura, attended by a benevolent nurse. She has just given each child an apple. Eva Duldig is in white in the centre of the front row. Gerald Seefeld stands to her left, Georgie Huppert to her right. Ruth Gottlieb stands behind Georgie's right shoulder. Grace Khuner stands behind Eva's left shoulder. To Grace's left is Georg Funk, and behind her is Eva Jacoby. Loretta and Doris Seefeld are near the back, slightly below and either side of the child with five buttons on her blouse (Doris is directly in front of the nurse). The names of the others in the photograph are unknown.

Many children remembered fun, friendship and good food in the camp, where they were able to lead secure lives with their families.

Source: Loretta Forsey.

Two brothers, Tatura

Gerhard and Helmut Seefeld stand next to each other in the front row. Gerhard is wearing a white shirt and dark shorts, Helmut long trousers and braces. They look different from the dashing men in the new year's eve celebrations a year before in Singapore (page 39).

For a time Gerhard was the leader of D compound, camp 3, at Tatura. He was popular with fellow internees, but not with camp officials, with whom he clashed. They deemed his conduct unsatisfactory and dismissed him as compound leader. He was guilty only of holding strong views and having a blunt manner.

Photographs of internees were prohibited, unless taken by an official photographer, and internees were forbidden from having cameras. There are few photographs of those held at Hay, Tatura and Orange.

Some internees did have cameras, however, and of those it seems most had come from Singapore on the *Queen Mary*. More photographs were taken of these men, women and children, for whom certain rules were policed less strictly, than of the *Dunera* internees. Helmut Neustaedter (Newton), a *Queen Mary* internee, taught photography at Tatura.

Source: Loretta Forsey.

'Laugh and forget' programme cover, Tatura, 1941

The *Queen Mary* internees were quick to develop their own entertainments in Tatura. The show 'Laugh and Forget', staged in 1941, mixed music, dance and comedy. At the end of the show the internees sang 'God Save the King', their rendition of the anthem a demonstration of loyalty. The show was organised by Hans Blau (Blair), a musician born in 1906 in Vienna.

Ludwig Meilich, an architect and builder from Holíč in the Austro-Hungarian empire, designed the artwork on the programme cover. This particular copy was hand painted specially for Blau. Meilich died of a heart attack at Tatura in September 1941, age 58.

Source: Duldig Studio. Copyright: Ilse Blair.

Karl Duldig, Tatura, 1941

Karl Duldig's self-portrait notes his unlikely journey from Przemyśl, the town of his birth, to internment.

The internees had more than enough time for introspection, the expression of which in self-portraits is a striking part of the visual record they left. A self-portrait was one way in which an interned man might preserve something of his identity.

Karl Duldig, *Self-portrait* 1941, pen and ink, 135 x 105 mm (Inv. No. 3781). Copyright: The Duldig Studio.

'Under guard', Tatura, 1940

Duldig presents an image of his wife, Slawa, and their daughter, Eva, looking troubled and uncertain. The Australian soldiers, one of whom is an officer, had come to search their hut.

Karl Duldig, *Under guard* c. 1940, pen and ink, 300 x 210 mm (Inv. No. 3740.b).
Copyright: The Duldig Studio.

SECTION 5C

INTERNMENT: ORANGE, 1941

INTERNMENT: ORANGE, 1941

'On the train Hay to Orange', May 1941

Fritz Loewenstein's two sketches on one page depict two internees on a train from Hay to Orange, and an Australian soldier in the same compartment, rifle by his side.

Loewenstein was a prolific artist who compiled a rich visual record of internment.

The two internees are Heinrich Eule and Heinz Kuehlenthal. Eule, a Jewish commercial traveller, was born in the Rhineland in 1908. Kuehlenthal, a Protestant, was ten years younger and had worked as a clerk. He was born in Hanover. His mother was Jewish and his father, a senior German naval officer, was a Protestant of Jewish descent.

Fred Lowen, *On the train Hay to Orange*, 1941. H94.190/7, Pictures Collection, State Library of Victoria. Copyright: Monica Lee Lowen and Jocelyn Lowen.

Orange internment camp, June 1940

Initially the camp, erected on the Orange showgrounds, held 113 German nationals living in Australia and interned in May 1940.

About 400 internees from Hay were sent to the Orange camp in 1941, most in May and a few in June. Some went to recuperate from illness. Others, older than most of their fellows, were given the chance to spend time in a climate less extreme than at Hay. Another reason for sending these men to Orange was to allow the army to reorganise internment camps in New South Wales and Victoria. An influx of prisoners-of-war was expected.

The internees sent to Orange stayed until July.

Source: National Archives of Australia, SP459/1, 420/30/92, Orange Internment Camp, 1940. Copyright: National Archives of Australia.

INTERNMENT: ORANGE, 1941

'Orange', 1941

This Ludwig Hirschfeld-Mack painting has soothing colours of brush and sky framing a peaceful landscape.

The use of watercolour and varnish gives a softer texture to this work than is found in Hirschfeld-Mack's lithographs and woodcuts.

In common with some Leonhard Adam paintings, nothing in this work tells of internment.

Ludwig Hirschfeld-Mack (1893–1965), *Orange (landscape)*, 1941, watercolour and varnish. The University of Melbourne Art Collection. Gift of Mrs Olive Hirschfeld 1982. 1982.0143. Copyright: Chris Bell.

'Camp Orange'

This woodcut by Ludwig Hirschfeld-Mack shows a daytime scene, his vantage point slightly above the camp. Internees had limited freedom to move under escort outside the enclosure of the camp.

The woodcut is evenly divided between the regimentation of camp life and the unrestricted freedom of the world beyond. This is the art of hope, not the art of despair.

Ludwig Hirschfeld-Mack, *Camp Orange* 1941, woodcut, printed in brown ink, from one block, printed image 13.4 x 18.6 cm, sheet 20 x 25.1 cm. National Gallery of Australia, Canberra. Gift of Olive Hirschfeld 1979.

INTERNMENT: ORANGE, 1941

Barbed wire, Orange

In this sketch Fritz Loewenstein, unlike Ludwig Hirschfeld-Mack, looks directly at the barbed wire enclosure, emphasising the predicament of the interned men.

Fred Lowen, Orange – through barbed wire, 23 June 1941. H91.350/7, Pictures Collection, State Library of Victoria.Copyright: Monica Lee Lowen and Jocelyn Lowen.

The cold of winter, Orange

Fritz Loewenstein's sketches catch the posture of men trying to stay warm any way they could. Even though Orange's climate is more temperate than that of Hay, the rigours of winter are severe.

Fred Lowen, *It Was Freezing*, 1941, pencil on paper. Jewish Museum of Australia collection 3115.

INTERNMENT: ORANGE, 1941

Characters at Orange

Fritz Loewenstein sketches characters around camp.

A man in a milk cart is about to pass a woman out for a stroll, probably outside of the camp.

The bottom part of the sketch shows three internees.

On the left is probably Max Marcus Klein, a Jew born in what was then the West Prussian town of Krojanke (now in Poland) in 1906. He had worked as a clerk.

In the centre is Fritz Kolm, a Catholic, born in Vienna in 1896. He had been a company director.

On the right is a man Lowen identifies as 'Ei-Weiss'. This possibly is a joke, playing on the English translation 'Egg-white'. The internee may be Hugo Weiss, a poultry farmer born in 1918 in Brno, or Joachim Guenter Weiss, an apprentice engineer from Bremen.

Fred Lowen, *Seen On A Walk Under Guard*, 1941, pencil on paper. Jewish Museum of Australia collection 3402.

Baron Martin von Koblitz, Orange

Fritz Loewenstein's sketch of Baron Martin von Koblitz shows how the nobility have fallen. A Viennese connoisseur of the arts, von Koblitz frequented aristocratic salons before the First World War and later. He opened the Salzburg office of Christie's auction house after the war, travelled between London and Vienna, and helped Austrian friends in his social circle to acquire art for their collections.

Fred Lowen, *Baron von Koblitz*, 1941, pencil on paper. Jewish Museum of Australia collection 3419.

INTERNMENT: ORANGE, 1941

Adolph Heilbronn, Orange

Fritz Loewenstein sketched Adolph Heilbronn.

Heilbronn was Jewish, born in 1899 in Homburg an der Efze in central Germany. He served in the German army during the First World War. He and his older brother Max were interned together. They died on 29 October 1942 when the MV *Abosso*, the ship on which they were returning to Britain, was sunk by a German U-boat.

Fred Lowen, No title, 1941, pencil on paper. Jewish Museum of Australia collection 3109.

Playing bridge, Orange

Fritz Loewenstein sketches internees playing bridge, while behind them another is absorbed in his reading.

    In Orange, Hay and Tatura, men devoted countless hours to reading and playing cards and board games. Some found a degree of solace in these activities, or simply a way of passing time.

Fred Lowen, *Studies of a group of internees playing bridge, and one reading,* 22 July 1941. H94.95/32, Pictures Collection, State Library of Victoria. Copyright: Monica Lee Lowen and Jocelyn Lowen.

INTERNMENT: ORANGE, 1941

Klaus Friedeberger, Orange

At Orange, Erwin Fabian drew this portrait of his friend and fellow artist Klaus Friedeberger on 8 July 1941. 75 years later, in 2017, Friedeberger (95) and Fabian (102) are still close friends.

In 1981, Fabian gave this drawing to Klaus's wife Julie.

Source: England & Co. Gallery, London. Collection: Julie Friedeberger. Copyright: Erwin Fabian.

Hut meeting, Orange

In this image Klaus Friedeberger developed the surrealist style he had begun to experiment with on board the *Dunera* and in Hay.

Source: England & Co. Gallery, London. Collection and copyright: Klaus Friedeberger.

INTERNMENT: ORANGE, 1941

Untitled, by Ludwig Hirschfeld-Mack

This lithograph, left untitled by Hirschfeld-Mack, is commonly called 'Desolation'. It is unclear who attached this title to the image, or when.

If there is 'desolation' in this image – the man with his hands in his pockets surrounded by barbed wire, the shadows, the unreachable stars – there is also hope. The man sees the world beyond and imagines regaining the freedoms he is presently denied.

Multiple versions of this print exist, one of which incorporates splashes of red and yellow. The versions done at Orange, of which this is one, are the best known.

Ludwig Hirschfeld-Mack (1893–1965), *Internment Camp: Orange, NSW 'Desolation'*, 1941, woodcut. The University of Melbourne Art Collection. Gift of Mrs Olive Hirschfeld 1979. 1979.0179. Copyright: Chris Bell.

INTERNMENT: ORANGE, 1941

Ludwig Hirschfeld-Mack, both untitled

The lithograph on page 221 had its origins at Hay. The original version, a print from a woodcut shown on page 222, is a more abstract and simplified composition, and all the more striking for it.

Above is a third variant on the same theme, this time with two individuals dwarfed by the indifference of the southern sky. Hirschfeld-Mack drew this picture in 1941, probably at Hay.

Image at left: Ludwig Hirschfeld-Mack, *Desolation, Internment camp, Hay, NSW.* 1940–41, woodcut, printed in black ink, from one block, printed image 21.8 x 13.1 cm, sheet 31.8 x 25.6 cm. National Gallery of Australia, Canberra. Gift of Olive Hirschfeld 1979. Copyright: Chris Bell

Above: Ludwig Hirschfeld-Mack, *not titled* (*Internment camp*) 1941, drawing in watercolour and black ink over black pencil; additions in varnish, image 19.7 x 28.7 cm, sheet 19.7 x 28.7 cm, backing board 25.7 x 36.2 cm. National Gallery of Australia, Canberra. Gift of Chris Bell 2015. Copyright: Chris Bell.

Untitled, by Ludwig Hirschfeld-Mack

This watercolour drawing dates from 1941. While the work was left untitled, the grandstand in the background indicates the internees are at Orange.

In this picture, a variation on the previous three images, the night has passed. The pink light in the distant sky is a suggestion of hope.

Hirschfeld-Mack, like Leonhard Adam (page 198), depicts a fence using poles but no barbed wire.

Internees in Australia were issued with, or could purchase, coats of a distinctive burgundy colour.

Ludwig Hirschfeld-Mack, *not titled* (*group of men looking out of Internment camp*) 1941, drawing in watercolour; additions in varnish, image 27.7 x 37.8 cm, sheet 27.7 x 37.8 cm. National Gallery of Australia, Canberra. Gift of Chris Bell 2015. Copyright: Chris Bell.

SECTION 5D

INTERNMENT: TATURA, 1941–1945

SECTION 5D.1
BETWEEN BITTERNESS AND HOPE

Tocumwal, 19 May 1941

Emil Wittenberg's sketch is of Tocumwal on the Murray River. While about 400 internees went from Hay to Tatura via Orange, the rest proceeded directly from Hay to Tatura in May 1941. The 400 internees who went via Orange arrived at Tatura two months later.

Trains in New South Wales and Victoria operated on different railway gauges. Internees changed trains at this 'bordertown', to use Wittenberg's description.

Source and copyright: Martin Burman.

Rushworth, May 1941

This photograph shows *Dunera* internees, on their way from Hay to Tatura, disembarking a train at Rushworth, the closest rail station to Tatura.

This is one of the few photographs of *Dunera* internees. It is thought to have been taken by the station master at Rushworth.

Source and copyright: Tatura Irrigation and Wartime Camps Museum.

Waranga Basin

When Julian Layton, Liaison Officer for the British Home Office, visited camps 7 and 8 at Hay in April 1941, he declared the town unfit for Europeans. The climate was too hot, dry and unforgiving. He recommended that the *Dunera* internees be moved to Tatura. This suited Australian authorities, who needed space at Hay to accommodate Italian prisoners-of-war.

There was more water at Tatura than at Hay. Waranga Basin was a plentiful source of fresh, clean water.

This picture of Waranga Basin on a moonlit night was drawn by Kurt Winkler, born in 1902 in Gransee, Germany. An artist and a Protestant, he was a survivor of the *Arandora Star* sinking.

Winkler was the most risqué of the *Dunera* artists. Did he give the tree at left a penis and the tree at right a vagina?

Kurt Winkler, *Waranga Basin*, c. 1942–45. H85.89/5, Pictures Collection, State Library of Victoria.

Internees and barbed wire

Emil Wittenberg arrived in Tatura on 19 May 1941. Four days later he painted this picture, which has strong similarities to work he produced at Hay. These forlorn figures are trapped behind thick barbed wire.

Source and copyright: Martin Burman.

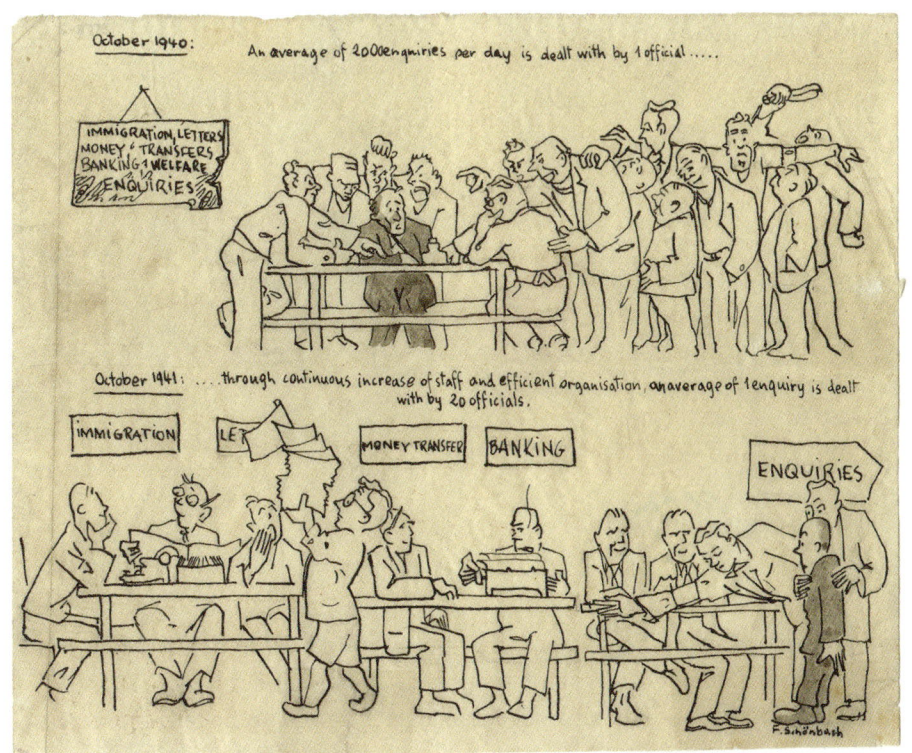

Immigration bureaucracy, 1940 and 1941

Fritz Schönbach's sketch depicts queues of internees waiting to speak with one immigration official in October 1940. A year later, two internees face '20 officials'.

By October 1941, British authorities accepted that the *Dunera* internees posed no threat. This allowed for the possibility of their emigration, within the constraints imposed by the war. Many internees hoped to go to the United States, but few reached their goal.

Fritz Schönbach, No title, 1941, pencil on paper. Jewish Museum of Australia collection 3558.2.

Christmas cards, Tatura, 1941

This lithograph on the left is part of Ludwig Hirschfeld-Mack's series of meditations on internment in a dark universe.

It represented hope beyond imprisonment, and faith as a resource in a world at war. The stars of the Southern Cross point to a better world to come.

The wider Christian community at Tatura offered an equally poignant reflection on the occasion of Christmas.

Its Christmas card (right) included a citation, in German, from Isaiah 9, 2: 'The people who walk in darkness see a great light; and of those who dwell in the dark land, it seems bright'.

Alfred Landauer, a Protestant, produced the print for the card. He too included the Southern Cross in his depiction of the night sky.

Image at left: Ludwig Hirschfeld-Mack, *Greeting card: Merry Christmas* 1941, woodcut, printed in black ink, from one block, printed image 9.6 x 7.8 cm, sheet 20 x 12.4 cm.

National Gallery of Australia, Canberra. Gift of Olive Hirschfeld 1979. Copyright: Chris Bell.

Image at right: Source: Anthony Lipmann.

SECTION 5D.2
DREAMS AND REFLECTIONS ON LIVING IN LIMBO

Oswald Volkmann, *Im Stachelkries: Gedichte* ('In the Circle of Thorns: Poems'), 1941

Many *Dunera* internees treasured the poems Oswald Volkmann composed during his internment. His poetry provided a link to the German poetic tradition which had marked their early lives: family poetry or doggerel was produced in German and Austrian households for birthdays and holidays. Volkmann wrote in both German and English, and on all aspects of camp life. Phrases such as 'His Majesty's Most Loyal Internees' became part of the *Dunera* lexicon. His work, which dwelt on the injustice of internment, was popular also with *Queen Mary* internees who shared his camp.

This image shows the cover of a collection produced at Tatura. Volkmann imitated the niceties of literary publications, including reserving all rights to the author. A bootlace was used to bind the volume.

Volkmann was born in 1889 in Liegnitz, Germany. In the First World War he flew aircraft alongside the 'Red Baron', Manfred von Richthofen.

Im Stachelkreis, Oswald Volkmann, 1941. Jewish Museum of Australia collection 4014.

Rubbish.

I found a piece of barbed wire
And formed it to a barbed ring
And then I made this barbed fire
Hang from the ceiling on a string.

I took a length of wiry copper,
Just salvaged from a heap of dirt
And bent the outlines of a proper
But somewhat undernourished bird.

Because the funny little creature
Appeared so poor and slim and pale
I added as a special feature
A coloured feather to its tail.

Within its ring the bird was swinging
And turning in my draughty den
Till, suddenly, it started singing
And busy got my fountain pen.

Do not expect my bird to flatter,
To sing exactly to your taste.
Remember, it is but a matter
Of mischief, made of metal waste.

... — — — ...

'Rubbish' by Oswald Volkmann

The poet puts together a handcrafted bird, trapped as he is in a barbed wire home.

Im Stachelkreis, Oswald Volkmann, 1941. Jewish Museum of Australia collection 4014.

HIGH POLITICS.

If I were the Prime Minister
Of Australia's Commonwealth
I would make out of sinister
Misery a source of health.

I would end the queer condition
That a shipload full of men,
Most of whom above suspicion,
Are interned without a plan.

I would take a pair of scissors,
Cut, with vigour, the red tape
And, in spite of certain hissers,
Give the thing a different shape.

I would ask the "enemy aliens"
Not - to write another list -
But ask Germans and Italians
If they're willing to assist.

Those who are, well, they could settle
On our empty continent,
Make munitions, rear the cattle,
Help the war with brain and hand.

As I'm not the Prime Minister
But a blooming internee
I keep writing to my sister:
Little hope of getting free.

oooooooooooo

'High Politics' by Oswald Volkmann

While all of Volkmann's poetry described the injustice of internment, this sentiment was expressed more strongly in some poems than in others. 'High Politics' lays bare the anger he felt about his and other internees' situation.

Im Stachelkreis, Oswald Volkmann, 1941. Jewish Museum of Australia collection 4014.

DREAMS AND REFLECTIONS ON LIVING IN LIMBO

'Yes sir'

Ludwig Hirschfeld-Mack carved this sculpture from a piece of red gum at Tatura in 1941.

An oversized internee stands at attention, surrounded by camp huts and a barbed wire fence. The internee is much larger than the space of imprisonment around him. Hirschfeld-Mack carved the words 'Yes' and 'Sir' into the base of the work.

Ludwig Hirschfeld-Mack, *Yes Sir*, 1941, sculpture, 37 x 22 x 22 cm, Australian War Memorial ART28158. Copyright: Australian War Memorial.

Joseph Ansbacher, artist unknown, c. 1941

This portrait belonged to Joseph Ansbacher, and it is thought that he is the man depicted: E39037 was his internee number. He was born in 1921 in Heilbronn, Germany, and was a furrier before the war.

The sketch, which may be a self-portrait, is in a different style to much of the art produced by *Dunera* internees. The meaning of the reference to the $10,000 reward is unclear. The dollar was not Australian currency, nor was Ansbacher a wanted man.

Wanted $10,000 Reward, c. 1941, pencil on paper. Jewish Museum of Australia collection 3595.

Birthday card for Joseph Ansbacher

Joseph Ansbacher turned 21 on 7 January 1942. This unsettling image, artist unknown, adorned a birthday card given to Ansbacher. A pig-faced Nazi walks on a tight rope strangling a naked woman, above an incomplete sketch perhaps of Hitler. Did the sketch tell of Ansbacher's mood at celebrating his coming of age in internment?

Birthday card of Joe Ansbacher, 1942. Jewish Museum of Australia collection 3608.

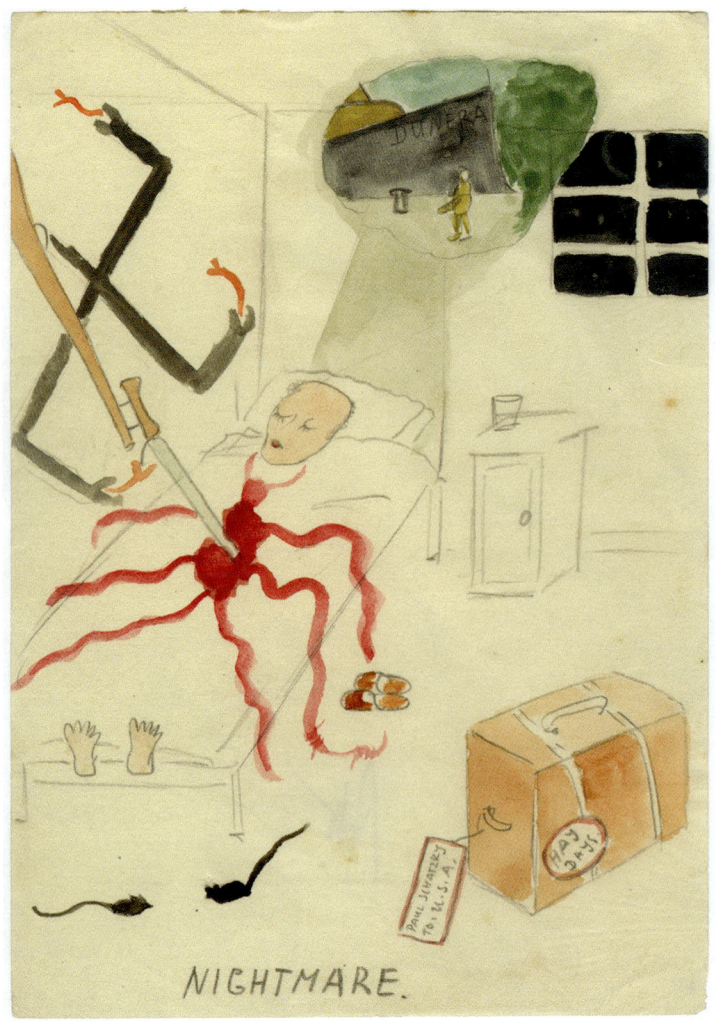

'Nightmare', 1942

In this watercolour sketch Dr Paul Schatzki provided a vivid and disturbing glimpse into his sub-conscious. Nazi vipers and insects come to kill him before he can escape internment in Australia and reach the United States. The United States was home to his mother and four brothers.

Schatzki was born to a Jewish family in Klarsfeld near Dachau in Bavaria in 1902. He had completed his medical studies in Italy before seeking refuge in Britain. He worked as a ship's surgeon in the British Merchant Marine before internment and deportation on the *Dunera*.

Paul Schatzki, *Nightmare*, 1942, watercolour and pencil on paper. Jewish Museum of Australia collection 4133.

'Tatura 3 October', 1941

Klaus Friedeberger sketches a spectral moment of mirth, when an internee dances to music on a gramophone to the amusement of his mates.

Source: England & Co. Gallery, London. Collection and copyright: Klaus Friedeberger.

'The Good Soldier Schwejk'

Schwejk, that master of survival and feigned incompetence in the First World War, has wandered into the Second World War. Fritz Schönbach puts Schwejk among the internees at Tatura, where he is confronted by road signs with nothing but question marks on them. He puffs on his pipe while reflecting on the uncertainties of the future.

Source and copyright: Schonbach family.

DREAMS AND REFLECTIONS ON LIVING IN LIMBO

'Souvenir from Tatura, 1942'

These six hand coloured drawings by Kurt Winkler appeared under the heading 'Souvenir from Tatura, 1942'. The titillating drawings of the semi-naked women replicate the 'pin-ups' painted by airmen on the fuselages of their aircraft. This form of art, which often was coupled with references to exotic places, as is the case here, was common also in magazines popular with servicemen in the Second World War. The presence of the bagpiper in Winkler's collection is harder to explain.

In a memoir published in 2003, Helmut Neustaedter purported to recall group sex among internees and orgiastic celebrations of Christmas and new year's eve: 'in the heat of the Australian night, the homosexual population of the camp embarked on a real Roman orgy under the stars. The couples were all over the parade ground.' Nobody else appears to recall these episodes. Did they happen or were they a figment of his virile mind, expressions of the urge to shock which helped to make his photography famous?

Kurt Winkler, *Souvenir from Tatura*, 1942, drawings, 26.5 x 16.2 cm, Australian War Memorial ART29565.002-007.

Many *Dunera* internees had liberal attitudes to sex. Germany under Weimar was a more permissive society than inter-war Britain, especially on the matter of homosexuality. In camp there were men known to be couples, and their relationships generally were regarded with acceptance or indifference. Werner Pelz, a Jew from Berlin born in 1921, wrote delicately of men exploring their minds and bodies, in the manner of the ancient Greeks. In a world of solitude, this process of exploration also drew men with homoerotic desires.

The majority of *Dunera* internees went months and years without sex. To be without female company was difficult, and for married men it was an especially bitter blow, for in 1940 authorities had made an unfulfilled promise that wives would be able to join their husbands in Australia.

DREAMS AND REFLECTIONS ON LIVING IN LIMBO

Thoughts of women and sex were constant. Among cultural amenities which flourished in the camps were societies for discussing issues large and small. One meeting in Hay considered the motion that 'ladies should be admitted to the debating society.' 'As we had not seen any "ladies" for many months', recalled Werner Oppenheim, 'that motion was acclaimed with great enthusiasm and a lot of unprintable witticisms.' Some internees sublimated their sexual energy in sport; some formed intense, platonic friendships; some devoted themselves to playing female characters in camp revues; and others, Winkler among them, painted and drew salacious images.

References

Alan Gill, *Interrupted Journeys: Young Refugees from Hitler's Reich*, (Sydney: Simon & Schuster, 2004), p. 196.

Helmut Newton, *Autobiography*, (New York: Nan A. Talese, 2003), p. 103.

Werner Pelz, *Distant Strains of Triumph*, (London: Victor Gollancz, 1964).

SECTION 5D.3
LANDSCAPES AND LONGING

LANDSCAPES AND LONGING

Barriers, 1942

Theodor Engel sketches a solitary figure looking through the barriers that deny his freedom.

Theodor Engel, No title, 1942, pencil on paper. Jewish Museum of Australia collection 13803.12.

'Tatura', 1941

This Ludwig Hirschfeld-Mack woodcut presents stooped figures going about their day. Internees move about the camp, sit quietly, or engage in conversation.

Ludwig Hirschfeld-Mack, *Tatura* 1941, woodcut, printed in brown ink, from one block, printed image 15.2 x 24.1 cm, sheet (sight) 16.5 x 25.3 cm. National Gallery of Australia, Canberra. Gift of Chris Bell 2015. Copyright: Chris Bell.

LANDSCAPES AND LONGING

Sunflowers, December 1941

Leonhard Adam's sunflowers offer a silent tribute to van Gogh. The subtle colours between the flowers hint at Australia's brilliant blue skies.

Sketchbook: drawings and paintings of Tatura Internment Camp and University of Melbourne, Leonhard Adam collection, University of Melbourne Archives, 1994.0060.00001, p. 21.
Copyright: Mary-Clare Adam.

Tatura, October 1941

Leonhard Adam configured freedom subtly as lying among the trees and hills beyond the camp.

Sketchbook: drawings and paintings of Tatura Internment Camp and University of Melbourne, Leonhard Adam collection, University of Melbourne Archives, 1994.0060.00001, p. 9. Copyright: Mary-Clare Adam.

LANDSCAPES AND LONGING

Eucalypts and flowers, February 1942

Eucalypts, with their seemingly infinite variety of silver, grey, green and blue colouration, fascinated many internee artists. These ancient trees, known commonly as gum trees, were the most popular subject among those who depicted the natural world. Internees left more images of eucalypts than of kangaroos, cockatoos and other Australian fauna and flora. This work is by Leonhard Adam.

Sketchbook: drawings and paintings of Tatura Internment Camp and University of Melbourne, Leonhard Adam collection, University of Melbourne Archives, 1994.0060.00001, p. 35.
Copyright: Mary-Clare Adam.

A hut and a tree, c. 1941

Robert Hofmann's landscape erases the boundaries of the camp, turning it into an image of peace and freedom.

Hofmann was an artist of considerable repute. He won the Prix de Rome in 1922, and in the 1930s worked as court painter for the Habsburg family. After moving to London in 1939, he was employed at Harrods department store. Customers paid him £50 per crayon portrait.

Robert Hofmann, No title, c. 1941, pastel on paper. Jewish Museum of Australia collection 7035.

LANDSCAPES AND LONGING

Watchtower among gum trees, 1942

Fritz Loewenstein's drawing of a watchtower and searchlights among the gum trees frames the poles in the foreground. Barbed wire is suggested, rather than added to the image.

Fred Lowen, *Watch tower with searchlights, barbed wire and gum trees*, 14 July 1942. H94.95/29, Pictures Collection, State Library of Victoria. Copyright: Monica Lee Lowen and Jocelyn Lowen.

Winter sunset, 1942

In Fritz Loewenstein's ink and watercolour picture, the sunset is seen through poles in the foreground, another motif of a world just out of reach.

Fred Lowen, *Sunset seen through [a] barbed wire fence*, 16 June 1942. H94.95/3, Pictures Collection, State Library of Victoria. Copyright: Monica Lee Lowen and Jocelyn Lowen.

LANDSCAPES AND LONGING

Camp huts and soil

Fritz Loewenstein's drawing of camp huts at Tatura in the winter of 1942 emphasises domestic calm. The huts are separated by clothes drying in the sun.

The deep reds of the soil catch the eye. The lands of the Goulburn Valley, the food bowl of Victoria, are far more fertile than the plains of Hay.

Fred Lowen, No title, 1942, gouache on paper. Jewish Museum of Australia collection 3117.

'Communication through barbed wire', c. 1942

Karl Duldig sketched a man and a woman, separated by barbed wire, waving at each other. The man is thought to be Uwe Radok, a *Dunera* internee, and the woman Anita Holper, a *Queen Mary* internee. They later married.

Karl Duldig, *Communication through barbed wire* c. 1942, pen and ink, coloured pencil, pastel, 300 x 210 mm (Inv. No. 3830). Copyright: The Duldig Studio.

SECTION 5D.4
FILLING TIME

'Happy Family'

Not all figurative work by internees was in the category of fine art. Kurt Winkler's woman looks as if she could have come directly from a fashion magazine.

The stylised woman and koalas suggest that Winkler was a satirist. The oddity of the 'happy family' could point to the mixture of different kinds of people in the camps.

Collegium Taturense Anniversary 1940–1941 booklet, Sir Thomas Karran Maltby collection, University of Melbourne Archives, 1961.0018.00001, p. 7. Copyright: Maltby family.

FILLING TIME

Gathering of internees, January 1942

Leonhard Adam sketches a gathering of men, summer 1942.

Sketchbook: drawings and paintings of Tatura Internment Camp and University of Melbourne, Leonhard Adam collection, University of Melbourne Archives, 1994.0060.00001, p. 23.
Copyright: Mary-Clare Adam.

Inside camp, c. 1942

Robert Hofmann's sketch dwells on an internee with what appear to be water containers. In the background are huts and other men at work. Here internment seems to have faded away.

Robert Hofmann, *Tatura internment camp, Victoria*, c. 1942, drawing, 22.5 x 30.2 cm, Australian War Memorial ART91993.

FILLING TIME

Workaday lives, 1941

These sketches by Fritz Loewenstein show men engaged in different activities. The man sawing wood is Bertold Kardegg, a Viennese Jew born in 1881, who had been a factory manager. The man typing is Ignaz Rosenbaum, born in 1887 in Odessa. He was Jewish and had been a manufacturer. The man at upper right is named Hamburger. He could be one of three who shared that last name in Tatura. The man at top left, looking through a card catalogue, is unidentified.

Fred Lowen, No title, 1941, pencil on paper. Jewish Museum of Australia collection 3403.

```
          The Board of Lecturers :

Rector: Dr.Bruno Breyer,Ph.D.,M.D.,M.A.,F.R.S.M.
Prorector: Dr.L.Adam,F.R.S.A.
Secretary: Dr.Felix Gutmann,Ph.D.

Rev.Padre Gierke (Bible - Exegesis)
Dr.L.Adam (Ethnology,Jurisprudence,Commercial Law,Chinese I & II)
Dr.A.Ehrenfeld (Theory of Music,History of Music)
Dr.Bruno Breyer (Chemistry I & II,Physical Chemistry)
Dr.W.Freund (Technical Chemistry)
Dr.F.Gutmann (Advanced Radio)
Mr.U.Radok,B.ENG.(Mathematics III)
Dr.F.Eichenberg (Mathematics II & II,English I,Chess)
Dr.A.Schiehsel (Anatomy)
Dr.J.Austerlitz (Microscopy)
Mr.L.Gottlieb,B.Eng. (Mechanics,Heat for Melb.Techn.Coll.,Metallography)
Mr.H.Littauer,B.Eng. (Gear Technique,Typewriting)
Mr.H.L.Baehr-Halbe,B.Eng. (Geometr.Drawing)
Dr.K.Regner (English Shorthand)
Mr.H.J.Will (Commercial English)
Dr.H.Graffunder,D.U.P. (Matriculation English Course)
Mr.H.K.Ruppin (English II & III)
Dr.A.Beck (Malay,Greek)
Dr.H.Jacobs (Spanish)
Mr.W.Wuerzburger (Counterpoint,Jazz,Arrangement,French)
Mr.J.Mundstein (Cost Accountancy,Bookkeeping)
Mr.H.Neustaedter (Photo Practice,English Circle)
Mr.K.Winkler (Fashion Drawing)

          The Council:

The Rector:Dr.B.Breyer            The Prorector:Dr.L.Adam
        The Secretary:Dr.F.Gutmann

Members:Dr.H.Graffunder,D.U.P.,Mr.U.Radok,B.Eng.,Mr.H.Littauer,B.Eng.,
       Mr.E.Blitz as Compound Leader.
```

Collegium Taturense: Board of Lecturers, October 1941

Tatura was home to an educational enterprise whose Latin title, *Collegium Taturense*, signalled a mission to carry the civilisation of Berlin and Vienna to the bush; 'to keep alive', as its makers proclaimed, 'the true spirit of European science and culture.' At first the *Collegium* was accommodated in camp 3, then moved to camp 4 in August 1941, then to camp 2 in early 1942. This last move brought together the Hay and Tatura educational practices, for camp 2 was home to the *Dunera* internees from Hay. Enterprises similar to the *Collegium* had flourished in the two camps at Hay, and were merged with activities at Tatura. Teaching materials – chalk, blackboards, paper, pencils, books – for the *Collegium* were supplied by well-wishers in Melbourne.

The Rector of the *Collegium*, Bruno Breyer, had trained in medicine in Padua and had a doctorate in chemistry from Bonn. The Pro-rector, Leonhard Adam, was trained in law in Berlin, and had taught art and ethnography in London. He lectured on a variety of subjects across the vast spectrum of his competence: ethnology, jurisprudence, commercial law, Chinese art and culture and language. Felix Gutmann, one of the instigators of the *Collegium* and its secretary, had a doctorate in chemistry from Vienna and was an authority on electrical phenomena. Father Franz Girke, a

Catholic priest and member of the Pallottine order, taught theology and scripture. Younger men, like Helmut Neustaedter, a *Queen Mary* internee, brought other skills to the *Collegium*; in his case, photography. Of the 23 lecturers, 15 were from the *Dunera* and eight from the *Queen Mary*.

To celebrate the first full year of the *Collegium*, on Sunday 26 October 1941 Adam delivered an anniversary lecture on 'The Practical Importance of Scientific Studies'. By that time the *Collegium* could report an average of 113 lectures a week, attended by nearly 700 students. Of 23 lecturers, 17 were graduates and the other six 'highly qualified', enabling 'a standard which is far above that to be expected under internment conditions.' The *Collegium* was preparing 17 students for the school leaving examinations of the University of Melbourne.

Collegium Taturense Anniversary 1940–1941 booklet, Sir Thomas Karran Maltby collection, University of Melbourne Archives, 1961.0018.00001, p. 11. Copyright: Maltby family.

References

Collegium Taturense Anniversary 1940-1941 booklet, Sir Thomas Karran Maltby collection, University of Melbourne Archives, 1961.0018.00001.

Collegium Taturense new year's card

This new year's card was the work of Leonhard Adam. The owl and cockatoo perch above the words *Eppur Si Muove*, attributed in legend to a defiant Galileo.

Sketchbook: drawings and paintings of Tatura Internment Camp and University of Melbourne, Leonhard Adam collection, University of Melbourne Archives, 1994.0060.00001, p. 3. Copyright: Mary-Clare Adam.

'Clearing the brain': Uwe Radok diary entry, 21 October 1941

In his diary Uwe Radok recorded his delight at solving a mathematical problem that had been troubling him.

Source and copyright: Radok family collection.

Poster advertising a lecture by Erich Lipmann on Japanese culture

This poster, designed by Bertold Meier, shows the rising sun behind Mount Fuji and the Torii Gate of Itsukushima Shrine, Miyajima, across from Hiroshima Bay. Brothers Bruno and Erich Lipmann shared an interest in Japanese language and culture. While Bruno was the more fluent in Japanese, Erich delivered the lecture.

Source and copyright: Anthony Lipmann.

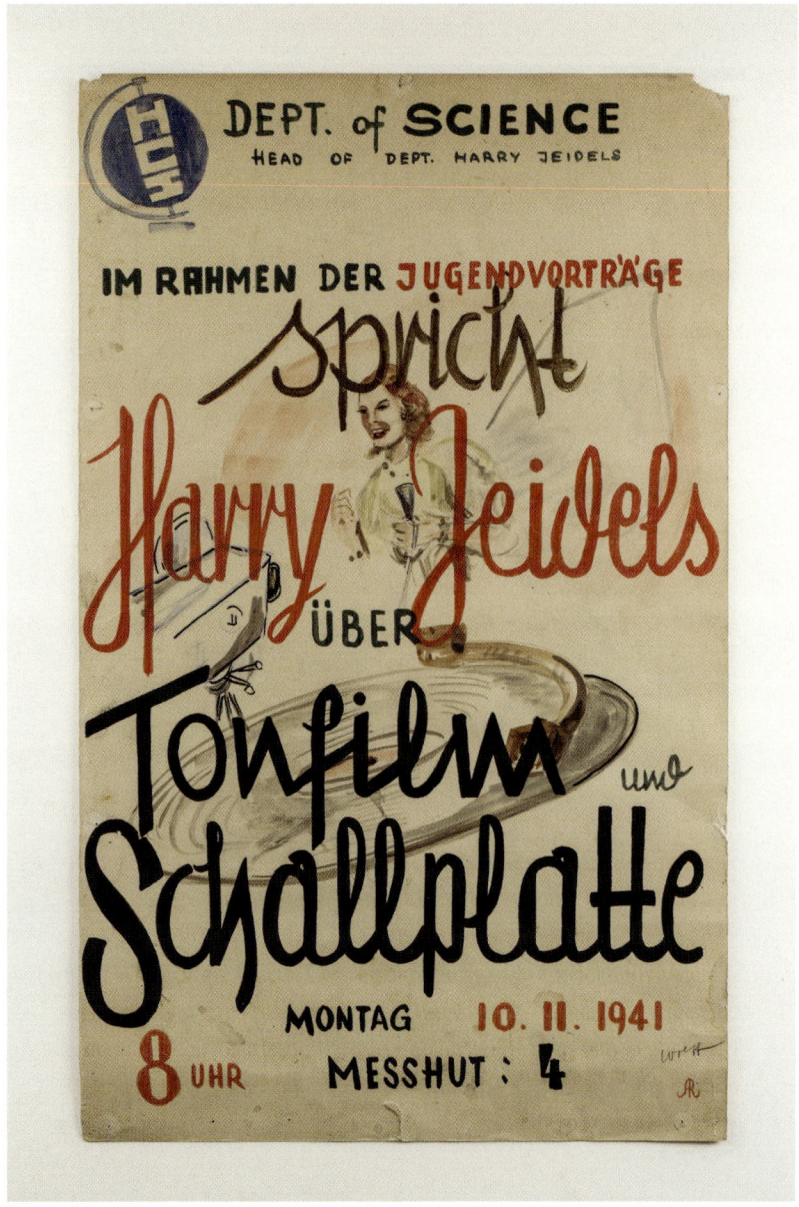

Poster advertising a talk by Harry Jeidels

Harry Jeidels (Harry Jay), Head of the Department of Science at Tatura, gave regular lectures on different topics. On this occasion his subject was the 'talkies' – early films with sound – and music records.

Jeidels was a photographer born in Berlin in 1905.

Poster for Jeidels talk at Tatura Camp, Harry Jeidels, 1941. Jewish Museum of Australia collection 3399.

FILLING TIME

Performance of Beethoven's Kreutzer Sonata, 8 March 1942

Leonhard Adam's pen and wash drawing of a performance of the 'Kreutzer Sonata' includes a Greek caption in which Adam salutes the soloists: 'one man is worthy of many'. The names of the violinist and pianist are not known.

In the camps, as on the voyage, internees made much music, and for all brows. The popular music of their own time, German, Austrian, English and American, was familiar to most internees, and crooners among them led the singing at evening concerts in a cabaret style reminiscent of Berlin or Vienna. These concerts were arranged by Kurt Kohn, who had studied at the Vienna Conservatorium, and who had been making a career on radio and stage in England under the name Ray Martin. If they cared to listen, guards might have heard their prisoners sing Duke Ellington's 'Solitude', Negro spirituals, songs by George Gershwin, and such recent American hits as 'South of the Border' and 'Ride, Tenderfoot, Ride', theme songs of films starring Gene Autry.

Leonhard Adam, *Kreutzer Sonata*, 1942, watercolour and ink on paper. Jewish Museum of Australia collection 4024.

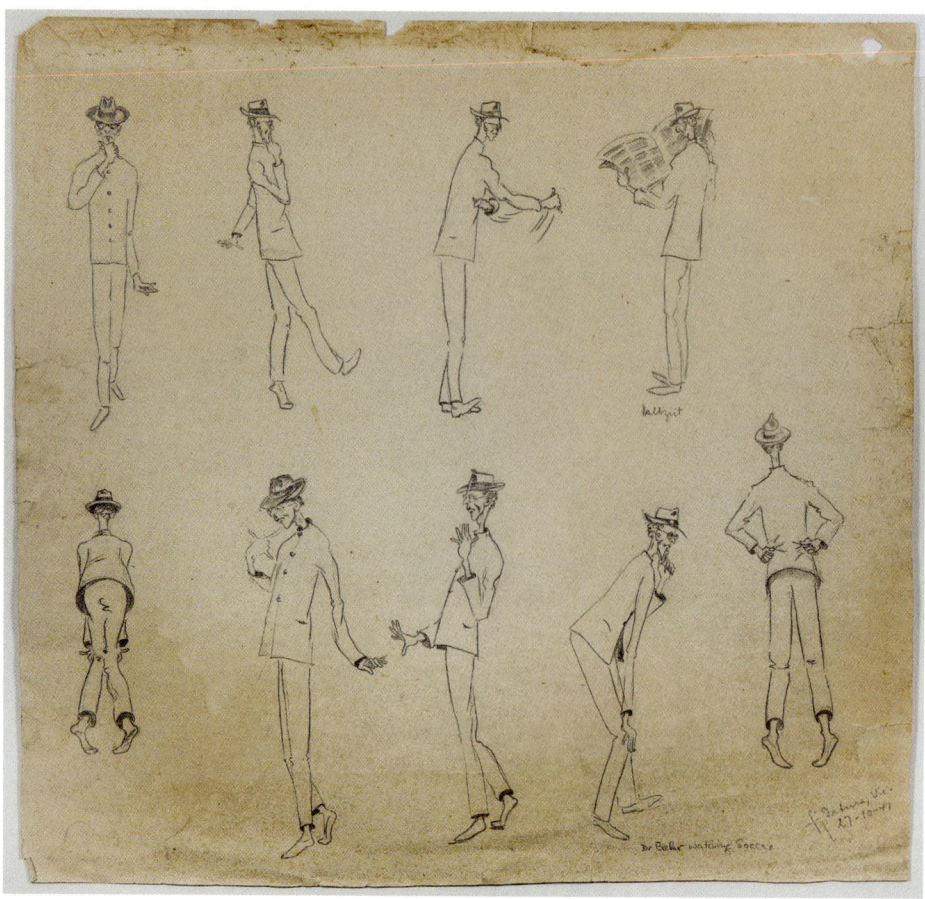

'Dr Behr watching soccer', October 1941

Fritz Loewenstein depicts a well-dressed observer at an internees' soccer match. He reads a newspaper at half time. The subject is thought to be Dr Walther Baer (not Behr, as Loewenstein had it), a Jewish man, born in Hamburg in 1894. He served in the German army during the First World War, and managed a copper plant before internment in England.

At Tatura, as at Hay, internees devoted much time and energy to sport, which was both a source of pleasure and a means to manage frustration. And at Tatura even more sports were on offer. On the initiative of Karl Duldig, person-in-charge of sports and amusements for D compound, camp 3, a tennis court was constructed in 1941.

Fred Lowen, *Dr. Behr watching soccer*, 1941, pencil on paper. Jewish Museum of Australia collection 3413.

Gardening, 1942

Fritz Loewenstein portrays the horticultural talents of internees. Growing flowers and vegetables was a popular pastime, and easily done in Tatura's rich soil.

Fred Lowen, *Gardening activities*, 10 June 1942. H94.95/1, Pictures Collection, State Library of Victoria. Copyright: Monica Lee Lowen and Jocelyn Lowen.

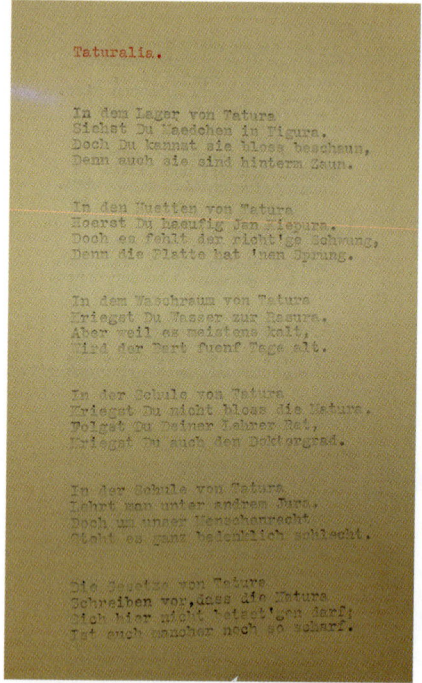
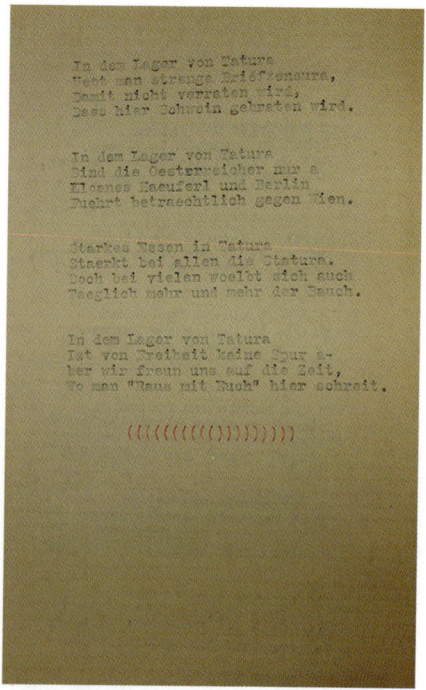

'Taturalia' by Oswald Volkmann

Volkmann filled his time by composing poetry. In 'Taturalia' and 'The Football or the Refugee' he mixed humour and protest while addressing facets of camp life.

Im Stachelkreis, Oswald Volkmann, 1941. Jewish Museum of Australia collection 4014. Translation by Kate Garrett.

> Next to the camp that's called Tatura
> Live the girls: bella figura.
> But you can't do more than stare
> They're beyond the fence – out there!
>
> In the huts around Tatura
> You'll hear songs by Jan Kiepura
> But one thing can't be ignored:
> We've just got one skipping record.
>
> Inside of Tatura's wash room
> Water runs to shave and groom.
> But the water's often cold,
> So our beards are five days old.

FILLING TIME

Inside of Tatura's school
They teach more than basic tools.
Just do what your teachers say,
Your doctorate's not far away!

Inside of Tatura's school
Law is studied, as a rule.
But not anyone highlights
Our own lack of human rights.

And there are Tatura's laws
That often make us think and pause.
For it is to all us clear:
Outside rules can't reach us here.

In the camp that's called Tatura
Mail is censored with bravura.
So people do not find out,
Here pigs are roasted – tail to snout.

The Austrians here in Tatura
When together only are a
Small percentage, yes indeed,
Deutschland's always in the lead!

In Tatura we eat dinner –
We're not getting any thinner.
Each day we grow just a little:
Now we're rounder round the middle!

In Tatura you will notice
Freedom's not something bestowed us,
So we wait for them to shout,
'Now it's time you all get out!'

Der Fussball
oder
Der Refugee.

Zwischen hartbeschuhten Füssen
Heftig hin und her getreten,
Muss das arme Leder büssen,
Bis es platzt in seinen Nähten.

Bald nach Süden, bald nach Norden
Kickt ihn jeder wie er kann.
Auf ihn stürzen sich die Horden
Und der Stürmer stets voran.

Manchmal flüchtet sich der arme
Aengstlich übern Seitenzaun,
Doch dann pfeift man zum Alarme
Und er wird zurück gehau'n.

Warum jagt man dieses Leder
Unbarmherzig übern Rasen?
Warum springt er wie 'ne Feder?
Weil er furchtbar aufgeblasen.

Sein Verhängnis ist das Pumpen.
Erst der Luftdruck macht ihn richtig.
Wäre er ein schlapper Lumpen,
Nähme keiner ihn so wichtig.

. . . — — . .

FILLING TIME

'The Football or the Refugee' by Oswald Volkmann

Im Stachelkreis, Oswald Volkmann, 1941. Jewish Museum of Australia collection 4014. Translation by Kate Garrett.

From side to side the poor ball goes
Each tough boot tries to kick it first.
Suffering is the life it knows
Until its seams give way and burst.

To the South and then back North
Why worry where they land their kick?
The hordes they chase it back and forth
The forward's known for being quick.

From time to time the poor thing springs
Right across the fence in fright.
But then of course the alarm rings –
They send it back with all their might.

Why is it that this ball gets chased,
Quite without mercy 'cross the field?
Why does it bounce off with such haste?
Because it's taut and will not yield.

It finds resilience at the pump
Restored again through re-inflation.
If it were just a droopy lump,
It wouldn't cause such agitation.

SECTION 5D.5
SEEKING GOD

Erwin Lamm and Orthodox Jewish internees, Tatura

This photograph, taken in 1941 or 1942, shows Erwin Lamm (white cap, centre of front row) and other Orthodox Jewish internees.

The collective nature of Jewish life, in its daily rituals and practices, was of benefit to observant internees, Orthodox and liberal. Some derived solace and motivation from study and teaching: Orthodox internees established a small *Yeshivah* (Talmudic college) at Tatura. Maintaining morale as an individual alone was difficult; maintaining morale in a collective was, for many, the path to emotional survival.

The needs of Orthodox Jews were catered for at Tatura. Initially they swapped their meat rations for the cheese rations of non-religious internees. Later a family from the Orthodox community in nearby Shepparton arranged a supply of kosher meat and other special foods.

Source: Ilse Lamm.

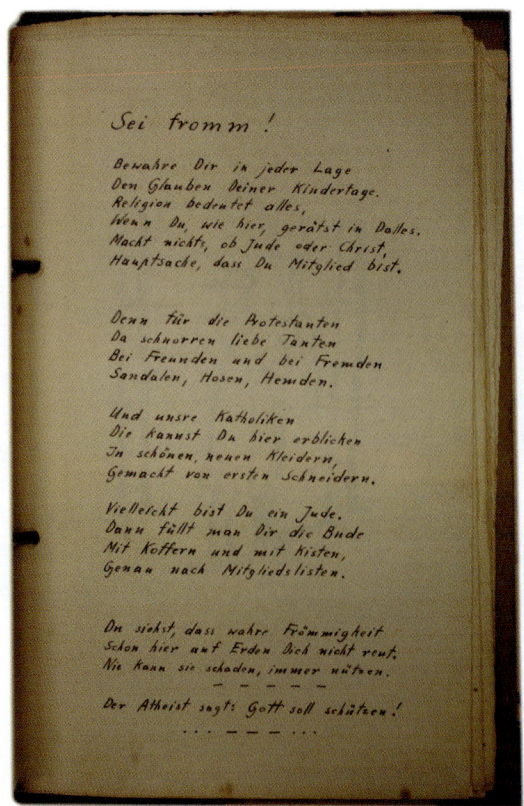

'Be Pious!' by Oswald Volkmann

In this poem Volkmann mused on the practice of religion at Tatura. The 'dear aunties' mentioned in the second stanza are Margaret Holmes and Constance Duncan. Duncan was director of the church-based Victorian International Refugee Emergency Committee, which solicited material and emotional support for the *Dunera* internees.

On both of Volkmann's internee forms the 'religion' section was left blank.

Im Stachelkreis, Oswald Volkmann, 1941.

Jewish Museum of Australia collection 4014. Translation by Kate Garrett.

SEEKING GOD

No matter where it is you are,
Don't let your faith wander too far.
Religion's something you must claim,
When here. No penny to your name.
You may be a Christian or a Jew
As long as you're a member too.

The Protestants have got it good
Dear aunties scour the neighbourhood.
They implore ev'ryone they know
Search for donations high and low.

We have the Catholics up next
Here you see them in their best.
Dressed perfectly down to the hem
Espec'ly tailored just for them.

Or p'raps you call yourself a Jew
There too are boxes just for you.
As long as your name's on the list,
I guarantee you won't be missed.

And so you see that piety
Will never cause anxiety.
Quite irrespective of the sect.

Atheists say, 'God will protect!'

Christian worship in the bush: Mass under corrugated iron, 1942

Theodor Engel's painting of a service at Tatura, 1942, is a reverent treatment of the act of faith. Though he was Jewish, and viewing the event at a tangent, Engel used warm colours to depict the scene.

Theodor Engel, No title, 1942, watercolour and pencil on paper. Jewish Museum of Australia collection 3666.

SECTION 5D.6
TATURA PORTRAITS

Fritz Gruen

Erwin Fabian's portrait of Fritz (Fred) Gruen shows a handsome and alert young man. Gruen was a Viennese Jew, born in 1921.

Fred Gruen 1941, by Erwin Fabian (b. 1915), gouache on paper. Collection: National Portrait Gallery, Canberra. Purchased with funds donated by Andrew Sayers and from the Basil Bressler Bequest 2002. Copyright: Erwin Fabian.

Kurt Baier

Erwin Fabian sketched this portrait in 1942, almost certainly at Tatura.

Baier was a Viennese Catholic born in 1917. He worked as a foreign correspondent in London before internment and deportation on the *Dunera*.

Kurt Baier 1942, by Erwin Fabian (b. 1915), conte on paper. Collection: National Portrait Gallery, Canberra. Gift of the artist 2002. Copyright: Erwin Fabian.

Adalbert Stern

Fritz Loewenstein portrays a pensive Adalbert Stern. A Jew and active socialist, born in the town of Themar in Thuringia, he fled Germany for Britain in 1939.

Fred Lowen, *Ada Stern*, 1941, charcoal on paper. Jewish Museum of Australia collection 3350.

TATURA PORTRAITS

Rainer Radok

While Theodor Engel painted and drew all aspects of camp life, he was especially interested in depicting his fellow internees. His portraits dwelt on facial features and expressions. A selection of his portraits follow.

This sketch is of Rainer Radok.

Theodor Engel, *Study of Rainer Radok, A Dunera boy at Tatura, Victoria, 1943*. Portraits of Dunera boys, 1941–1943, National Library of Australia.

Julius Spier

Julius Spier was born in 1922, and was two years older than his brother Alfred, also interned at Tatura. They were born to a Jewish family in Rauischholzhausen, 80 kilometres from Frankfurt. They fled to Scotland in 1938, where both worked in farming, before their internment and deportation on the *Dunera*.

Theodor Engel, *Portrait of Julius Spier, approximately 1942*. Portraits of Dunera boys, 1941–1943, National Library of Australia.

David Teichmann

David Teichmann was born in 1912 in Kozova in Galicia, then in Poland, now in Ukraine. His family was Jewish. He was a physician, living in Vienna, when he fled to England in 1938.

Theodor Engel, *Study of Dr Teichmann, a Dunera boy, 1942*. Portraits of Dunera boys, 1941–1943, National Library of Australia.

Hugo Gottlieb

Hugo Gottlieb was a Jewish merchant born in Vienna in 1894. He left Austria for England in 1938.

Theodor Engel, *Study of Hugo Gottlieb, a Dunera boy, Tatura, Victoria, 1942.* Portraits of Dunera boys, 1941–1943, National Library of Australia.

Sally Cohn

The orthodox Jew depicted in this Theodor Engel sketch is thought to be Sally Cohn. Born in Hamburg in 1900, he had served in the German army in the First World War. He was a solicitor.

Theodor Engel, No title, 1943, pencil on paper. Jewish Museum of Australia collection 3931.

Norman Bleiweiss

Norman Bleiweiss, born in 1885, was one of the oldest *Dunera* internees. He was a Jewish bookseller, born in Breslau, then in Germany, now in Poland.

Theodor Engel, *Study of Norman Bleiweiss, a Dunera boy, May 1943*. Portraits of Dunera boys, 1941–1943, National Library of Australia.

SECTION 5D.7
HERMANN VALENTIN:
TREES AND TATURA

Hermann Valentin, July 1942

Hermann Valentin was born in 1895 in Seemühlen, Germany. He was a builder's labourer, and a Protestant. He was interned in Aberdeen in 1940, probably the northern-most point of arrest among internees.

On arrival in Australia, he was among the internees who were disembarked at Port Melbourne and sent directly to Tatura.

Valentin returned to Britain in July 1942. This sketch, by Fritz Loewenstein, was done that month.

Fred Lowen, *Hermann Valentin*, 8 July 1942. H94.95/23, Pictures Collection, State Library of Victoria. Copyright: Monica Lee Lowen and Jocelyn Lowen.

HERMANN VALENTIN: TREES AND TATURA

Tatura landscapes (1–2)

Valentin spent nearly two years interned at Tatura. The images in this section give a glimpse of how he saw the landscape of his internment.

When Valentin left Tatura, he gave these watercolour, ink and pencil pictures to Fritz Loewenstein.

Image at top: Hermann Valentin, *View of hills and red roofed houses*, 1941. H94.95/38, Pictures Collection, State Library of Victoria.

Image below: Hermann Valentin, *Landscape with gum trees*, 1942. H94.95/37, Pictures Collection, State Library of Victoria.

Tatura landscape (3)

Valentin uses a gully with road tracks to divide the landscape near Waranga Basin. The texture of wood is mottled into the exposed gully.

Hermann Valentin, *Landscape with road, Tatura*, 1942. H94.95/34, Pictures Collection, State Library of Victoria.

HERMANN VALENTIN: TREES AND TATURA

Camp scene

Valentin's horizontal tree has something of a human face in it.

Hermann Valentin, *The camp at Tatura*, 1941. H94.95/40, Pictures Collection, State Library of Victoria.

Watch tower

Valentin's composition is vigorously vertical. Even when unguarded, the camp's barbed wire, traced between the poles, describes the limits of hope and release.

Hermann Valentin, *Watch tower and barbed wire fence at Tatura*, 1941. H94.95/41, Pictures Collection, State Library of Victoria.

HERMANN VALENTIN: TREES AND TATURA

Eucalypts (1–2)

Valentin was among the internee artists, amateur and professional, who were fascinated by eucalypts. The tree on the left has some of the lush transparency of the jungle foliage in Douanier Rousseau's paintings.

Image at left:

Hermann Valentin, *Eucalyptus tree and barbed wire fence*, 1941.

H94.95/36, Pictures Collection, State Library of Victoria.

Image at right:

Hermann Valentin, *Gum trees*, c. 1941–1942. H94.95/39, Pictures Collection, State Library of Victoria.

Eucalypts (3)

Valentin's focus here is on the bark and texture of the tree in the centre. The beauty of eucalypts is often more in the bark than in the foliage. The trees in the background stand like courtiers.

Hermann Valentin, *Tall gums*, c. 1941–1942.

H94.95/35, Pictures Collection, State Library of Victoria.

SECTION 5D.8
TO THE END

Waranga Basin, 8 August 1943

By the end of 1942, many of the *Dunera* and *Queen Mary* internees had been released. For images of the Tatura camps beyond this time, we rely on Kurt Winkler, who was interned until May 1945.

It is thought Australian officials were suspicious of Winkler's loyalties. His family remained in Germany, untroubled by the regime; two of his sisters were married to German officers; and he was disinclined to do the bidding of camp authorities. None of this was evidence that Winkler held Fascist sympathies. At Tatura he chose to live with non-Fascist internees.

Winkler gave this painting to Theodor Engel a day or two before Engel's release.

Kurt Winkler, No title, 1943, watercolour on paper. Jewish Museum of Australia collection 3870.

'Walking party', 2 June 1943

Winkler's 'walking party' proceeds around what appears to be an animal run, though in this case it is the internees who are enclosed.

'Kurwin' [Kurt Winkler], *Walking party*, 2 June 1943. H85.89/1, Pictures Collection, State Library of Victoria.

Tatura at night, 1944

'Kurwin', as Winkler came to sign his art, returned time and again to settings of the camp at night.

Source: Stocky family.

Camp 2 at night, Tatura, 1944

Winkler's drawing provides a contrast between the barbed wire on the right and the almost bucolic scene of tree and huts on the left. The black cat appears in a number of his pictures.

'Kurwin' [Kurt Winkler], *Camp No 2 Tatura, Vic.*, 1944. H85.89/2, Pictures Collection, State Library of Victoria.

'Hut 18', camp 2, Tatura, 1945

Kurt Winkler's painting of hut 18, camp 2, captures some of the stasis and lassitude of camp life. By 1945, the camp was almost empty.

His signature black cat accompanies these internees like a bad dream.

'Kurwin' [Kurt Winkler], *Tatura No 2 'Hut 18'*, 1945. H85.89/3, Pictures Collection, State Library of Victoria.

Section 6

AFTER INTERNMENT

INTRODUCTION

In late March 1941, Major Julian Layton arrived in Australia. He was a Jewish stockbroker turned Home Office official in London. His mission marked the beginning of the end of internment for those who had been sent to Australia on the *Dunera*. The policy of enemy alien internment had been recognised as an error, though freeing these men was easier said than done.

Where could these internees go? Where would they agree to go? Australia had accepted them as British internees, not as candidates for Australian residence or citizenship. Many internees had tried to get visas to the United States in the 1930s. When that option failed in Germany or Austria, they fled to Britain. In early 1941, the United States, still neutral, maintained a detached position with respect to virtually all refugees, especially those arrested in Britain as enemy aliens. Ludwig Hirschfeld-Mack was one internee who found that American officials in Australia simply did not reply to his enquiries about the possibility of obtaining an American visa.

Under these circumstances, the simplest choice for British officials was to return the internees to Britain, from where they had come. Many internees opposed this option. Some were embittered by their treatment on the *Dunera*, while others had no one in Britain. Joining the British army's Pioneer Corps, a possibility offered to internees, did not always appeal: men harboured memories of being welcomed to Britain and then arrested for being German. Others saw a return to Britain in pragmatic terms, a first step in their plan to go elsewhere. But there too the risks were high, since German U-boats challenged Allied military and passenger shipping on the Atlantic throughout the war. U-boats attacked and sunk two ships making for Britain with *Dunera* internees on board: the MV *Abosso* in October 1942 and the SS *Waroonga* in April 1943.

The first major release of internees took place in June 1941, after Major Layton's visit, when 198 men were freed. A further 440 left internment in

October, 434 of whom returned to Britain. The exodus from internment continued in 1942. In January, 285 internees were freed, followed by 88 in March, and another 429 from July through September. These men left the country, joined the Australian army, or were released to work or because of age or illness. By early 1943, 1812 internees had left the camps.

Over the next two years, releases continued, though at a slower pace. Those who remained in Tatura were not a homogenous group. Among them were German nationals who were unable or did not seek to convince officials they could be released safely; Jews who did not trust Australian authorities to provide an environment in which they could observe their faith; and men who believed they should be released on principle rather than as a quid pro quo for subsequent war service. The final wave of releases was in May 1945 when peace came to Europe and the last *Dunera* men at Tatura were transferred back to Britain. Appendix 2 to this volume documents the many ways in which internment came to an end.

In this section of our visual history, we see the faces of some of those who returned to Britain, before focusing on those who stayed in Australia. The men who stayed may be divided into two groups. The first was composed of those who joined the 8th Employment Company, a non-combatant labour battalion of the Australian army. That escape route from internment had opened up partly owing to the accession late in 1941 of a Labor government readier than its predecessors to think fresh thoughts about internees, but mainly to the entry of Japan into the war and the consequent drive to mobilise national resources as never before. An alien unloading ships at the port of Melbourne or moving supplies from a railway system of one gauge to those of another at Albury or Tocumwal could be seen as releasing an Australian man for military duties.

The second group was made up of those who took civilian jobs or found places in schools and universities in Australia. From February 1944 the men in both groups were deemed 'refugee aliens' rather than 'enemy aliens', though their new status did not confer the right of permanent residence or citizenship. When individuals applied for citizenship, their cases were decided on their merits. Here we reach the intersection of the history of internment and the wartime and post-war history of Australia.

In effect, once the *Dunera* and *Queen Mary* internees were no longer incarcerated, they entered a different world. Men in the 8th Employment Company were under military discipline. But they had chosen freely to put on Australian uniforms. Just like the ex-detainees who went directly to civilian employment or study, they had lives to build. That story is the subject of the remainder of this volume.

SECTION 6A

RETURNERS

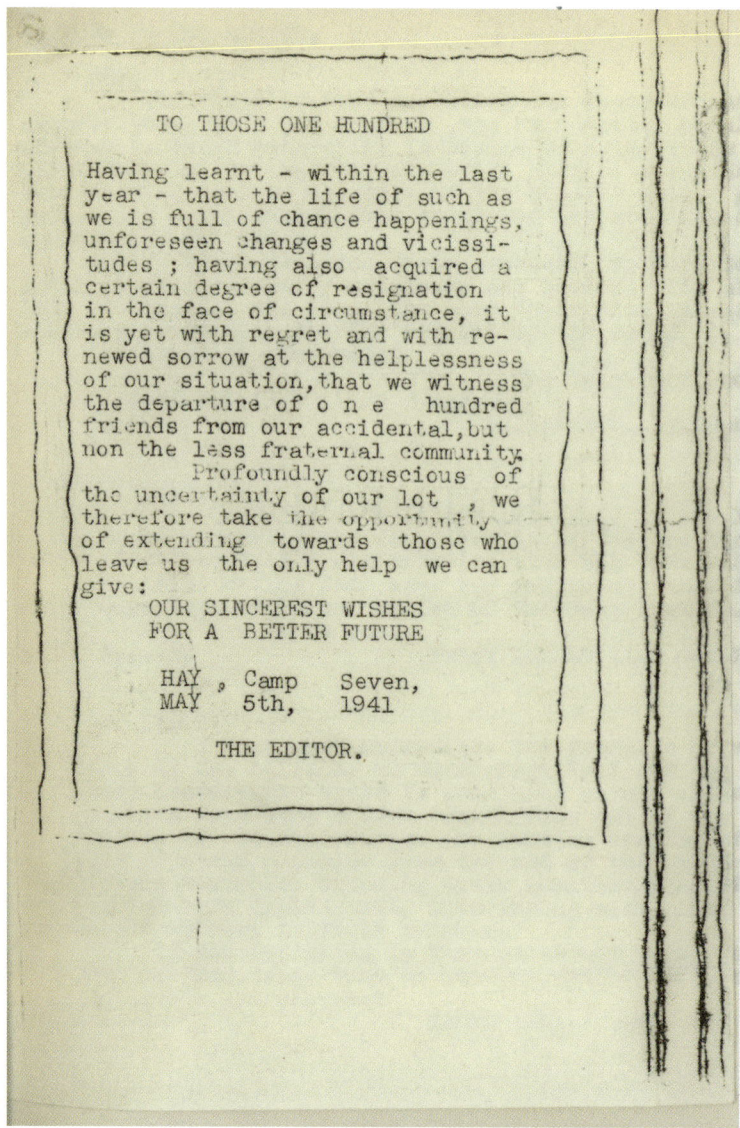

'To those one hundred', *The Boomerang*, 5 May 1941

Issue number 11 of *The Boomerang* included this message to 100 internees who were leaving Hay camp 7. About half returned to Britain over the next two years, 19 made for Palestine, and 34 stayed in Australia.

The editor addressed those who remained in confinement, 'Profoundly conscious of the uncertainty of our lot', and the 100 men who were leaving, offering them good wishes for a better future.

The Boomerang, 1941. Jewish Museum of Australia collection, 4173.

> 4th June 1941.
>
> After 26 years,
> It now appears,
> That of all careers,
> You chose pioneers;
> So three hearty cheers,
> As liberty nears,
> No doubt destiny steers,
> Towards many beers,
> Times without fears,
> And never tears,
> In your future years.
>
> Werner Goldschmidt

Werner Goldschmidt poem, Tatura, 4 June 1941

Werner Goldschmidt penned this farewell to a friend who had chosen to return to Britain to join the British army's Pioneer Corps. Four months later, in October, Goldschmidt did the same. Later in the war he served as a British commando.

Untitled poem, Werner Goldschmidt, 1941. Jewish Museum of Australia collection 3441.

> **TO OUR LEAVING FRIENDS.**
>
> Tell them in London that we are
> Still in the blooming Camp so far.
>
> We hope, however, that one day
> We may as well be on the way.
>
> Or that the time is very near
> When we are called free people here.
>
> At first, quite out of our senses,
> We hoped for Prime Minister Menzies.
>
> Then our hopes, all of a sudden,
> Turned round to his successor Fadden.
>
> To-day —and some are even certain —
> All our hopes are set on Curtin.
>
> ... --- ...

'To our leaving friends' by Oswald Volkmann

Oswald Volkmann wrote this wistful poem at Tatura, probably after the election of John Curtin's Labor government in October 1941.

Volkmann's wish for his own freedom was soon realised. He left Tatura for Britain in November 1941.

Im Stachelkreis, Oswald Volkmann, 1941. Jewish Museum of Australia collection 4014.

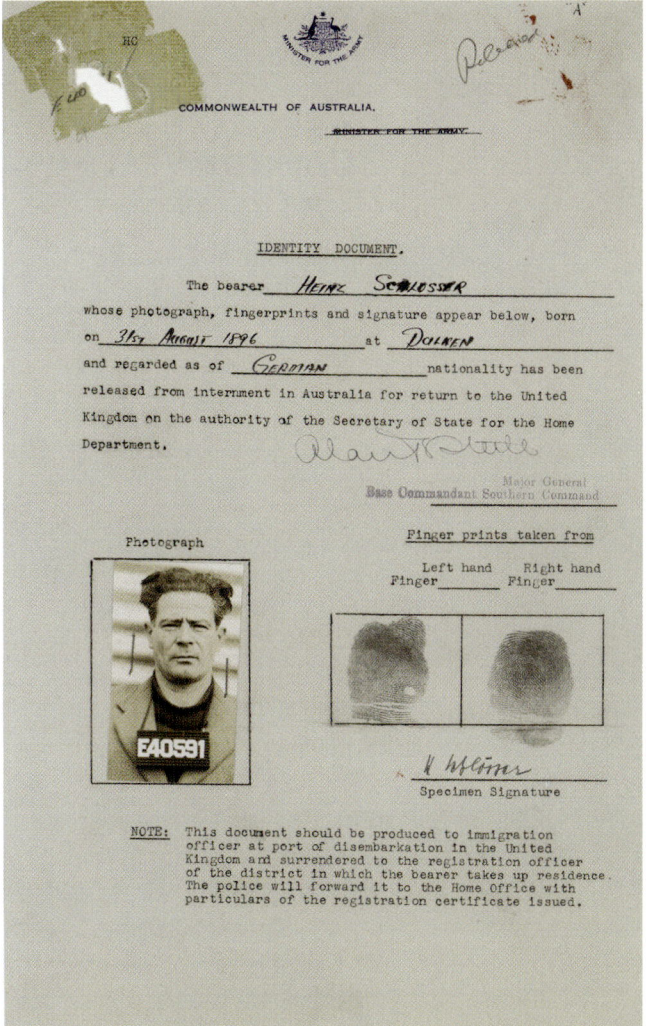

Heinz Schlösser, identity document

When Heinz Schlösser sailed on the *Dunera*, his companion Fay Jackson was left behind in Britain. She obtained passage to Australia and then engaged in a relentless effort to have him freed from internment, even threatening suicide. He left Tatura in March 1942 and married Fay in Melbourne on 7 April that year.

Documents such as that shown here were compiled to replace the identity papers internees had lost, and were given to men intending to return directly to Britain in wartime. As it happened, Schlösser did not make this journey. The alphanumeric number on his chest is his internee number.

Source: National Archives of Australia, A367, C81257, Schlosser Heinz Hans, 1940–45. Copyright: National Archives of Australia.

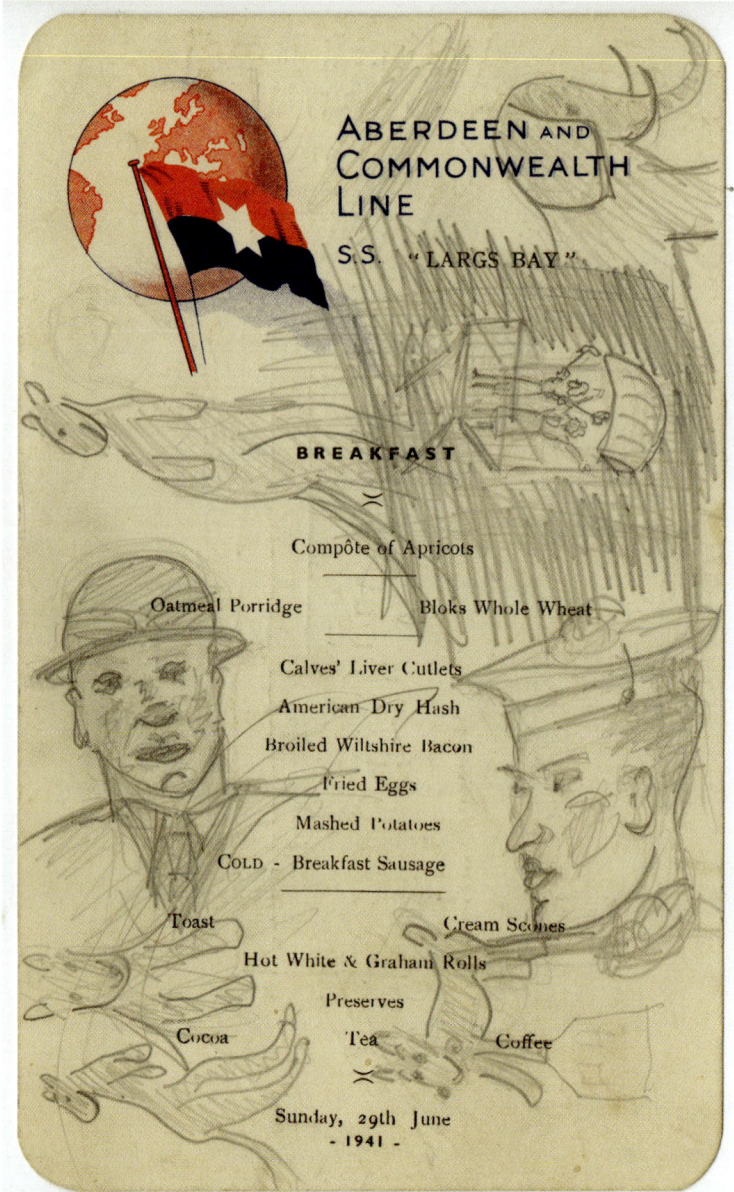

Breakfast menu, SS *Largs Bay*, 29 June 1941

In June 1941, Leonhard Posner, who had worked as a hairdresser in camp 8 at Hay, returned to Britain, where his wife and child lived. While at sea he passed some time by doodling, including on menu cards. On this menu he sketched a soldier, sailor, elephant, dogs and kangaroos.

Aberdeen and Commonwealth Line menu, illustrated by Leonhard Posner, 1941. Jewish Museum of Australia collection 3808.3.

> **AUSTRALIAN MILITARY FORCES.—SOUTHERN COMMAND**
>
> 3rd Forestry Coy., R.A.E., A.I.F.,
> S.S. "THEMISTOCLES."
> 12th June, 1941.
>
> **WOOD ; ITS CHEMISTRY AND ITS USES IN ENGINEERING AND INDUSTRY.**
>
> Lecturer - Mr. Haim.
>
> Structure of Wood.
> What Chemistry Is.
> How dyes, drugs and foodstuffs are made out of wood.
> How Paper is Made.
> Explosives from Wood.
> Artificial Silk and Plastics.
> Preservation of Wood against Decay.

Georg Haim lectures, June 1941

Georg Haim left Australia for Britain on the SS *Themistocles* in June 1941. On the ship he perpetuated the educational traditions of Hay and Tatura by giving a series of lectures to the 3rd Forestry Company, Royal Australian Engineers, on the chemistry and uses of wood.

Haim's wife, Marguerite, awaited him in Britain.

Source: John Haim.

 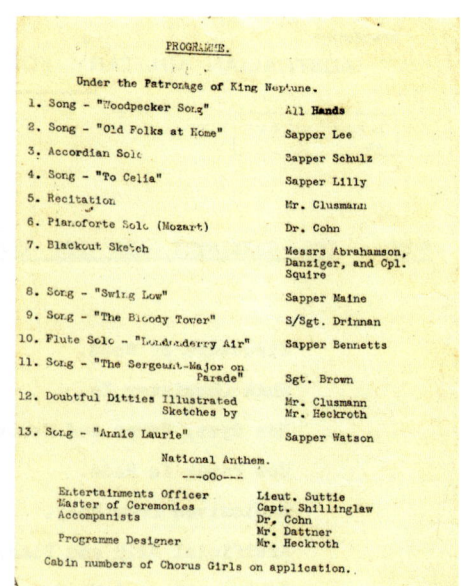

Programme for 'South Sea Sappers Serenade'

The educational traditions of Hay and Tatura were not the only echoes of camp life aboard the *Themistocles*. Former internees joined with sappers (army engineers) to stage a revue entitled 'South Sea Sappers Serenade'.

Source: John Haim

Baron Alexis Vivenot

Baron Alexis Johannes Maria Vivenot was born in Vienna in 1909. He was a diplomat and a Catholic with Jewish ancestors. He was interned in London on 2 July 1940, then deported to Australia on the *Dunera*.

In August 1942 he left Tatura for Britain; he never got there. On 29 October 1942, the MV *Abosso*, sailing from Cape Town, was sunk by a U-boat north-west of the Azores. Vivenot was one of 362 people who died when the ship went down.

Vivenot's mother, Countess Alice Kuenberg, never recovered from her son's death. She wrote to a British Home Office official in April 1943: 'With his death all the light has gone out, all and every interest in life is dead, and only one wish, to join him as soon as possible remains. The knowledge of what he has suffered, is agony.'

Source: National Archives of Australia, B6531, AUSTRIAN/VIVENOTALEXIS, 1941. Copyright: National Archives of Australia.

Quotation from The National Archives (United Kingdom), HO 214/64, Kuenberg to Bluett, 29 April 1943. Underlining in original.

Hans Spira's Service and Casualty Form

Hans Spira was born to a Jewish family in Vienna in 1922. He escaped to Britain on the last *Kindertransport* to leave the Continent.

In Australia he made use of his time in internment, working in the camp kitchens and studying Chinese under the tutelage of Leonhard Adam. Spira had wealthy relatives in Australia, but they offered him no help. He disliked Australia and never thought of settling in the country.

Spira left Tatura on 22 July 1942 to return to Britain. He worked in a factory in Scotland that produced aircraft propellers. In November 1943 he enlisted in the Royal Army Service Corps. Later he served in a Scottish unit under the name Henry Herbert Stewart. He may have seen combat, possibly in Belgium.

After the war, Spira, who reverted to using his original name, returned to Vienna. He was a member of the Communist party. He never spoke about his war experiences. He died in 1979.

Spira was one of many *Dunera* internees who regarded their time in Australia as an unfortunate interlude in their lives. For these men, Australia was to be endured and then left behind.

Source: National Archives of Australia, MP1103/1, E40704. Copyright: National Archives of Australia.

Horst Blumenthal, 93rd Company, Pioneer Corps, Southampton, 1943

Horst Blumenthal was born to a Jewish family in Berlin in 1920. He managed to leave Germany and find a job in Britain, working in the clothing trade in Bradford, Yorkshire. He was interned there on 16 May 1940.

He left Australia for Britain on the *Stirling Castle* in October 1941, joining the Pioneer Corps on his return. The name of the man to his right in the middle photograph is not known.

Source: Sharon Barnett.

Horst Blumenthal (Barney Barnett), Lübeck, Germany, 1946

In 1943 the British War Office ruled that non-British men could join fighting units. Blumenthal was one of a number of former *Dunera* internees who took this path; he left the Pioneer Corps for the 8th King's Royal Irish Hussars. At this time he changed his name to Horace Abraham (Barney) Barnett. The War Office advised men in Barnett's position to change their names as a precaution to hide identity should they be taken prisoner by Germany.

Barnett landed at Normandy on 7 June 1944 (D-Day+1). In October the tank he was in was hit by a missile and he was captured: once again he found himself behind barbed wire, though this time as a POW. As Horst Blumenthal, German Jewish refugee in the uniform of an enemy country, he likely would have been killed by his captors; as Barney Barnett, he was one British soldier among many.

Barnett stayed in the army and worked in Germany for a time after the war. This sketch of Sergeant Barnett was done in Lübeck in 1946. The artist was a local, name unknown.

In 1948 Barnett returned to Australia to live, acting on a decision he had made while a POW.

Source: Sharon Barnett.

Anton Walter Freud

Anton Walter Freud was born in 1921. He and other family members, including his grandfather Sigmund, escaped Vienna in 1938 through the intervention of friends and allies, including William Bullitt, the American ambassador to France, Dr Ernest Jones, a British psychoanalyst, and Princess Marie Bonaparte. In Britain both Anton Walter and his father Martin were interned and sent to the Isle of Man, but only Anton Walter was deported.

Anton Walter returned to Britain in July 1941 to join the Pioneer Corps. He signed up later that year. In early 1943 he transferred to the Special Operations Executive (SOE). In 1945 he parachuted into Austria, behind enemy lines.

At least two other former *Dunera* internees served in the SOE. Heinz Guenther Spanglet (Stephen Patrick Dale) was captured in northern Italy in late 1944 and spent six months as a POW of Germany. Six years earlier he had been imprisoned in Sachsenhausen concentration camp.

Peter Ernie Weisz went missing in the Netherlands in April 1945 while on an SOE operation. He was awarded, posthumously, The King's Commendation for Brave Conduct. Like Freud, Weisz served under his birth name, though unlike Freud he was not Jewish.

This photograph was probably taken in 1944 or 1945. The wings on Freud's breast pocket indicate he had qualified as a parachutist.

In August 1945, Freud was posted to the Control Commission for Germany. His work as an interpreter brought him into contact with Nazi war criminals.

Anton Walter's son, Baron David Anthony Freud, is a Conservative politician and member of the House of Lords.

Source: Rt. Hon. Lord Freud.

SECTION 6B

FRUIT-PICKING AND THE 8TH EMPLOYMENT COMPANY

FRUIT-PICKING AND THE 8TH EMPLOYMENT COMPANY

Fruit-pickers, Kyabram, c. March–April 1942

On 21 January 1942, Frank Forde, Minister for the Army, announced that internees would be able to join a labour company of the Australian army. This decision opened the gates of Tatura for those prepared to work in support of the Australian war effort. Over the next 10 weeks, about 415 *Dunera* and *Queen Mary* internees volunteered for the labour company.

While the army worked to form the proposed labour company, the internees who had signed up were dispatched across the Goulburn Valley to pick the stone fruit crop. Japan's entry into the war had taken men from the land to the front, diminishing the rural work force. The men from the *Dunera* and *Queen Mary* replaced them. Gunter Sondheim was among the men who went fruit-picking on his way to the army. It is thought he is the man on the bicycle.

The 8th Employment Company was formed on 7 April 1942. Its men, most of them citizens of countries with which Australia was at war, did not carry arms.

Source: Clive Sondheim and Jeanette Eforgan.

Fruit-picking, Shepparton, March 1942

Jules Stocky kept these photographs of himself and friends. The top image shows the men in fruit-picking garb. The bottom image shows a group of sophisticated young Europeans. Once their day was over, the men were free to enjoy their time as they pleased. For many, this meant exploring Shepparton and the delights it offered, including milkshakes, steak, and female company. Stocky is at right in both photographs.

Source: Stocky family.

FRUIT-PICKING AND THE 8TH EMPLOYMENT COMPANY

Friends go fruit-picking, early 1942

The photograph at top shows Hans Mannheim (second from left) and Gerd Sostheim (second from right). After meeting in England (page 30), they stuck together through captivity – at Hay, Orange and Tatura – and beyond. In the bottom photograph, Sostheim is at left. Here, as in the two previous photographs, we see men dressed for work and for leisure.

It is thought these photographs were taken in early 1942 when Mannheim and Sostheim were picking fruit on their way to the army. The length of the grass and the nature of the dwellings are indications that the pictures were not taken in an internment camp.

Source: Linda Mannheim.

Fruit-pickers at McNab orchard, Ardmona, 1942

Here members of the McNab family stand alongside former *Dunera* internees.

Herbert McNab and his wife Olga (nee Lenne), who was originally from Germany, offered a warm welcome to the men sent to labour in their peach and pear orchards. Enduring friendships were formed.

Franz Feuerstein, a talented musician, asked Mrs McNab if he might use the piano in her home to practise. His playing brought her such joy that she invited him to use the piano whenever he wished.

Herbert McNab stands closest to the truck. The small boy at his feet is his son Colin.

Source: Tom Firestone and Walter Firestone.

FRUIT-PICKING AND THE 8TH EMPLOYMENT COMPANY

Farewell to Tatura, 1942

The opportunity to join the 8th Employment Company remained open to internees through the war, with those who joined the unit after its formation in April 1942 going directly into the army. Only the men who volunteered between January and April 1942 were sent to pick fruit. The last internee to join the 8th Employment Company did so in September 1944.

Erich Tichauer left Tatura for the army in November 1942. This farewell card, given to him by Ulrich Laufer, covers the internees' journey from freedom to internment to freedom, via London, Cape Town, Sydney and Hay.

Laufer, born to a Jewish family in Berlin in 1923, had trained to be a commercial artist before internment. In 1943 he drowned in a swimming accident. Erich Tichauer was older, born in 1898 in Ratibor in Germany, now Racibórz in Poland. Friendships between men of different generations brought a familial element to the camps. The image to the right of the card suggests that Tichauer and Laufer may have worked together in a camp kitchen at Hay or Tatura.

Farewell card for E. Tichauer, Ulrich Laufer and Wolfgang Steinmetz, 1942. Jewish Museum of Australia collection 3295.

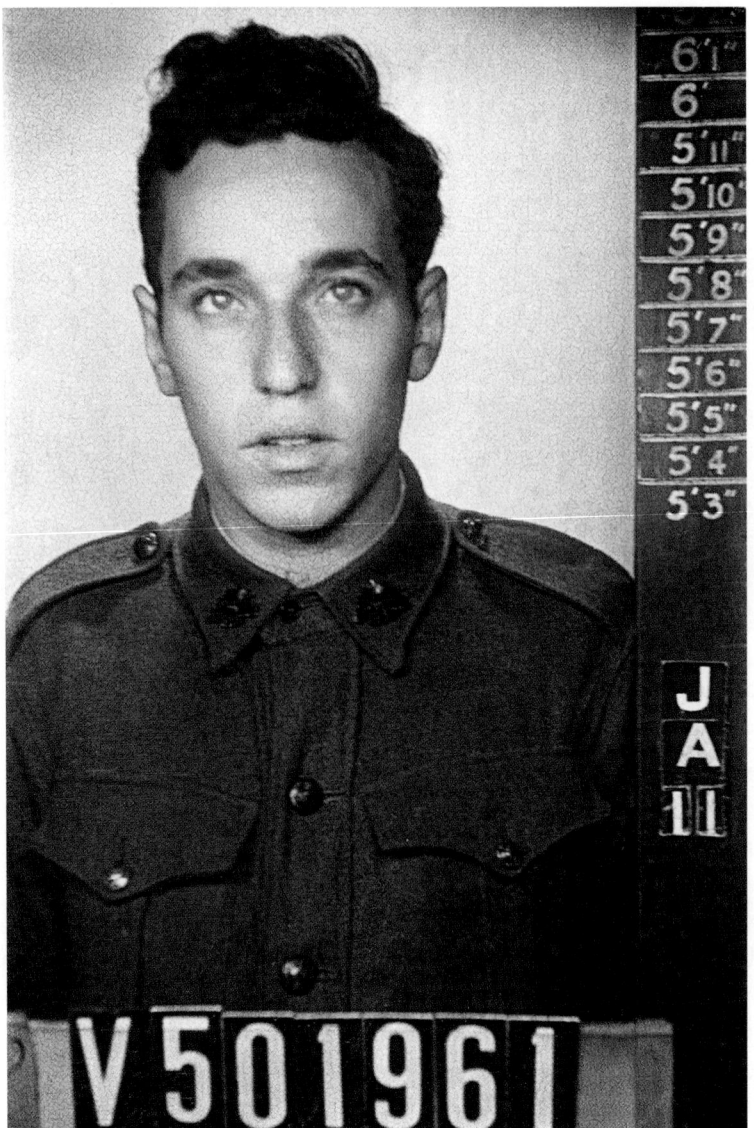

Erwin Lamm enlists

Erwin Lamm enlisted in the army at Royal Park, Melbourne, in September 1942. He did not sign up until he was sure the army could and would provide for his needs as an Orthodox Jew.

Lamm left the army in October 1944 to help lead an Orthodox Jewish community in Melbourne. He was a learned man, and though not a rabbi, he had an excellent voice and found a home among Melbourne's observant Jews.

Source: National Archives of Australia, B884, V501961, Lamm Erwin, 1939–48.

Copyright: National Archives of Australia.

FRUIT-PICKING AND THE 8TH EMPLOYMENT COMPANY

Erwin Fabian enlists

Fabian enlisted in the army in March 1942. He remained in the services until June 1946, when he was discharged.

Fabian's artistic talents developed during his army career. He contributed pictures to *Salt*, a wartime education journal published by the army for its soldiers, and designed covers for the *Current Affairs Bulletin*, a fortnightly publication of the Army Education Service.

His work also attracted attention beyond the army. In 1943 an exhibition of his drawings was held in Sydney, Adelaide and Melbourne, and that same year the National Gallery acquired his monotype entitled *Showerbath in camp*.

Source: National Archives of Australia, B884, V377518, Fabian Erwin, 1939–48. Copyright: National Archives of Australia.

Fritz Schönbach enlists

Fritz Schönbach was one of the most prolific artists among the *Dunera* internees. He provided a rich visual archive of life in captivity and beyond.

He enlisted in the army in April 1942, and like Erwin Fabian used his artistic talents to decorate army publications. His drawings occasionally brought financial reward. One of his works published in *Salt* earned him £1/10/-, and for another he won a canteen order.

Schönbach was discharged in August 1946.

Source: National Archives of Australia, B884, V377433, Schönbach Fritz, 1939–48. Copyright: National Archives of Australia.

FRUIT-PICKING AND THE 8TH EMPLOYMENT COMPANY

Fritz Gruen enlists

Fritz Gruen enlisted in the army in March 1942. From early October 1945 to the end of January 1946 he served in Lae, New Guinea, with the Australian Army Education Service. He was discharged in February 1946.

Gruen became one of the most distinguished economists of his generation.

Source: National Archives of Australia, B884, V377485, Gruen Fritz Henry Georg, 1939–48. Copyright: National Archives of Australia.

Helmut Neustaedter enlists

Helmut Neustaedter was born in Berlin in 1920, the son of a Jewish button factory owner. He developed an interest in photography while still at school. He was arrested briefly after *Kristallnacht*. His parents fled to South America, while he boarded the *Conte Rosso* at Trieste, heading for China. He disembarked at Singapore and there worked as a photographer. Interned in September 1940, he was sent to Australia on the *Queen Mary*.

In January 1942 Neustaedter signalled his intention to join the army. He picked fruit before donning an Australian army uniform three months later. He was discharged in August 1946.

Source: National Archives of Australia, B884, V377945, Neustaedter Helmut, 1939–48. Copyright: National Archives of Australia.

FRUIT-PICKING AND THE 8TH EMPLOYMENT COMPANY

Hans Mannheim, enemy alien and member of the Australian military forces, c. 1942

Hans Mannheim, German enemy alien, wore the famous slouch hat of the Australian army with pride.

He and other members of the 8th Employment Company remained 'enemy aliens' until February 1944, when they were granted 'refugee alien' status by the Australian government. It was a significant moment for it meant the *Dunera* men had a future in Australia, should they opt to stay.

Source: Linda Mannheim.

8th Employment Company coat of arms

Two of the main tasks of the 8th Employment Company were unloading cargo from ships docked at Port Melbourne, and working in towns along the Victoria–New South Wales border to transfer goods between trains.

The Latin tag on this coat of arms translates roughly as 'work and more work'. The design shows two railway gauges meeting over the red and white badge worn by members of the Australian army's employment companies, including the 8th. Emil Wittenberg designed the coat of arms.

Source and copyright: Martin Burman.

FRUIT-PICKING AND THE 8TH EMPLOYMENT COMPANY

8th Employment Company on parade, Royal Park, 1942

Royal Park in Melbourne was the site of a large military camp in the Second World War. At different times, Camp Royal Park, later named Camp Pell in honour of an American air force officer, was home to members of the 8th Employment Company.

The varied shapes of the men on parade confirm that the 8th was an unusual unit, made up of men whose ages and physical abilities sometimes differed greatly.

Franz Feuerstein marked his place in the photograph with an 'X', lest he forget.

Source: Tom Firestone and Walter Firestone.

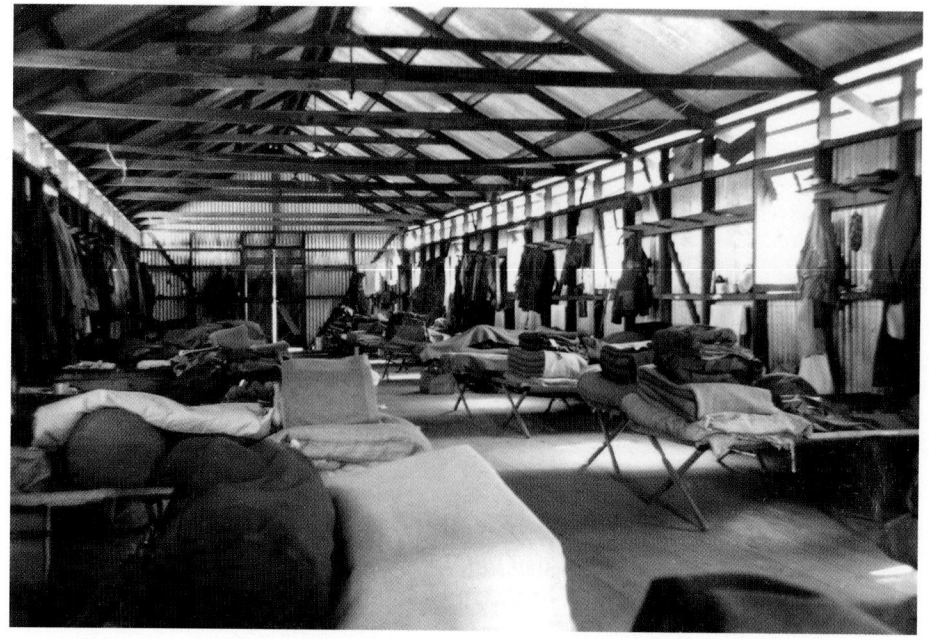

8th Employment Company barracks, 1942

The location of these barracks is not known, though Royal Park is likely.

One member of the 8th Employment Company, Franz Philipp, believed that rising from bed at a time dictated by the army was an infringement of his liberty.

Source: Kurt Liffman.

FRUIT-PICKING AND THE 8TH EMPLOYMENT COMPANY

The Duldig family, St Kilda, Melbourne, 1942

Private Karl Duldig stands with his wife Slawa and their daughter Eva outside their home in Park Street, St Kilda. Karl visited his wife and daughter whenever he could get a pass to leave barracks.

Karl had joined the army in April 1942. Slawa and Eva were released the next month. When an internee enlisted, it was usual that his wife and any of their children who remained in internment were freed soon after. Some school age children were released before their parents.

Karl in his army uniform, Slawa and Eva Duldig on the front verandah, Park St, St Kilda, 1942, black and white photograph (Inv. No. 6144). Copyright: The Duldig Studio.

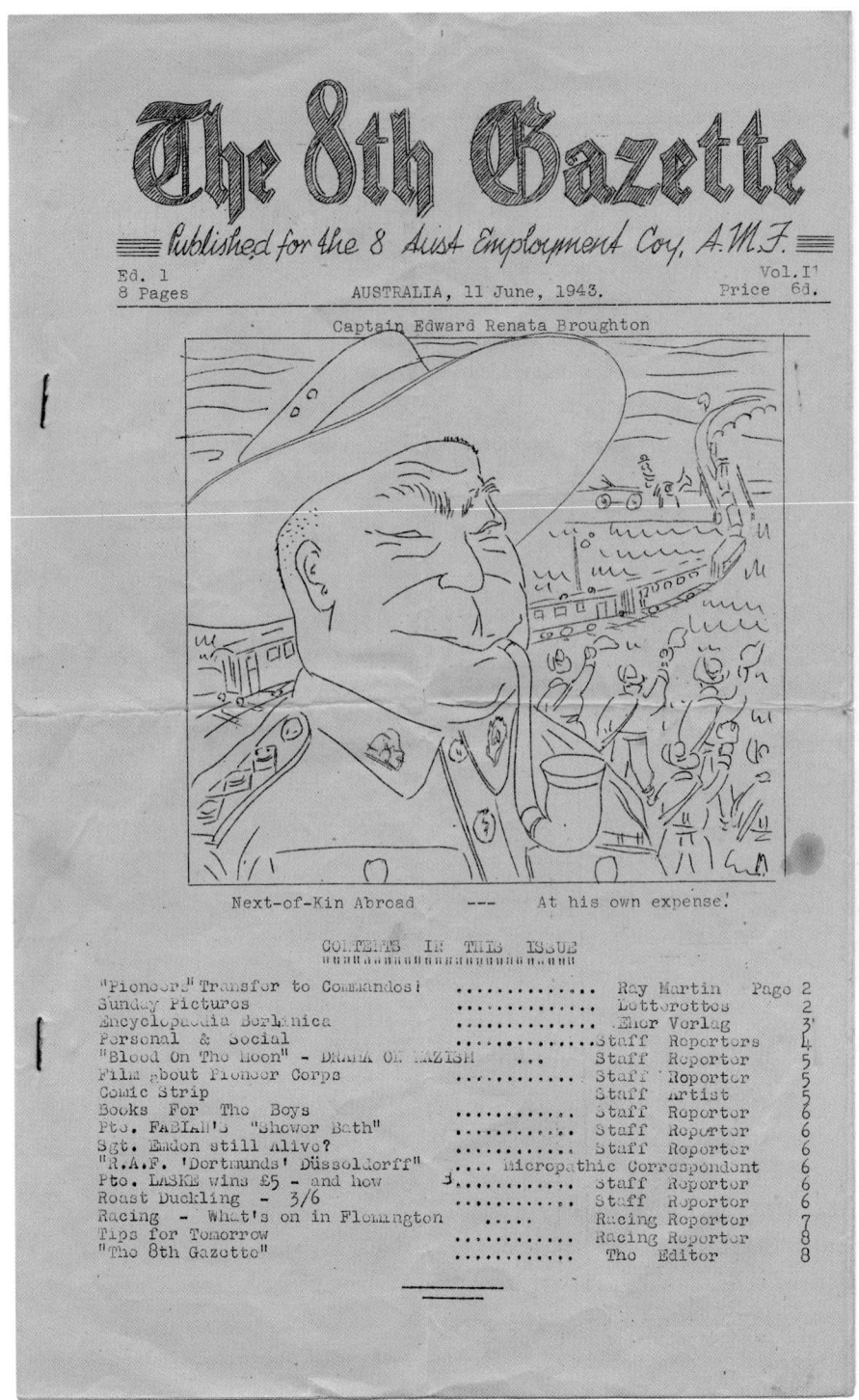

FRUIT-PICKING AND THE 8TH EMPLOYMENT COMPANY

Cover of *The 8th Gazette*, 11 June 1943

Camp newspapers filled time, and flourished even after the end of internment. This image shows the cover of the first edition of *The 8th Gazette*, 'Published for the 8 Aust. Employment Coy.' Corporal Bernhard Meier was editor and publisher, and Major Layton its first regular subscriber. Meier was a newspaper reporter who had been involved in editing and producing *The Boomerang*. *The 8th Gazette* included tips from a 'racing reporter', a sign that former internees were embracing aspects of Australian culture.

The caricature is of the avuncular Captain Edward Renata (Tip) Broughton, who commanded the 8th Employment Company until his retirement on 24 May 1944. Behind him a train snakes away, presumably after having its cargo loaded or unloaded by members of his unit. The name of the artist is unknown.

Broughton came from New Zealand, and was of mixed Maori and European parentage. He had put his age up to get to war in South Africa at the turn of the century, served on Gallipoli in the First World War, and put his age down to enlist for the Second World War. He was a Catholic, though perhaps not a very observant one. The majority of his men – possibly as many as 80 per cent – were Jews. It has been suggested that the 8th Employment Company was the most Jewish army unit in the world. He was responsive far beyond the call of duty to the dietary and other ritual requirements of the most Orthodox among them, and sympathetically curious about their faith and traditions. He was also a strict disciplinarian, with a sharp eye for humbug. Woe betide any man in the company who professed to be a Jew on Saturday and a Christian on Sunday. He was proud of his men, and they revered him. Fritz Schönbach wrote of Broughton: 'he knew everyone by name and all about our families.'

The 8th Gazette, 1943, Melbourne. Jewish Museum of Australia collection 3322.

Quotation from Schonbach to Howard E. Paine, National Geographic Magazine, 1988. Letter in possession of Gabriela Schonbach.

Eva Duldig with bronze cast of Captain Broughton, c. 1943

Karl Duldig rendered Captain Broughton in bronze, fashioning a cast of his head. Eva Duldig stands in front of her father's work.

The photograph was taken in Melbourne, most likely in early 1943.

Karl Duldig, *Eva Duldig with bronze cast of Captain Broughton c. 1943*, black and white photograph (Inv. No. 6229). Copyright: The Duldig Studio.

FRUIT-PICKING AND THE 8TH EMPLOYMENT COMPANY

```
8 AUST EMPLOYMENT COY MARCH

                    Words & Music by Sgt. L O H D E.

We know the world from Norway down to Greece
We left our homes and sailed the Seven Seas;
We answered the call, when they asked for volunteers
For the Home Defence as Pioneers
In Austra - li - a - a - a.

When a ship comes in then we take the freight ashore,
And we work like hell as we've never done before.
We shift bales and cases and we handle them with skill,
And enjoy the daily drill
In the e - ve - ning, ching, ching,
In the e - ve - ning.

We are fond of marching and we always "shake it up",
Trotting like the horses at a rainy Melbourne Cup.
Smartly we jump out when the morning bugle goes
And there roar those N.C.O's
Those N - C - O - oh - ohs
Those N - C - Os!

Give us our Leave Pass and we give you a fair go
Give us a long spell and let us have a blow;
Then you'll be surprised how efficient we can be
The Employment Company
The Eightth Employ-oy-oy-
- Ment Company.

We have lots of fun, when we flirt and when we dance;
We don't like C.B., when we go in for romance,
But Absent Without Leave does not enter our minds,
When we serve in our lines
With stew and bullybeef
With bullybeef.

Ev'rybody thinks we're a funny looking crowd,
Being in the Army makes us feeling mighty proud.
We adore the Skipper and salute the Rising Sun,
Until Victory is won.
For Peace and Victory,
FOR    VICTORY!
```

The 8th Employment Company march

Sergeant Sigurd Lohde (Sydney Loder), a stage and screen actor from Weimar, composed a march for the 8th Employment Company. His lyrics attest to the pride he and his comrades felt in serving Broughton and Australia.

8th Australian Employment Company March, Sigurd Lohde, 1940s. Jewish Museum of Australia collection 4466.

8th Employment Company posters, 7 April 1943

These 1943 posters (above and right) celebrated the first anniversary of the 8th Employment Company. The posters were the work of Lance Corporal Friedrich Oschinsky, a member of the unit.

This first poster tells that the 8th Employment Company was doing its bit to bring about American President Franklin Roosevelt's four freedoms. The patriotic tag at the bottom suited former internees well: 'The great things [sic] in this life is not so much where we are standing as in what direction we are moving'.

FRUIT-PICKING AND THE 8TH EMPLOYMENT COMPANY

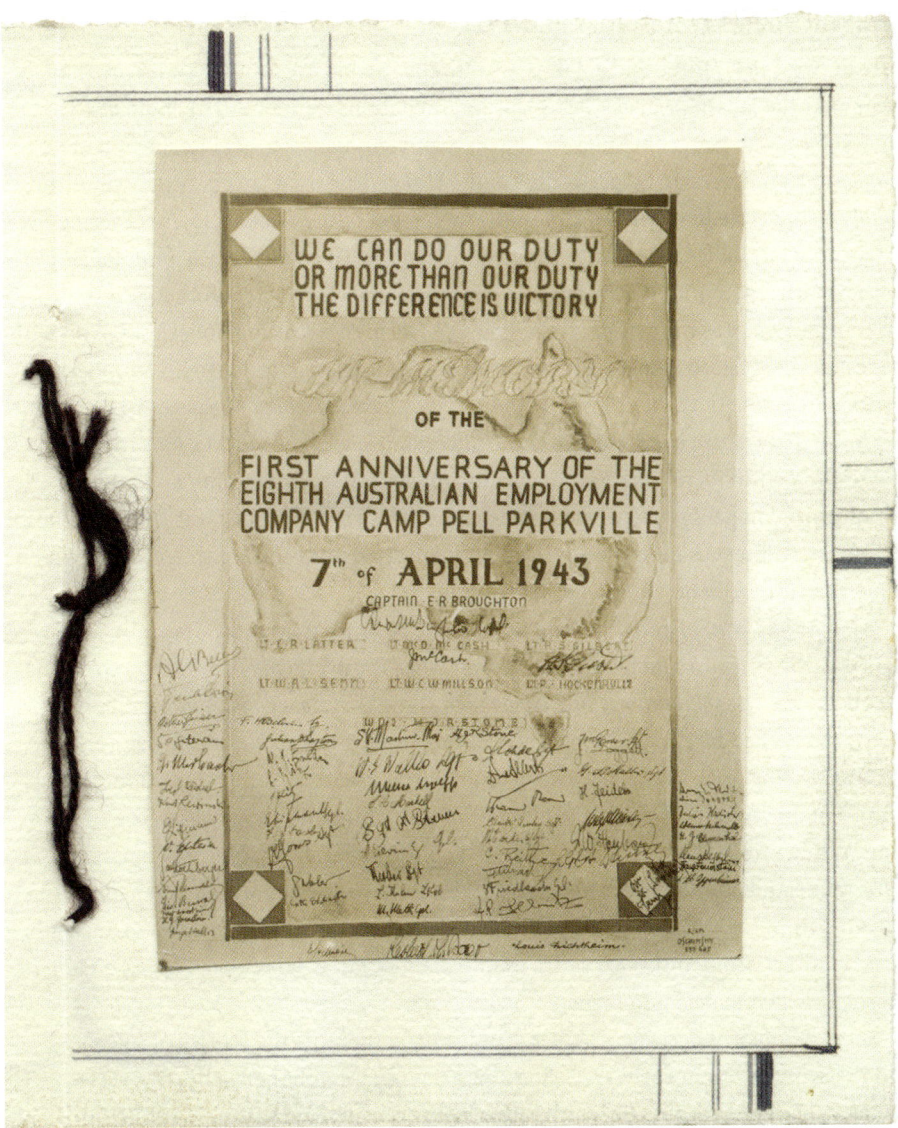

The poster above, which carries the signatures of Captain Broughton and other members of the 8th Employment Company, confirms the unit was proud to contribute to the war effort. This kind of wartime public art mixes swagger with a trace of self-mockery.

Werner Hirschfeld collection, Sydney Jewish Museum, M2015/018:017.

'Sergeant Snow White' programme (1)

Early in April 1943, three and a half years into the Second World War and more than a year after the Japanese struck Pearl Harbor, invitations went out in Melbourne to a remarkable event. 'Sergeant Snow White', a 'happy-go-lucky Musical Revue of Bad Old and Good New Times' to be performed at the Union Theatre, University of Melbourne, would celebrate the first anniversary of the formation of the 8th Employment Company.

The folk tale collected in early nineteenth century Germany by the philologist brothers Grimm, telling the story of the princess, the wicked stepmother and the seven little men, was known in virtually every German-speaking household. And with the rest of the western world Germans and Austrians were familiar with a modern version of the tale in the medium of cinema. Walt Disney's film released in 1938, the first animated feature ever made in the United States, was the world's most profitable film in the year of its release, and its formula of sugary sentimentality and gothic horror proved hugely popular wherever the film was shown. Hitler was known to be an enthusiast. Audiences in England included many, perhaps most, of the refugees who were to be interned and shipped to Australia.

Snow White was admired by film makers far beyond its country of origin, among them Charlie Chaplin and Sergei Eisenstein. Also among Disney's admirers was Kurt Sternberg, known as 'Doc', his nickname signalling that he was a Doctor of Law. The 'Doc', who turned forty in September 1939, had made films in Germany before 1933 and then in England, where he worked as producer and director for Gaumont British Films. For an accomplished practitioner of popular film and theatre arts, the story of Snow White provided an attractive template, anchored in both the traditional culture of his homeland and the international and modern world, into which fate had now delivered him. Into this accommodating vessel he could include whatever elements he chose to insert, from anti-Nazi satire to knockabout farce. His experience as a *Dunera* internee yielded material in plenty.

Snow White had become a *Dunera* tradition by the time the release of internees into the army began in early 1942, Sternberg having brought her to life in a series of revues in Hay and Tatura. 'Sergeant Snow White' owed most to 'Snow White Joins Up', first performed at Tatura on 31 December 1941. It incorporated songs and music by *Dunera* internee Kurt Kohn, a composer and entertainer who liked to work under pseudonyms, most commonly Ray Martin.

By the end of 1942, Corporal Sternberg of the 8th Employment Company had set to work composing an enriched version of his show incorporating the now conceivable prospect of a victorious outcome, to which he and other former *Dunera* internees were making their own, albeit modest, contribution. Erich Liffmann was cast as Prince Charming, the star of the show. Sternberg had heard him sing in London before the war and had sought to cast him in a film, and they had worked together since joining the army. In July 1942 Liffmann had sung at a concert organised by Sternberg in Dandenong, east of Melbourne.

FRUIT-PICKING AND THE 8TH EMPLOYMENT COMPANY

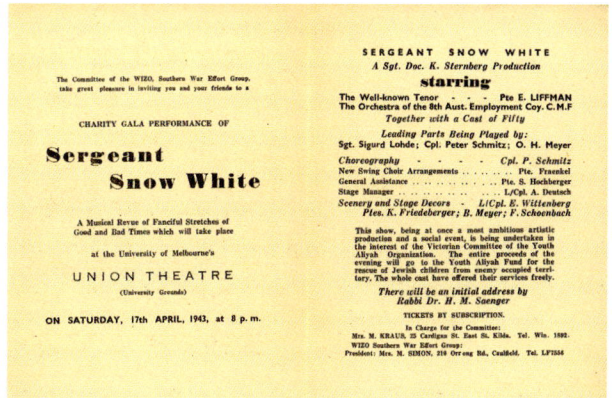

In his theatrical pursuits Sternberg had the blessing of Captain Broughton. He made it possible for Sternberg and his comrades to combine military duties with rehearsals, and was evidently untroubled by lines in the script which made the unit the 8th *Enjoyment* Company – a term that stuck. Broughton even had a part in the show, playing himself in a scene celebrating the unit's anniversary.

'Sergeant Snow White' invitations and programmes turn up in many collections of *Dunera* memorabilia. Different versions were printed for performances of the revue in April and May 1943. This particular invitation, with artwork by Erwin Fabian, was for a performance on 17 April.

Invitation to Sergeant Snow White charity gala performance, 1943.
Jewish Museum of Australia collection 7039.

Reference

Radio Times, May 17-23, 1942, Vol. 9, No. 20.

"Sergeant Snow White"

A HAPPY-GO-LUCKY MUSICAL REVUE OF BAD OLD AND GOOD NEW TIMES
A SERGEANT DOC. K. STERNBERG PRODUCTION.

Union Theatre on May 11th, 12th and 13th, 1943.

Programme

Act 2.
"Europe Calling"

1. OUVERTURE
2. PROLOGUE
   Grandma .. .. Pte. J. Feder
   Child .. .. Pte. L. Oppenheimer
3. EUROPE ON THE AIR
4. ENGLAND:
   R. C. Sherriff's "Journey's End"
   Capt. Stanhope .. Sgt. S. LOHDE
   Lieut. Hibbert .. Pte. F. Gruen
5. FRANCE: BAL TABARIN
   The Chansonier .. Pte. H. Blau
   The Musician .. Sgt. W. BAER
   Les Jeunes Filles du Bal Tabarin }
   Les Spectateurs } The Ballet
6. RUSSIA: MELODIES OF RUSSIA
   Ivan .. Pte. ERIC LIFFMANN
   6 Russians Sgt. W. BAER and 5 Accordionists
7. AUSTRIA: PRATER DREAM
   Alois Lerchengruber .. Pte. H. Blau
   Hederl .. ? ? ?
   4 Admirers—The Ballet
8. CZECHOSLOVAKIA:
   J. Hazek's "The Good Soldier Schweyck"
   Imperial Medical Officer Sgt. S. LOHDE
   3 Czech Patients
   Palivets .. Pte. S. Hochberger
   Pokorny .. Pte. H. Fleischer
   Schweyck .. Pte. L. Komorner
   Her Imperial Highness .. E. Hutterer
   Medical Orderly .. Pte. F. Weidenbaum
9. ENTRE ACT: The Witch at Work
   The Witch .. Cpl. A. P. SCHMITZ
   Wolf .. Pte. H. Reiss
10. GERMANY:
    THE GESTAPO OFFICE
    Nazi Party Secretary .. Sgt. S. LOHDE
    Solicitor .. Pte. K. Lowenstein
11. THE COSMOPOLITAN
    Pte. L. Oppenheimer
12. POLAND: CHOPIN'S NOCTURNE
    2 Polish Barons .. Ptes. J. Chlumecky
    F. H. Feuerstein
    2 Nazi Soldiers .. L/Cpl. H. Davidson
    Pte. F. Gruen
13. THE EUROPEAN
    Sgt. S. LOHDE
14. THE GHOSTS OF EUROPE
    The Ballet—Ensemble
    Soloist, Cpl. A. P. SCHMITZ
    INTERVAL

Act 1.
"Snow White"

1. Ouverture
2. Prologue
   Grandma .. Pte. J. Feder
   Child .. Pte. L. Oppenheimer
3. The Mirror
   Queen .. O. H. MAYER
   Master of the Bedchamber Sgt. S. LOHDE
4. Fairy Wood
   Snow White .. Snow White
   Prince Charming Pte. ERIC LIFFMANN
   Long Nose } .. Pte. H. Reiss
   Wolf }
   The Witch .. Cpl. A. P. SCHMITZ
5. The Banquet
   Queen .. O. H. MAYER
   Master of the Bedchamber Sgt. S. Hochberger
   2 Ambassadors .. Pte. S. Hochberger
   E. Hutterer
   Wolf .. Pte. H. Reiss
   The Witch .. Cpl. A. P. SCHMITZ
   Prince Charming Pte ERIC LIFFMANN
   The King of the Gypsies PAUL STEINER
   Master of the Tappers } Pte. C. Begach
   Captain of the Guard }
   The Seven Dwarfs The Swing Choir
   The Ballet
   INTERVAL

Act 3.
"Snow White in Camp"

1. Ouverture
2. Prologue
   Grandma .. Pte. J. Feder
   Child .. Pte. L. Oppenheimer
3. The Dwarfs at Home
   Prince Charming Pte. ERIC LIFFMANN
   The Seven Private Dwarfs
   The Swing Choir
4. Orderly Room
   The C.O. .. O. H. MAYER
   Sergeant Staff .. Sgt. S. LOHDE
   2 Soldiers .. Ptes. F. Weidenbaum
   F. Gruen
   The Committee Lady .. E. Hutterer
   The Toys .. The Ballet
5. The Sergeant Major
   W/O. H. J. R. STONE
   The Seven Private Dwarfs
6. On Arguing the Point
   Pte. L. Oppenheimer
7. The Dwarfs at the Wharves
   Sergeant Staff .. Sgt. S. LOHDE
   Private Charming Pte. ERIC LIFFMANN
   The O.C. .. O. H. MAYER
   The Seven Private Dwarfs
8. Calling All Cobbers
   The Ensemble

AT THE PIANOS: L/Cpl. H. PORTNOJ, Ptes. E. FRAENKEL, H. FICHMAN, H. VOSS, S. COHN, R. LAQUEUR

SEVEN DWARFS	SWING CHOIR	BALLET	ACCORDIONISTS
H. Goldstein	W. Hirschfeld	C. BEGACH	Sgt. W. Baer
F. Weidenbaum	H. Hermansohn	F. Rosenthal E. Schieinger	L/Cpl. K. Blach
O. Stiwelband	A. Landauer	O. Stiwelband J. Feder	L/Cpl. K. Wuerrzburger
W. Hirschfeld	O. Stiwelband	M. Klein H. Goldstein	Pte. S. Cohn
M. Reichwald	M. Reichwald	O. Gabler K. Tichauer	Pte. H. Loewe
H. Hermansohn	H. Fraenkel		Pte. G. Brandt
A. Landauer			

"Sergeant Snow White"
Written and Directed by SERGEANT DOC K. STERNBERG
CHOREOGRAPHY: CPL. A. PETER SCHMITZ
Ballet and Dances arranged by Cpl. A. P. Schmitz, M. Lewinsky.   Musical Arrangements by Ptes. S. Cohn and H. Fichman
SPECIAL MUSICAL ARRANGEMENTS BY RAY MARTIN
In Charge of Swing Choir: Pte. E. Fraenkel.   Schrammel Quartet: Sgt. W. Baer, Ptes. A. Landauer, Reiter, O. Silberstein
Chansons by E. Lehrburger, F. Gottfurcht, R. Popper, A. Gray, F. Hollaender.   Poem, "Listen Brothers," by Pte. S. Hochberger
STAGE MANAGER: L/CPL. A. DEUTSCH
In Charge of Light: L/Cpl. H. Davidson
Make Up: Make Up Artist Pte. Carlos Beer.   Masks for Ballet "Ghosts of Europe" by Pte. E. Fabian
Costumes by Courtesy of Messrs. J. C. Williamson, Ltd.   Wiggs by Messrs. L. Barnett & Sons
SCENERY AND STAGE DECORS: L/Cpl. EMIL WITTENBERG,
Pte. K. FRIEDEBERGER, Pte. B. I. MEIER, Pte. F. SCHOENBACH
Chairman of Committee: W/O. H. J. R. STONE   Secretary and Business Manager: Pte. H. E. FLEISCHER
Assistant: L/Cpl. E. LIPMANN

Riall Bros. Pty. Ltd., Printers, 212 Bay St., Port Melbourne

'Sergeant Snow White programme' (2)

This version of the 'Sergeant Snow White' programme, produced for performances on 11, 12 and 13 May 1943, lists the acts, scenes, cast, musicians and crew.

The revue told of Sergeant Snow White and her dwarves leaving the land of make believe, escaping occupied Europe, and joining the Australian army. Snow White herself remained an unseen presence. As one critic observed, 'Sternberg's plot puts Snow White in a concentration camp because of doubtful Aryan origin of her creators, Brothers Grimm.' Later Snow White is said to be in Australia. Where is Sergeant Snow White, the Queen asks of the seven dwarves at the end of the revue. On ten days' home leave in Sydney, they reply. 'Probably asleep again', thunders the Queen. 'I'll court martial her … take off her stripes'. Meanwhile, Prince Charming, or rather 'Private' Charming, informs the Queen that he is to be 'discharged for work of national importance': he has a relationship to conduct with Sergeant Snow White. The quirks of the script are many. Sternberg rendered Hitler as 'Shitler' and Mussolini as the 'Italian Crime Minister'.

'The Ghosts of Europe' scene centred on a ballet which told of nations under Nazi rule deposing 'The Witch', played by Peter Schmitz, a corporal in the 8th and a sometime professional ballet dancer.

In act 3, scene 4, Private Fritz Gruen and Private Fritz Weidenbaum (Fred Carter) played two soldiers. Their post-war lives would place them on more formal stages. Gruen advised Prime Minister Gough Whitlam on economic affairs, while Weidenbaum worked as a butler at Government House, Melbourne.

Sergeant Snow White, Erwin Fabian, illustrator, 1943. Jewish Museum of Australia collection, 3362.

References

'Alien Soldiers' Show Twits Nazis', *Pix*, Vol. 11, No. 26, 26 June 1943.

Sergeant Snow White script, Dr K. Sternberg, 1943, Jewish Museum of Australia collection, 3685.

Performance of 'Sergeant Snow White', Union Theatre, University of Melbourne, 1943

These photographs of a 'Sergeant Snow White' performance were taken by Harry Jeidels. Some of his photographs of the revue were published in the illustrated magazine *Pix* under the headline 'Alien Soldiers' Show Twits Nazis'.

The rollicking and sophisticated show, redolent of pre-Nazi Berlin and Vienna, might have heralded a new form of entertainment in Australia. The reviewer for *Pix* thought this 'Continental ... blend of revue, farce and satire' would 'stimulate a taste for flesh-and-blood stage, swelling its audience.' Catherine Duncan, a left-wing playwright writing in *The Listener In*, declared the show an absorbing mix of the 'gay and tragic'. Here was Melbourne's 'first taste of European wit blended with the Australian idiom', she wrote. As it was, the revue left no legacy other than fond memories in the minds of cast, crew, and audience.

A complete script for 'Sergeant Snow White' survives in carbon copy, a precious record of what the men from the *Dunera* were thinking and imagining nearly three years into their internment.

Performers in Sergeant Snow White, Harry Jeidels, 1943. Jewish Museum of Australia collection 3442, 3443, 3444.

References

'Alien Soldiers' Show Twits Nazis', *Pix*, Vol. 11, No. 26, 26 June 1943.

Catherine Duncan, 'Snow White Joins the Army', *The Listener In*, 22-28 May 1943.

Kurt 'Doc' Sternberg, 1943

'Doc' Sternberg was born in 1899 in Zielenzig, Germany, to Jewish parents.

The uniform he wears is not that of the 8th Employment Company, or any Australian unit. He may have been dressed for a part in one of his revues.

Doc. K. Sternberg, 1943. Jewish Museum of Australia collection 3473.

Kia Eriki Riiwhimana
E Hoa Tena Koe. He kupu aroha enei mo nga
ra e heke mai ana te tumanakotanga o te
ngakau kia tae koe ki te tihi o te maunga
waiata ki reira tu ai a ake tonu. Heoi
ma te Kai Hanga koe e awhina a nga
wa katoa. Na Muhunga.
Translation. Edward Broughton. Capt.
To Erich Liffmann
My Son Salutation! These the words of
affection founded on thoughts emanating from
the depths of my Soul that some day you
will ascend to the peak of the mountain
of Song and there dwell for ever. May the
Creator bless you and guard you always
Edward Broughton
CAPTAIN EDWARD R. BROUGHTON
O.C. 8 AUST. EMPLOYMENT COY.
20 MAY 1943 Camp. Pell - Australia.

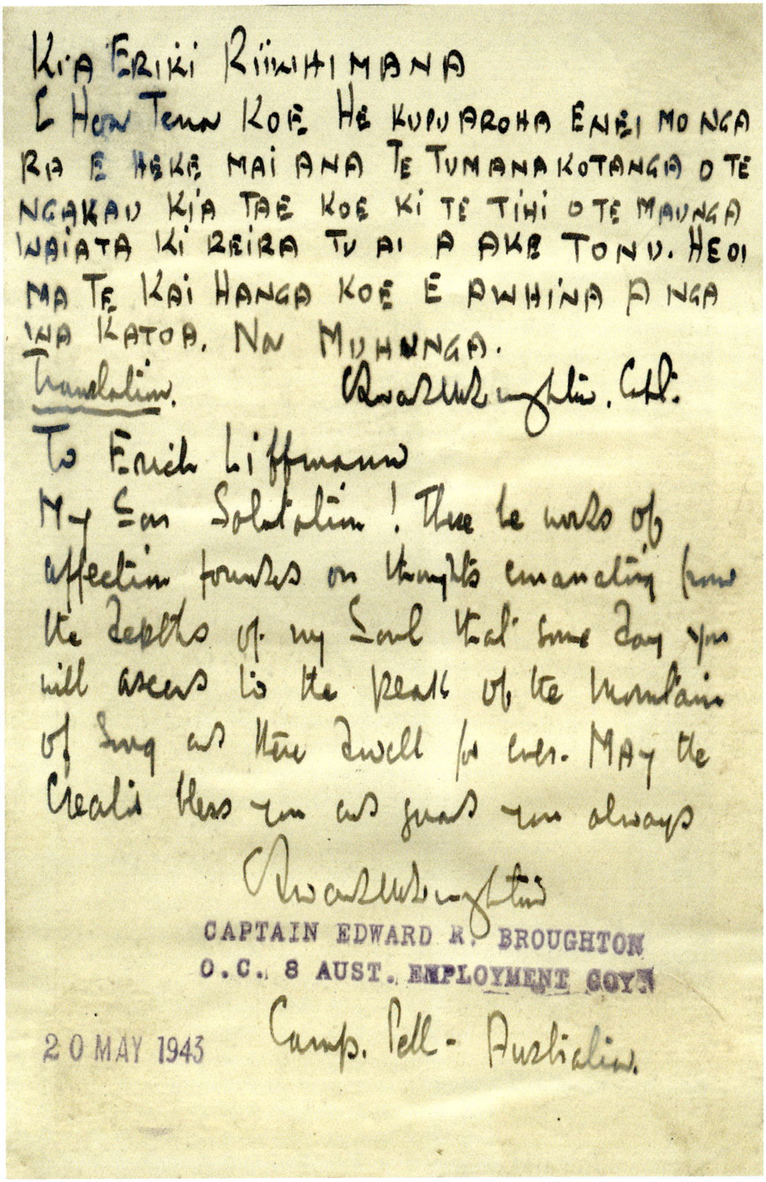

Letter from Captain Broughton to Erich Liffmann, 20 May 1943

In May 1943 Captain Broughton sent a letter to Erich Liffmann. He wrote in Maori, which he then translated. The translation (edited) reads:

'These words of affection are founded on thoughts emanating from the depths of my soul that some day you will ascend to the peak of the mountain of song and there dwell forever. May the creator bless you and guide you always.'

Source: Kurt Liffman.

Erich Liffmann, soldier and tenor

Erich Liffmann is shown standing by a poster advertising one of his musical performances. On 19 June 1944, he performed 'Songs the people love' at the Assembly Hall, Collins Street, Melbourne, in aid of the Australian Comforts Fund. The poster used an Anglicised version of his name. On stage at least, Erich Liffmann had already become Eric Liffman.

Another member of the 8th Employment Company and former *Dunera* internee was involved in the recital. Herbert Voss, a pianist, was one of the 'associate artists'.

Source: Kurt Liffman.

FRUIT-PICKING AND THE 8TH EMPLOYMENT COMPANY

'Black Rock, Melbourne', 1942

Klaus Friedeberger joined the Australian army in March 1942. In his free time, he explored Melbourne and its art scene. He formed friendships with artists Sidney Nolan and Arthur Boyd, and John Reed, whose Contemporary Art Society promoted modernist artists and their works. To these relationships Friedeberger brought thoughts and ideas about art derived from his time in camp: he had studied art history with Franz Philipp and Ernst Kitzinger, colour theory with Ludwig Hirschfeld-Mack, and surrealism with Hein Heckroth.

Friedeberger's surrealist painting is set in Black Rock, a suburb of Melbourne, where Friedeberger and a girlfriend spent time at the beach. The Australian army hat appears to cover the arousal, and longings, of the figure at left.

Source: England & Co. Gallery, London. Collection and copyright: Klaus Friedeberger.

References

Email from Klaus Friedeberger to Seumas Spark, 7 March 2017.

[Jane England], *Klaus Friedeberger: Works 1940-1970*, (London: England & Co, undated), pp. 8-9.

Eureka Youth League outing, c. 1942–1943

These men and women are members of the Eureka Youth League on an outing to Sherbrooke Forest in the Dandenong Ranges east of Melbourne. Fritz Heymann and his future wife, Mirjam (Miriam) Lobatz, are pictured. He is third from the left in the middle row; Mirjam is second from the right in the same row, with her arms crossed. She and her family were German Jewish refugees who arrived in Australia in June 1939.

Fritz, born to a Jewish family in 1922 in Euskirchen in western Germany, left Tatura for the army in July 1942. He was discharged in February 1946. In the photograph he wears army uniform, as do some of the other men. They too may have been members of the 8th Employment Company.

The Eureka Youth League, founded in 1941, was affiliated with the Communist Party of Australia. The League sought to attract enthusiastic men and women committed to building socialism in Australia.

Source: Colin Heymann.

FRUIT-PICKING AND THE 8TH EMPLOYMENT COMPANY

Wedding of Jules Stocky and Jean Nicol, 13 March 1943

On 13 March 1943, Jules Stocky married Jean Nicol at the Sacred Heart Catholic church in Kew, Melbourne. He was among the first men from the *Dunera* to marry in Australia. Frank Maher, a prominent Melburnian and Catholic intellectual, was best man. He is second from right, and his wife Molly is to his right in the white hat. Jules and Jean had met at the Mahers' home in Kew in 1942. Captain Broughton is second from left.

Jean came from a prosperous and well-established Gippsland farming family. Marked 'German by marriage', her travel was even more restricted than her husband's. He at least was in the army.

Source: Stocky family.

Wedding of Franz Feuerstein and Posy Kloot, 14 September 1943

Franz Feuerstein and Mathilde Kloot, always known as Posy, married in the Toorak Road synagogue, Melbourne, on 14 September 1943. The best man was Gerd Feuerstein, Franz's brother and fellow member of the 8th Employment Company. Captain Broughton granted Franz leave for the wedding and honeymoon.

Posy's family had come to Australia from England in 1919. The Jewish fathers of both bride and groom fought on opposite sides in the First World War.

Source: Tom Firestone and Walter Firestone.

Walter Kaufmann and Barbara Dyer

Walter Kaufmann left Tatura in March 1942 to join the Australian army. While in the army he met Barbara Dyer, originally from Strahan in Tasmania, and they married at Tocumwal, on the New South Wales-Victoria border, on 20 October 1944. She was an army sergeant engaged in secret work, coding and decoding cypher messages. They later divorced.

These photographs date from Walter's time in the 8th Employment Company. The image above was taken in 1943, the image below in 1944.

After being discharged from the army in February 1946, Walter began a long career as a writer. He has lived and worked in Australia, East Germany, and, since the fall of the Berlin Wall, in unified Germany.

Source: Walter Kaufmann, via Volker Dittrich.

8th Employment Company soldiers

The photograph at top, probably taken in Royal Park in 1942, shows eight soldiers of the 8th Employment Company, aglow with camaraderie. Their uniforms do not sit well.

Top row, from left: Alfred (Fred) Katz, Ernst Wolf, Kurt Leiser, Erich Strauss. Bottom row, from left: Gerd May, Walter Epstein, Guenter Hartwich, Albert Katz.

The photograph below, taken two years later at Tocumwal, shows three of the same men: from left, Ernst Wolf, Albert Katz, and Gerd May. The contrast between the images is striking. Now the men are comfortable in the attire of the Australian army Digger.

Source: Anna and Andrew Wolf.

FRUIT-PICKING AND THE 8TH EMPLOYMENT COMPANY

Erich Liffmann, almost in uniform, December 1944

Erich Liffmann relaxes in his army slouch hat, St Kilda beach, December 1944. Captions in his photograph album refer to St Kilda as 'the home for Yanks and prostitutes'. Another caption reads 'The fighting tenor'.

Source: Kurt Liffman.

Gerd Bernstein, 8th Employment Company soldier, c. 1943–1944

Gerd Bernstein joined the 8th Employment Company in April 1942. These photographs give glimpses of his army life.

In the top photograph Bernstein is second from right. He and others are leaving Camp Pell on the back of an army truck. The photograph was taken by Helmut Neustaedter.

In the bottom photograph Bernstein is at right.

Source: Bern Brent.

FRUIT-PICKING AND THE 8TH EMPLOYMENT COMPANY

The 8th Employment Company at Tocumwal, 1945

In the top left photograph, the last but one soldier waiting for food is Helmut Neustaedter. In the top right photograph, Gerd Bernstein is furthest left, and on his right are Manfred (Mike) Klein and Kurt Gert Treitel (Gary Trent). The bottom photograph was taken on a Sunday, rest day for the men of the 8th. After cleaning out his tent, Bernstein caught up on his reading. He was studying International Economics as part of an army correspondence course.

Though not allowed to carry guns, members of the 8th Employment Company were ordered to hump boxes of ammunition from one train to another. As the men recalled with amusement, they fought 'the battle for Albury', or Tocumwal in this case, at the break of gauge.

Source: Bern Brent.

Alfred Rosenthal, Tocumwal, 2 April 1945

Fritz Schönbach sketched Alfred Rosenthal at Tocumwal, surrounded by flies. Five years on from his arrival in Australia, Schönbach was still drawing flies.

Fritz Schönbach, No title, 1945, ink on paper. Jewish Museum of Australia collection 3386.

FRUIT-PICKING AND THE 8TH EMPLOYMENT COMPANY

'Tocumwal landscape, NSW', c. 1945

Klaus Friedeberger painted this surrealist vision of Tocumwal in 1945. His intention was to convey the impression made on him by the 'surrealistic' landscape of Australia. He found the space and light unfamiliar.

His depiction of Tocumwal differs markedly from that sketched by Emil Wittenberg (page 227).

Source: England & Co. Gallery, London. Private collection. Copyright: Klaus Friedeberger.

Reference

Email from Klaus Friedeberger to Seumas Spark, 7 March 2017.

'In the Park (Botanical Gardens, Melbourne)', 1945

Klaus Friedeberger's painting has everything missing in Tocumwal: spectacular and lush plants and vegetation.

In the artist's words, the painting derived from a 'sort of vaguely oneiric surrealism' and owed a debt to Rousseau. The painting was displayed in a Melbourne exhibition organised by the Contemporary Art Society.

Friedeberger was still in the army when he painted this picture. He was discharged in August 1946.

Source: England & Co. Gallery, London. Collection and copyright: Klaus Friedeberger.

Reference

Email from Klaus Friedeberger to Seumas Spark, 7 March 2017.

Hans Mannheim and malaria research

From 1943 the Australian army conducted research into malaria, which was having a devastating effect on its soldiers in New Guinea. A specialist team working in Queensland was responsible for the research.

Army units, including the 8th Employment Company, were canvassed for volunteers to take part in clinical tests to help develop treatments for malaria. Gerd Bernstein volunteered but was rejected. 'Thank God', he later wrote. The task of the men who were accepted was to be bitten by mosquitoes.

Hans Mannheim was one former *Dunera* internee who joined the research programme. He was involved both as a subject and as a laboratory assistant. After the war he moved to the United States, qualified as a doctor, and worked in the field of medical research.

This photograph was taken in 1944. Mannheim was part of the malaria research programme from December 1944 to January 1945.

Source: Linda Mannheim.

Reference

Email from Bern Brent to Seumas Spark, 20 October 2015.

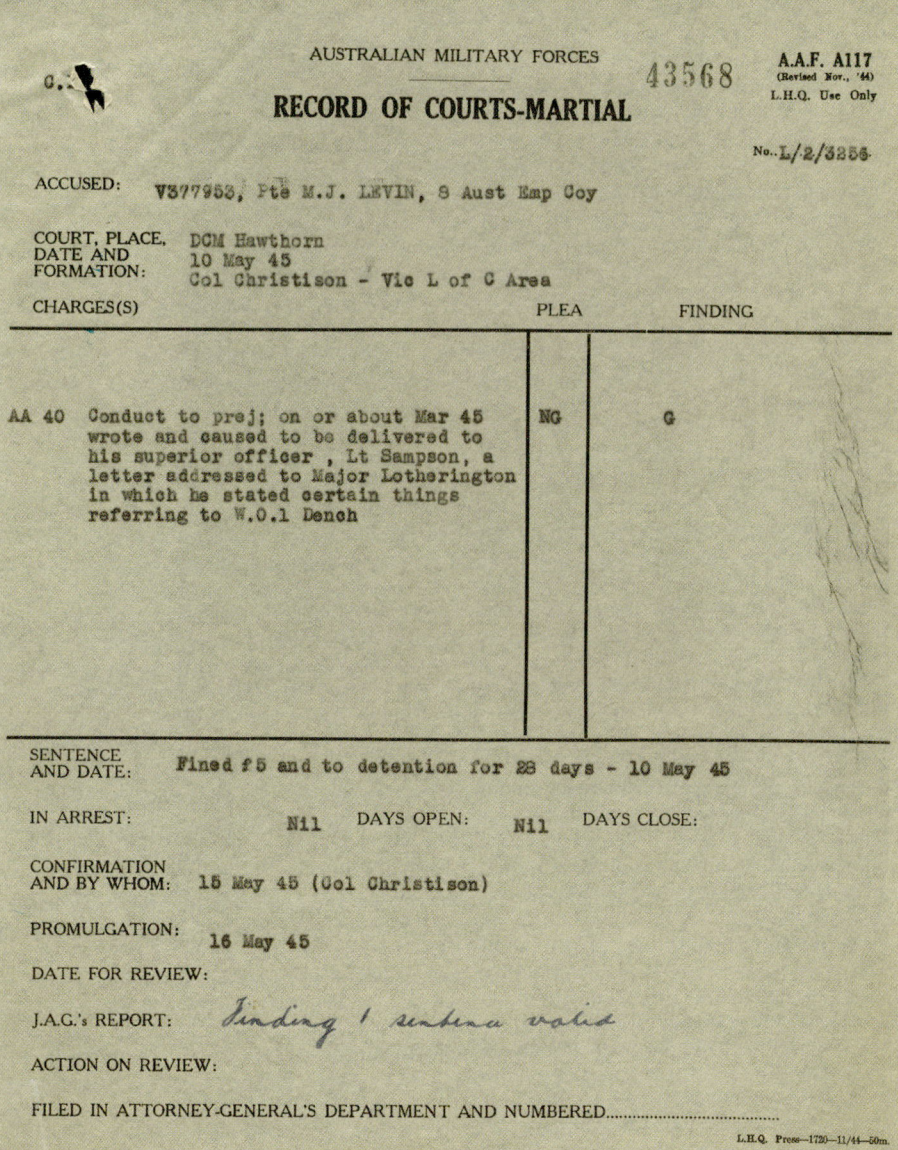

FRUIT-PICKING AND THE 8TH EMPLOYMENT COMPANY

Record of courts-martial, Private Michael Levin, May 1945

At least four 8th Employment Company soldiers faced courts-martial: Wolfgang Stekel in 1943, Franz Altschul in 1944, and both Michael Levin and Gerd Bernstein in 1945. Altschul, Levin and Bernstein were court-martialled after Captain Broughton had retired and left the unit.

In each case the charges were minor, and all four soldiers were found guilty, though Altschul was given no formal punishment. After being charged for being absent without leave, he had spent 43 days in 'close arrest awaiting trial', an unofficial punishment which the Judge Advocate General ruled was improper and excessive. Altschul was sick at the time, and was medically discharged from the army six days after his trial.

Stekel was accused, among other things, of being 'improperly in possession' of some shirts, one of which belonged to Erich Liffmann. Stekel told the court: 'I will take any punishment of any sort but please don't send me back to the internment camp.'

Bernstein was court-martialled for being absent without leave. To celebrate Japan's surrender in August 1945, the men of the 8th were given twenty-four hours leave. Bernstein left Tocumwal, went to Sydney to see his girlfriend, and returned to camp five days later.

The image at left shows the charge against Levin, who was accused of insubordination. At Tocumwal in early 1945, he had written to Major C. A. Lotherington, his commanding officer, demanding a discharge from the army and listing various concerns, one of which involved Company Sergeant Major Dench: 'In this unit I am being treated like a schoolboy, herded about the parade ground by a professional soldier whose only ambition in life seems to be bigger and better wars, who has used, countless times in my hearing, obscene and vulgar language, and who once actually had the impertinence to call me a 'queen' – just because I am in the habit of wearing my hair rather longer than customary. My manliness does not, thank God, depend on the shortness of my hair.'

Levin's letter to Lotherington revealed a sensitive man tired of the tyrannies of army life. By 1945, he had lost whatever faith he may once have had in religion and politics. 'Others may be ready to suffer and die for the love of Christ or Stalin's pipe, [obscured] love of Jehova or Churchill's cigar, or just for the love of dying. But I intend to live, to use my wits to prevent if possible the next war.' Not for Levin was it the '8th *Enjoyment* Company'.

Source: National Archives of Australia, A471, 69525, Court Martial of Michael Jakob Levin, 8th Employment Company, 1945. Copyright: National Archives of Australia.

References

NAA, A471, 32543, Court Martial of Wolfgang Stekel, 8th Employment Company, 1943.

NAA, A471, 56967, Court Martial of Franz Altschul, 8th Employment Company, 1944.

NAA, A471, 69525, Court Martial of Michael Jakob Levin, 8th Employment Company, 1945.

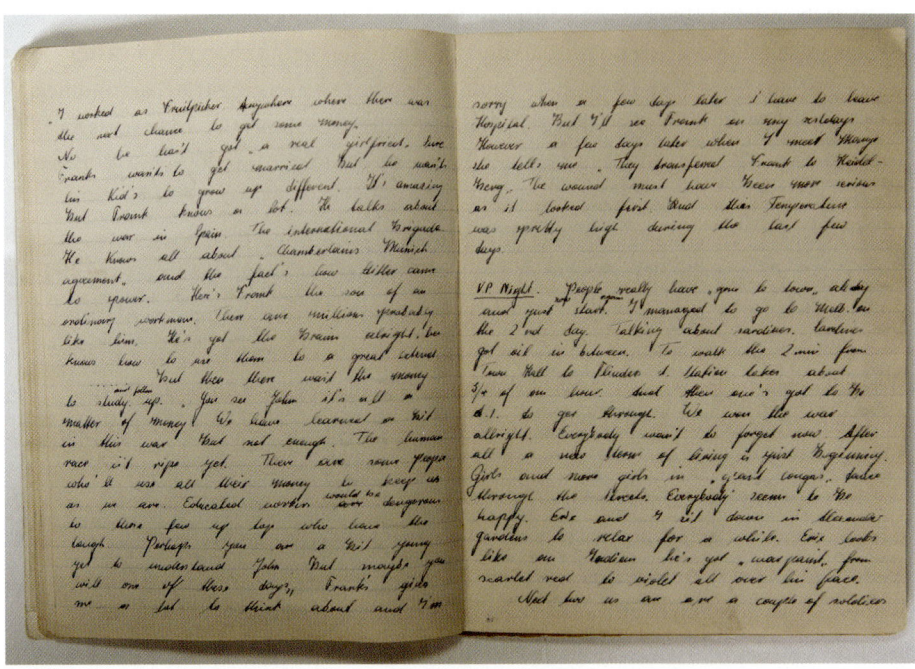

Hans Neuwahl's diary entry for 'VP Night', 1945

This entry was written the night the Pacific war ended. On Swanston Street in Melbourne, Neuwahl is surrounded, like a sardine, by delirious crowds. It took 45 minutes to edge his way one block from the Town Hall to Flinders Street Station, through throngs of 'Girls and more girls'. How sweet it was.

Source and copyright: Rosemary Newall, Karin Morrison and Susanne Platt.

SECTION 6C

CIVILIAN LIFE

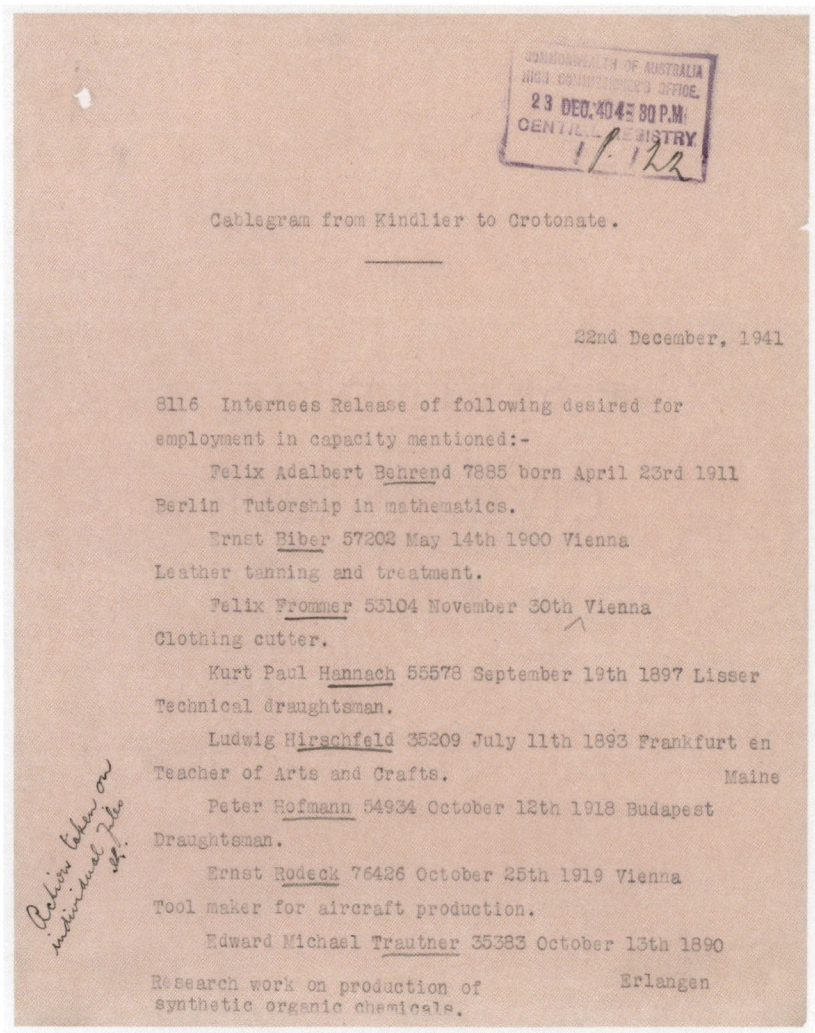

Release

From mid-1941 Australian and British authorities began to discuss the release into Australian civil society of internees with particular skills useful to the war effort. In some cases their talents were directly relevant. Ernst (Ernest) Rodeck, for instance, was released to work in aircraft production. Others were released to replace men who had gone to the front. When the war deprived Geelong Grammar School of its art teacher, James Darling, the school principal, recruited Ludwig Hirschfeld-Mack to fill this role.

Source: National Archives of Australia, A2908, P22 Part 7, Internees ex 'Dunera', 1941–42. Copyright: National Archives of Australia.

> Kindlier to Crotonate.
>
> 1st April, 1942.
>
> 2762. Internees Following have been released on the dates indicated for employment specified.
>
> Your telegram 6th February 1072 Felix Adalbert Behrend 9th March for employment as tutor in mathematics at the University of Melbourne.
>
> Your telegrams 16th February 1398 and 18th February 1464 George Eduard Kaufmann and Abram Zajac 19th March for employment as loom weaver with Century Weaving Mills Melbourne.
>
> Arthur Weisinger born 11th October 1916 at Vienna approved applicant for Australian Labour Unit also permitted to accept employment as a loom weaver with same firm on 19th March.
>
> Your telegram 26th January 673 Edward Trautner 19th March for employment on research work in production of synthetic organic chemicals with Mendelsohn & Company Melbourne.
>
> Your telegram 23rd January 607 Ludwig Hirschfeld 27th March for employment as teacher at Geelong Church of England Grammar School Corio Victoria.
>
> Your telegram 18th February 1464 Georg Drach 27th March for employment as Mechanical Draughtsman with K.M. Steel Products Limited Melbourne.
>
> Conditions of release for all seven internees follows. They will not change approved place of employment or residence without prior approval of Military authorities. They will register with Aliens Registration Officers nearest place of residence and report to them at short intervals.

The Prime Minister's Department in Canberra, and the Australian High Commission in London, acting in concert with the British Home Office, discussed the proposed releases via cablegram, usually over a period of several months. Approvals, and sometimes disapprovals, were issued from London in the name of the Home Secretary, who was responsible for the internees. In practice, the individual with the most agency in this process was the Australian Minister for the Army.

These particular cablegrams date from December 1941 and April 1942. As stated in the cablegram above, conditions were attached to the release of internees.

Source: National Archives of Australia, A2908, P22 Part 8, Internees ex 'Dunera', 1942. Copyright: National Archives of Australia.

'After lunch, Queen's College', University of Melbourne, 2 August 1942

Leonhard Adam was released in May 1942 to live and work at the University of Melbourne. As a free man, he continued to sketch and paint people and scenes that caught his eye. This pencil and watercolour drawing shows students emerging from lunch at Queen's College. Adam's lodgings were in the college.

Sketchbook: drawings and paintings of Tatura Internment Camp and University of Melbourne, Leonhard Adam collection, University of Melbourne Archives, 1994.0060.00001, p. 39.
Copyright: Mary-Clare Adam.

Queen's College, 1942

Under Dr Raynor Johnson, master since 1934, Queen's became the most diverse and international college at the University of Melbourne. Johnson, wearing robes, is in the large chair in the middle of the front row. Leonhard Adam is two places to his left.

In 1943 another former *Dunera* internee, Georg Duerrheim, took up residence at Queen's. After brief service in the 8th Employment Company, he enrolled at the University of Melbourne with the aim of completing the medical degree he had very nearly finished in his native Vienna before the *Anschluss* intervened. Duerrheim's place at Queen's was tribute to Johnson's worldly interests and religious pluralism. Duerrheim was a Roman Catholic, classified Jewish by the Nazis, living in a Methodist institution.

Duerrheim was 35 in 1943.

Source and copyright: Queen's College Archives, University of Melbourne.

Newman College, 1943

This 1943 photograph of the residents of Newman College, a Catholic residential college at the University of Melbourne, includes three former *Dunera* internees: the Austrian brothers Christoph and Oswald von Wolkenstein, and Gerhard Schaefler from Czechoslovakia. Christoph is eighth from the left in the back row, Oswald sixth from the left in the third row. Schaefler, an engineering student who had studied at the University of Edinburgh before the war, is immediately to the left of Oswald.

Before their internment and deportation, the von Wolkensteins had been at Ampleforth College, a distinguished Catholic college in Yorkskire. They were released from Tatura in February 1942 and sent to Xavier College, a Catholic boarding school in Melbourne, to continue their education. When they finished at Xavier, the boys moved to Newman College.

During the war, Daniel Mannix, the Catholic Archbishop of Melbourne, helped extricate Catholic internees, including the von Wolkensteins, from internment. When the brothers arrived in Melbourne from Tatura, Mannix met them personally at Raheen, his stately residence. He acted as their guardian during school holidays and provided for their maintenance. This included finding ways, direct and indirect, to ensure the brothers' fees at Xavier and at Newman were covered. The cost of their education was likely borne by the Jesuits.

Source and copyright: Newman College, University of Melbourne.

CIVILIAN LIFE

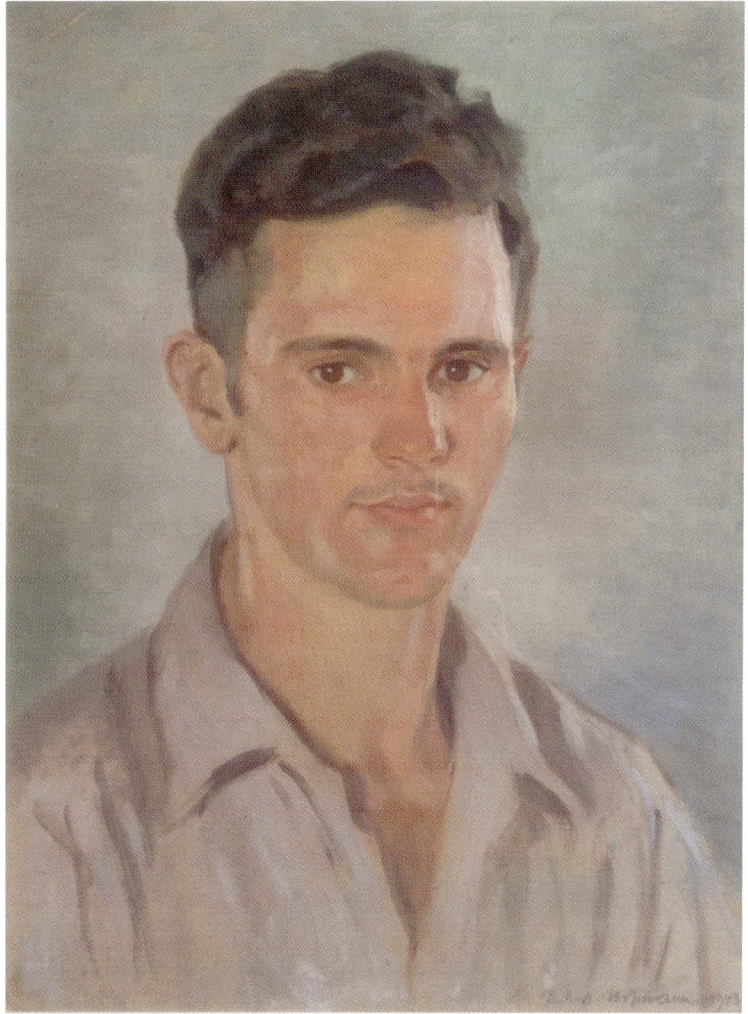

Herbert Barber, 1943

Robert Hofmann's painting of Herbert Barber, done at Tatura, shows a young man with delicate features. While most internees had left camp by 1943, Barber chose to bide his time until he could take up a place at the University of Melbourne.

Barber was a Viennese Jew born in 1921, who had left school at 14. In camp he returned to his education, studying English, mathematics and German; he took his school leaving certificate and completed the first year of a University of Melbourne Arts degree while interned at Tatura. He was released in March 1943 to pick fruit at Ardmona in the Goulburn Valley, then moved to Melbourne where he took up a scholarship at the university to study electrical engineering and continue his Arts degree.

Source: Muriel Barber.

'Toorak Road, South Yarra', 6 September 1943

Leonhard Adam's sketch of Toorak Road describes one of the most fashionable districts in Melbourne. In the background is the spire of Christ Church, South Yarra, the Anglican church where Adam himself and the Buchdahl brothers, Gerd and Hans, celebrated their respective marriages.

Source: Tatura Irrigation and Wartime Camps Museum. Copyright: Mary-Clare Adam.

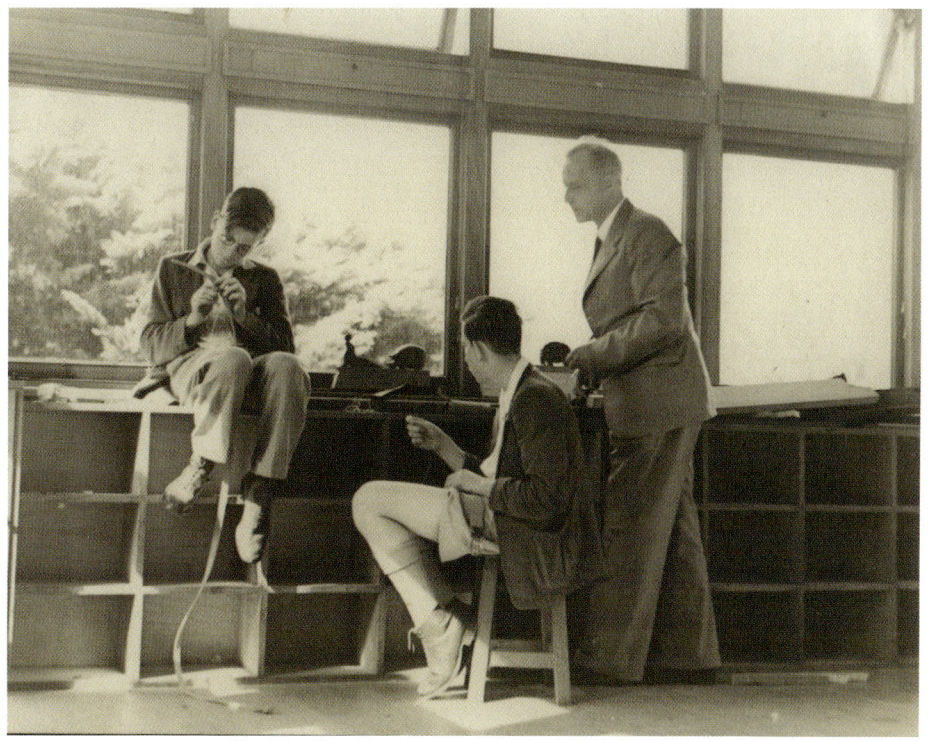

Ludwig Hirschfeld-Mack and students, Geelong Grammar School, 1942

This photograph of Ludwig Hirschfeld-Mack and two students was published in the 1942 Geelong Grammar magazine under the title 'Scene in the art school'.

In that year, the school principal, James Darling, needed to replace an art master who had joined the army. With Darling acting as sponsor, Hirschfeld-Mack was released from internment on 27 March 1942.

Hirschfeld-Mack found a congenial environment in Geelong. His pacifist beliefs, dating from his Quaker associations in Germany and in England, were shared by some in the school.

Ludwig Hirschfeld-Mack and two students, Art School, Geelong Grammar, 1942, Ludwig Hirschfeld-Mack collection, University of Melbourne Archives, 1971.0009.00002.

'Corio (Road to the You Yangs)', c. 1943

This Ludwig Hirschfeld-Mack woodcut depicts the You Yangs, which rise from the Werribee Plains. The You Yangs are visible from Geelong Grammar School in Corio, Geelong.

The print offers a remarkable vision: a master of the modernist Bauhaus depicting a site important to the Wadawurrung people for thousands of years.

Source: Geelong Grammar School. Copyright: Chris Bell.

CIVILIAN LIFE

Mural of the Life of Christ by Ludwig Hirschfeld-Mack, 1943

In autumn 1943, Hirschfeld-Mack and several of his students created a mural depicting the life of Christ. The mural, a frieze in oils on the walls of the upper story of the art department at Geelong Grammar School, remains there to this day. The first twelve images were prepared in classes led by Hirschfeld-Mack, in the spirit of the collective work he had done in the Bauhaus. Among those who joined him in this endeavour were students John Court, Mark Kellaway, and, possibly, Ian Bassett. Working with Hirschfeld-Mack was a privilege his students never forgot. The thirteenth image, Christ Pantocrotar, was the work of Hirschfeld-Mack alone.

Annunciation (above), Nativity (below). Source: Geelong Grammar School. Copyright: Chris Bell.

CIVILIAN LIFE

The flight into Egypt (above left), Jesus in the synagogue (below left), Healing of the lame man (above), Jesus preaching to a crowd (below).

Christ and the fishermen (above), The Last Supper (below), The kiss of Judas (above right), The trial (below right).

At the end of his frieze on the life of Christ, Hirschfeld-Mack leaves us with Christ Pantocrator, Christ the All Powerful, the master of a world unified, purified after total destruction. Here Hirschfeld-Mack returns to the German Renaissance, and images of hope triumphant in the work of Grünewald and other German masters.

Notice the figures linking hands traversing the globe. This symbol of world peace became Hirschfeld-Mack's motif for the gates at the entrance to Geelong Grammar School.

The way of the cross (above left), The crucifixion (below left), Christ Pantocrator (above).

"A BIT OF SWEDEN"

55 SWANSTON STREET

Your Favourite Rendezvous for

LUNCHEON :: DINNER :: SUPPER

Phone: Cent. 2426

MENU

SOUPS:
- MINESTRONE — 9d.
- CREAM OF TOMATO — 6d.

SPAGHETTI:
- SPAGHETTI NAPOLITANA — 1/-

FISH:
- GRILLED WHITING — 2/9
- FRIED WHITING — 2/6

CONTINENTAL SPECIALTIES:
- VEAL a la SWEDEN — 2/6
- VIENNESE CUTLETS — 2/6
- SWEDISH HAMBURGER — 2/-

GRILLS:
- MIXED GRILL — 3/-
- PORTERHOUSE STEAK — 2/6
- RUMP STEAK — 2/6
- LAMB CHOPS — 2/3
- FRENCH CUTLETS — 2/3
- PORK SAUSAGES & BACON — 2/-

(Extras: Egg 6d., Tomatoes 6d., Onions 6d., Salad 6d.)

OMELETTES:
- PLAIN OMELETTE — 2/-
- CHEESE OMELETTE — 2/3
- TOMATO OMELETTE — 2/3
- HAM OMELETTE — 2/6

EGGS:
- POACHED EGGS — 2/-
- EGGS AND BACON — 2/6

COLD BUFFET:
- SWEDISH SPRING SALAD — 2/3
- COLD COLLATION — 2/3

SWEETS:
- JAM OR LEMON PANCAKE — 9d.
- BANANA FRITTER — 9d.
- FRUIT SALAD & CUSTARD — 6d.
- BANANAS & CUSTARD — 6d.
- APPLE JUICE — 6d.

(One Cup of Coffee or Tea included with every dish except with Soups, Spaghetti or Sweets. Extra cup 3d.).

MINIMUM CHARGE 2/-.

- Rumpsteak with Mushrooms — 3/6
- Lobster Mayonnaise — 3/-
- Continental Roast — 2/-
- Baked Sausages & Bacon — 2/-

"A BIT OF SWEDEN"
for
A BIT OF SUPPER

JUST A LITTLE DIFFERENT

Menu, 'A bit of Sweden' restaurant, Swanston Street, Melbourne, c. 1944–1945

After his discharge from the army on medical grounds in February 1944, Jules Stocky ventured into the café and restaurant business. Among his business partners was another former *Dunera* internee, Karl Hans Nathan Strauss. 'A bit of Sweden' restaurant offered local fare and meals with 'Continental' touches; 'just a little different' was how the menu put it. Keeping the business alive was a struggle. As a newcomer to the food trade, Stocky fell victim to hard-headed suppliers.

Source: Stocky family.

CIVILIAN LIFE

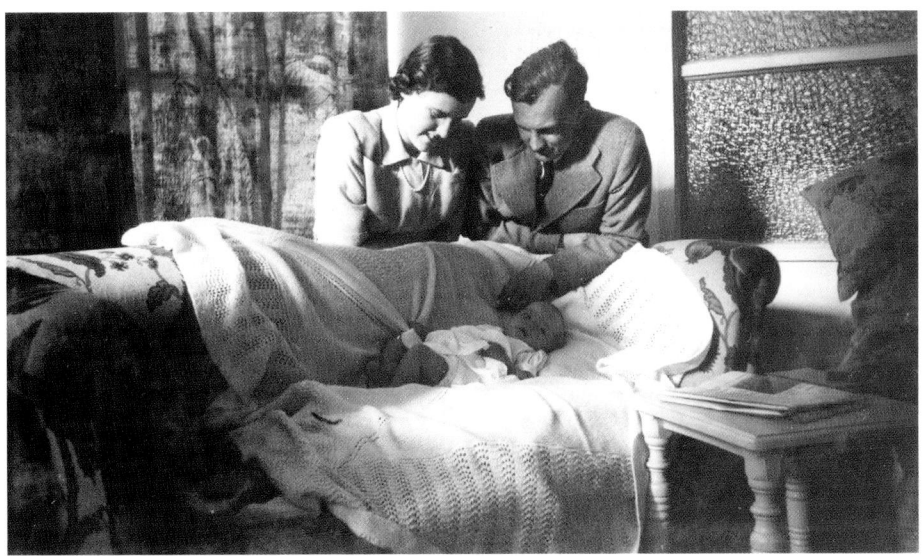

Jean and Jules Stocky with child, March 1945

Jean and Jules Stocky dote over their first-born, Anna, five months old. The photograph captures a moment in the young parents' new lives.

Source: Stocky family.

Bruno Lipmann, translator

Bruno Lipmann is pictured on the front page of the Melbourne *Herald*, 13 August 1945. The caption above his photograph reads 'Listening Post records what Tokyo radio has to say'.

Lipmann had studied Japanese in Vienna before the war. Interned in Australia, he continued to study the language, teaching himself with the aid of a Japanese-English dictionary provided by Margaret Holmes.

Men and women with Japanese language skills were in demand in wartime Australia, and Lipmann was no exception. Translators were needed to decipher information intercepted from Japanese sources. But Lipmann's background was a difficulty. How could the Australian government engage an 'enemy', a man it had imprisoned, to help in the fight against the enemy? Once the bureaucratic obstacles were cleared, Lipmann began work as a translator. He was a member of the Allied Translator and Interpreter Section, part of General Douglas MacArthur's headquarters, and worked with the 'Listening Post' of the Department of Information translating Japanese radio broadcasts into English.

The Herald, Melbourne, 13 August 1945, p. 1. Source: National Library of Australia.

Section 7

TOWARD THE FUTURE

INTRODUCTION

In the post-war years the men who had sailed on the *Dunera* and who decided to remain in Australia left the war behind. Their first step was securing residency and citizenship. Until 1949, when Australian nationality was made possible by an act of parliament, they became British subjects. From 1949, they were Australians.

Then came finding lodgings and a job. Here the difficulties were real but transitory, since these newcomers – mostly young and unmarried – appeared just in time for a huge demographic boom. This was an auspicious moment to found a family. Turning their backs on war, many decided to marry and to get on with their lives. Many *Dunera* internees married local girls of all faiths. Others sought Jewish wives. There were German and Austrian Jewish communities in Melbourne and Sydney happy to welcome educated and talented young men into their families.

Australian universities absorbed those who wished to study, with financial assistance through the Commonwealth Reconstruction Training Scheme available to those who had served in the army. These older undergraduates added a dimension to cultural life that reflected the languages and experiences they had brought with them. Many excelled in their studies and soon found their way into academic posts, becoming pioneers and innovators in different disciplines. Others moved into the world of business, or the arts, which had its own renaissance in these years.

There were disappointments and failures alongside success stories. Some men encountered insurmountable barriers when they sought to return to their pre-war occupations. Some marriages endured, others foundered. The story of these years is not one of uniform achievement, but of striking variety. Among the variations was the decision of a considerable number of men to return to Britain or Europe. When we survey this group, we find every conceivable choice. Most chose to start a life in Britain or the United States

– about 550 in the former and 230 in the latter. Some returned to Germany, at least 25 to the East and 35 to the West. Roughly 120 chose to help build the Jewish state in the making. Others went to Canada and Austria, a few to South America: the men from the *Dunera* spread around the world. And once again we find evidence that they had substantial educational and cultural capital which they used to their benefit and that of their circle. They were part of the German and Austrian diaspora whose absence reduced German social and cultural life during the war, and whose presence enriched the societies in which these emigres found refuge.

One part of this story is hidden. Some emigres paid a personal price for the dislocation of their lives. The loss of family ties was one blow; the loss of a mother language and points of cultural reference was another. The presence of others in similar straits in the camps had helped some; others felt acutely the loss of privacy, and of female companionship. Some withdrew into themselves and never recovered from these upheavals.

One facet of assimilation which is captured in this visual history is the way these newcomers took to the Australian landscape. We know that eucalypts seemed to fascinate many of the artists among them, and so did the blue green beauty and wild and ancient topography they came to know and, in many cases, to love. Those internees who stayed in Australia gained access to employment, education, the public service, politics, and the judiciary, and to an enchanting natural world, very different from the European and British environments in which they had lived before the war. How far they had come from the sadness of the Hirschfeld-Mack lithograph to which others attached the word 'Desolation'. Landscape as consolation is part of the *Dunera* story too.

Work and play, September–December 1945

In late 1945 Johnny Newall was still in the army, working along the New South Wales–Victoria border. However, the war had been left far behind.

He writes of weekends spent in the town of Corowa on the banks of the Murray River. The people were welcoming and there were girls to meet. 'Lot's [sic] of girls alright and they sure can mix Singapore Slings'. Life was good.

Newall's diary entries were now written in English.

Source and copyright: Rosemary Newall, Karin Morrison and Susanne Platt.

TOWARD THE FUTURE

Henry Talbot, naturalisation application, 1946

Henry Talbot was born in 1920 to a Jewish family in Hindenburg in Oberschlesien (now the Polish town of Zabrze), a town in Silesia. From his teenage years, he dreamed of becoming a photographer. His family gave him a Rolleiflex camera as a bar mitzvah present. He studied graphic art in Berlin, before fleeing to England after *Kristallnacht* in 1938. He was deported to Australia on the *Dunera*.

He joined the army in early 1942, and was discharged in June 1946. In the same year, he applied for and received naturalisation as a British subject. This document, an alien registration form filed in Birmingham in 1939, was part of his Australian application for naturalisation. The name 'Israel', an appellation forced on Jewish men in Nazi Germany, followed him to Britain and beyond.

He worked in various trades after the war, and from 1948 spent two years with his parents in Bolivia. On his return to Australia in 1950, he devoted himself to photography.

Source: National Archives of Australia, A435, 1948/4/3968, Tichauer Heinz, 1946. Copyright: National Archives of Australia.

Felix Werder, alien registration document, Australia

Werder left Tatura in May 1943 to join the Australian army. He had no interest in joining up, but did so because his chronically ill father, Boaz, with whom he had been deported on the *Dunera*, would receive better care as a soldier's dependant than as an internee at Tatura. Boaz was freed in September 1943.

Felix's inglorious army career ended on 26 June 1946 when he was discharged. Boaz, who never recovered his health, died two days later.

That same year Felix applied for naturalisation, and his application was approved on 21 October 1947. With a few strokes of a red pen, a government official updated Werder's alien registration form created at Hay in February 1941. The alien was now an Australian.

Source: National Archives of Australia, B6531, NATURALISED/1946–1947/GERMAN/BISCHOFSWERDER FELIX, 1946. Copyright: National Archives of Australia.

Father Walter Koenig

From the time the *Dunera* arrived in Australia, the Catholic Church lobbied politicians and government officials to release Fathers Walter Koenig and Franz Girke from internment. Girke was released in July 1942 and went to live with fellow members of the Pallottine order in Kew, Melbourne. Koenig had to wait another year for his freedom. British and Australian officials had raised doubts about his loyalties; they knew he was not pro-Nazi, but worried he was anti-British. His release was secured when Daniel Mannix, the Catholic Archbishop of Melbourne, vouched for him and pledged to be responsible for his welfare and whereabouts. Mannix had done the same for Girke.

On his release, Koenig went to live at Loyola, the Jesuit seminary in Watsonia, Melbourne. In November 1949 he left the country and returned to Germany.

Source: National Archives of Australia, B78, GERMAN/KOENIG WALTER HERMANN, 1939–1972.
Copyright: National Archives of Australia.

Peter Herbst

In 1948 Peter Herbst applied for naturalisation as a British subject. This photograph was submitted with his application, which was approved in 1950.

On his application Herbst listed his employment as university tutor and research scholar. He was on his way to becoming a distinguished philosopher. In 1962, he succeeded Kurt Baier, another former *Dunera* internee, as professor of philosophy at the Australian National University. Herbst came to that position from the University College of the Gold Coast, now Ghana.

Source: National Archives of Australia, B78, 1950/HERBST P, 1948–1950.
Copyright: National Archives of Australia.

Fred Lowen at work, Melbourne, 1946

Fred Lowen stands in his workshop shaping wooden salad bowls and salad servers. The photograph catches him at the start of a brilliant career as a designer and craftsman.

Source: Monica Lee Lowen and Jocelyn Lowen.

Ernest and Sheila Rodeck, c. early 1950s

Ernest Rodeck and Sheila Thonemann married in Melbourne in October 1948. Ernest was from a Viennese Jewish family; he was non-observant. Sheila was a local girl from a well-established, non-Jewish, family. Her father was a stockbroker and had served as member for Toorak in the Victorian parliament. Ernest's best man was Fred Lowen, his business partner and close friend.

Source: Sheila Rodeck.

The FLER Company, Richmond, Melbourne, c. October 1952

On 1 January 1946 Fred Lowen and Ernest Rodeck formed the FLER furniture company. The name of their company was composed of their initials. FLER designed and made what is now called Scandinavian furniture – tables, chairs, couches – in wood and metal, with clean lines and a 'modern look'. In providing the stuff of domestic lives to Australian families, FLER helped to transform Australian interiors.

Source and copyright: Monica Lee Lowen and Jocelyn Lowen.

Two friends, c. 1946–1947

Bern Brent (left) and Peter Danby stand in the Botanic Gardens, Melbourne.

Brent spent much of his post-war career as a public servant with the New South Wales and Commonwealth departments of education.

Danby established a business making and installing fittings for shops, hospitals and hotels. His nephew Michael Danby, a Labor member of the Australian parliament, was elected member for Melbourne Ports in 1998.

Source: Bern Brent.

TOWARD THE FUTURE

Professeur **Bern Brent and students, Saigon University, 1961**

For much of the 1950s Bern Brent taught English, mostly to migrants and displaced persons arriving in New South Wales in search of a new life in Australia. In 1958 he responded to an advertisement, issued by the Australian Department of External Affairs, calling for people to go to Vietnam to train budding English teachers. Instruction would be delivered primarily at Saigon University, with the programme overseen by the South Vietnam Ministry for Education. Bern's application was successful, and he became a member of the university's Faculté de Pédagogie. The students in this photograph were training to be French and English teachers in Vietnamese secondary schools.

    Bern lived in Saigon from 1958 to 1962. In early 1963 he started another role with the Department of External Affairs, this time in Jesselton (now Kota Kinabalu in Malaysian Borneo), where he spent five years as head of the English department at a teachers' college.

Source: Bern Brent.

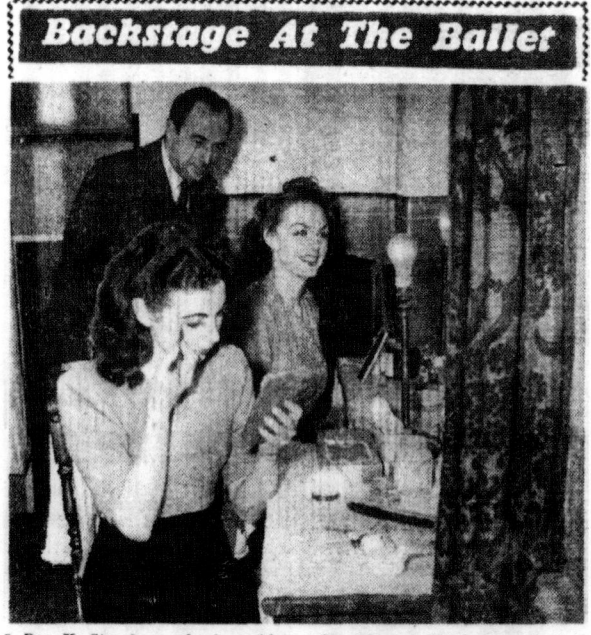

Doc. K. Sternberg, who is making a film about ballet for the Dept. of Information, arranging a dressing room shot backstake at the Borovansky Ballet last week. The girls are members of the corps de ballet. The film will be shown at city theatres on completion.

'Backstage At The Ballet', *Truth*, 24 August 1947

In early 1944, 'Doc' Sternberg was seconded to the Film and Photographic Unit of the Netherlands Information Service, based in Melbourne. As editor-in-chief of the unit, Sternberg made documentary films about Allied military operations in the Dutch East Indies.

After the war Sternberg made several films for the Australian Department of Information. These films, which promoted Australian industries and tourism to the world, were regarded highly by the Commonwealth government.

But his success did not last. His film 'The Theatre in Australia', made for the Department of the Interior and completed in 1952, was never released by the government. Independent companies organised and sponsored its release in some theatres, but not until 1955. Sternberg's career stalled. It may be that the government objected to the cost of making the film, reported to be £10,000, and the time it took. Sternberg worked on the film for three years and visited every Australian state. It was his most ambitious work.

Moreover, the times were conspiring against Sternberg. The coming of television to Australia in 1956 diminished the appeal of documentary films made for cinema.

Little is known about Sternberg's life and work after the mid-1950s. We do know he settled in Sydney and died in 1971.

Truth, Sydney, 24 August 1947, p. 64. Source: National Library of Australia.

George Nadel and other Queen's College students, University of Melbourne, 1948

These eight residents of Queen's College, University of Melbourne, achieved first class results in their university examinations in 1947. George Nadel is second from left in the top row.

Nadel, born in Vienna in 1923, was discharged from the army in September 1945. The next year he enrolled in History at the University of Melbourne, and took up residence at Queen's. He was awarded a first-class degree in 1948.

In 1949 he moved to the Australian National University in Canberra, where he started a Master of Arts thesis on Australian political thought in the period 1840 to 1860. He spent two years at Harvard University conducting comparative research for his thesis, and returned there from Canberra in 1954. The following year Nadel was awarded a PhD for a thesis entitled 'Adaptation and Social Culture in Early Colonial Australia'. A version of his thesis, entitled *Australia's Colonial Culture*, was published in 1957. In 1960 he founded the historical journal *History and Theory*, to which he attracted such eminent scholars as Isaiah Berlin and Raymond Aron.

Max Corden is on the right of the front row. He and his family, refugees from Nazi Germany, arrived in Australia in 1939. He became a distinguished economist. Ken Inglis is next to Corden.

Source: Ken Inglis.

The Seefeld family, 1949

On 7 April 1949 the Seefeld family celebrated the 70th birthday of Arthur Seefeld. The celebration was held in Arthur's home in East Malvern, Melbourne.

Gary Seefeld, Arthur's son, is at the centre of this photograph. Rosie, Gary's second wife, is top left. They pose with the three children of Gary's first marriage. Freddy is in the back row, Doris to the right of her father, and Loretta to his left.

Source and copyright: Loretta Forsey.

Sydney Loder in 'Eureka Stockade', 1949

Sigurd Lohde was discharged from the army in August 1945. As Sydney Loder, in 1948 he won a role in the film 'Eureka Stockade', which Harry Watt was making for Ealing Studios. Loder played a German character, Vern. The Australian actor Chips Rafferty played Peter Lalor, the lead role. The film, released in January 1949, also starred Peter Finch and the British actor Gordon Jackson.

In this image, a still from the film, Loder is second from right. Chips Rafferty is the tall man in the centre, Gordon Jackson is at right, and Peter Illing, who played Italian Rafaello Carboni, is at left.

In 1955 Loder moved from Australia to west Berlin, where he opened a tavern called 'Das Känguruh'. He continued to act, securing minor roles in films and television productions.

Source and copyright: StudioCanal Films Ltd, United Kingdom. Our thanks also to the National Film and Sound Archive of Australia for help in identifying and obtaining this image.

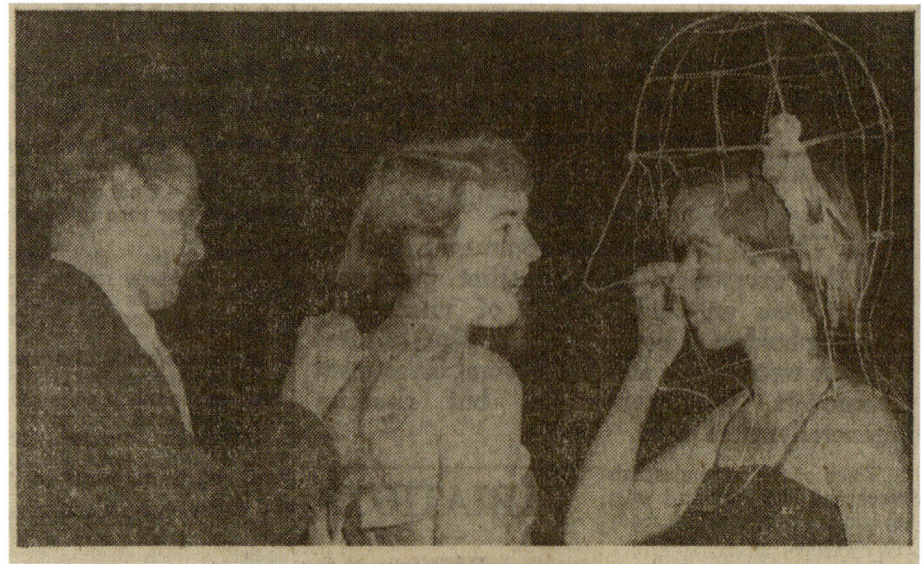

MR. KLAUS FRIEDEBER-GER used his partner's lipstick to sketch a few extra surrealistic symbols on MISS DIANA MEDWORTH'S bare shoulders while her sister, MISS SALLY MEDWORTH, in the wire bird cage she made, watched.

Body art, November 1949

Klaus Friedeberger uses lipstick to draw on the back of Diana Medworth at the Trocadero dance hall, Sydney, November 1949. Diana and her sister Sally (with bird cage) were artists and illustrators.

Friedeberger had first visited Sydney in 1944, when on leave from the 8th Employment Company. After his discharge from the army in August 1946, he moved to Sydney to study painting at the East Sydney Technical College. His studies were supported by the Commonwealth Reconstruction Training Scheme. Frank Medworth, the director of the art department at the college, and the father of Diana and Sally, declared it the premier art school in the southern hemisphere. Friedeberger's fellow students included the painters Guy Warren and Tony Tuckson and the sculptor Oliffe Richmond.

Sydney Morning Herald, 30 November 1949, p. 9. Source: National Library of Australia.

Reference

[Jane England], *Klaus Friedeberger: Works 1940-1970*, (London: England & Co, undated), pp. 9-12.

TOWARD THE FUTURE

Hans Buchdahl and Pamela Wann, Hobart, February 1950

Hans Buchdahl and his fiancée Pamela Wann are pictured in his office in the Department of Physics, University of Tasmania, February 1950. Hans had just won a Nuffield Foundation Dominion travelling fellowship, enabling him to spend twelve months in England.

A copy of this photograph, published in the *Hobart Mercury* on 18 February 1950, appeared in Buchdahl's Australian Security and Intelligence Organisation (ASIO) file. The Buchdahls were being watched. The loyalties of an English-speaking German-born scientist, thought to be a Communist, who worked on the physics of thermodynamics and general relativity, were matters of concern in the early days of the Cold War. As one spy reported, 'he would probably be a very dangerous type if the opportunity arose.'

Source: Pamela Buchdahl.

Quotation from NAA, A6119, 1280, Buchdahl, Hans Adolf, 1941-1963.

The Buchdahl brothers and the Wann sisters

Gerd Buchdahl married Nancy Wann in Christ Church, South Yarra, Melbourne, in December 1947 (above). The bride and groom, centre, are flanked by Hans Buchdahl and Pamela Wann, Nancy's younger sister.

Hans and Pamela wed in the same Anglican church in April 1950 (right), having first met at Gerd and Nancy's wedding. Hans and Pamela are at left and Gerd at right. Jeannie Jones, Pamela's bridesmaid, is on Gerd's arm. Nancy was heavily pregnant and unable to attend the wedding.

It was common for assimilated and well-educated Jews in Germany and Austria to marry out of the faith. But marrying into established Australian families was another step again. It signified a setting down of roots in Australia, at least for a time.

The Wann sisters came from Benalla in Victoria, where their family had owned and worked land since the 1860s. Nancy, Pamela and their brother Lex were educated at prestigious Melbourne schools: the sisters at Melbourne Church of England Girls' Grammar School and Lex at Scotch College, a Presbyterian institution. Some members of their extended family were opposed to Nancy marrying a Jewish man. Pamela faced no such resistance. By the time she wed, the family saw the Buchdahl brothers as having 'good prospects'.

Source: Pamela Buchdahl.

Reference

Email from Pamela Buchdahl to Seumas Spark, 18 September 2017.

Douglas Boerner and goanna, 1 January 1950

Douglas Boerner was born in Frankfurt in 1919 to an English mother who failed to have him naturalised British. He lived only his first six weeks in Germany, making him possibly the least German of the *Dunera* internees. He was interned with his brother, Herbert Boerner, a hairdresser. Douglas was an automobile mechanic.

Douglas soon developed an unusual appreciation for the Australian landscape and its history. In December 1942, while still interned at Tatura, he corresponded with the Director of the National Museum of Victoria about donating a collection of indigenous stone artefacts he had found in camp.

In August 1943 Douglas joined the Civil Alien Corps, one of very few *Dunera* internees to do so. Members of the corps laboured in support of the war effort, but as civilians: unlike the men of the 8th Employment Company, they did not wear military uniform. Douglas was posted to Alice Springs, where he remained after the war and lived until his death in 2011. He became an expert on the flora, fauna and history of central Australia.

Herbert returned to Britain in October 1941.

Doug Boerner and Goanna, PH0764/0460, http://hdl.handle.net/10070/214630. Copyright: Northern Territory Library.

Gary Sostheim, c. late 1940s–early 1950s

In early 1939, when he was 15, Gerd Sostheim fled Germany on a *Kindertransport*. His brother Heinz, three years his junior, remained in Düsseldorf with their parents, Ernst and Erna. Heinz, Ernst and Erna were killed in the Holocaust, as were Gerd's grandparents and several other close relatives. He lost his entire family to genocide.

Gerd had nothing and no one to return to in Europe. He stayed in Australia, adopted the name Gary, and slowly and patiently built a new life. For a long time this meant avoiding all things German. He lived a quiet and dignified existence, the pain of his past hidden from family and friends.

Source: National Archives of Australia, B78, GERMAN/SOSTHEIM GERD SALLI, 1939–1972.
Copyright: National Archives of Australia.

Fred Schonbach on Mt Isa

After Fred Schonbach was discharged from the army in August 1946, he moved to Sydney to study art at the East Sydney Technical College. Like Klaus Friedeberger, who followed the same educational path, Schonbach's studies were supported by funds from the Commonwealth Reconstruction Training Scheme.

As he had done in the army, Schonbach earned money by illustrating newspaper and magazine articles. This article on Mt Isa in Queensland was published in the Sydney newspaper the *Sunday Herald* on 24 April 1949. In this case, he was both author and illustrator.

In April 1950 Schonbach married June Heydon, a photographer from a working-class Sydney family.

Source: Schonbach family.

Fred Schonbach in Buenos Aires

In 1950 Fred Schonbach and his wife June left Sydney for Europe on a tramp steamer. After hitchhiking around the Continent they made for London, where they planned to settle. Fred's parents, however, wanted their son and his new bride to come to Argentina. Fred had not seen his parents, who had fled from Hitler's regime to South America, in over a decade. Fred and June sailed for Argentina in January 1951.

They spent the next eight years in Buenos Aires, with Fred scraping together a living as a freelance illustrator and graphic designer. Their first two children, Michael and Gabriela, were born in Buenos Aires.

TOWARD THE FUTURE

Fred took to depicting Buenos Aires street scenes. The image at left was painted in 1955. The image above is captioned 'Death of Evita – crowds'. The date is given as 1955, though Eva Perón died in 1952.

Argentina in the 1950s was an autocratic state, and Fred and June eventually tired of the instability of daily life in Buenos Aires. In 1959 they moved to the United States, where Fred found work near Washington, DC.

Source and copyright: Schonbach family.

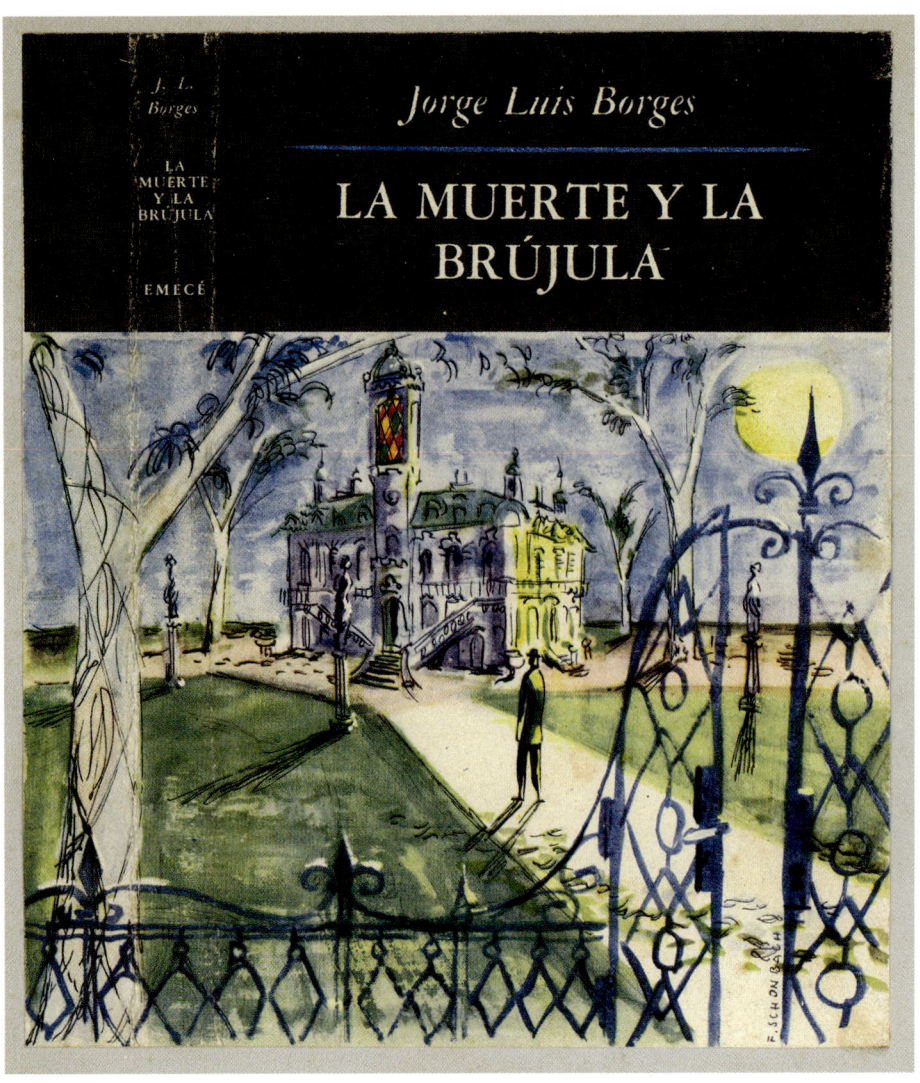

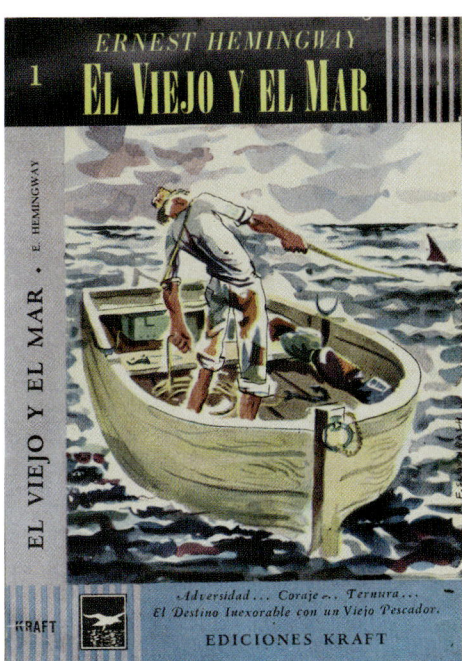 

Fred Schonbach book covers

Schonbach drew and painted the illustrations for these book covers in Buenos Aires.

Source and copyright: Schonbach family.

Fred Schonbach in North America

Fred and June Schonbach lived in the United States from 1959 to 2000, when they moved to Vancouver, Canada. June died in 2011 and Fred in 2012.

Fred sketched a bird's eye view of Philadelphia (above) in 1970. The watercolour of Lonsdale Quay in Vancouver (right) was painted in 1993. Careful attention to detail, and bright and attractive colours, characterised much of the art he produced decades earlier at Hay and Tatura.

In 1988, at the age of 68, he wrote: 'I see the curve of my life and fortunes as U-shaped: A carefree and privileged childhood and adolescence; some tough times as refugee, so[l]dier and penniless artist and, finally a relatively settled old age.'

Source and copyright: Schonbach family.

Quotation from Schonbach to Howard E. Paine, National Geographic Magazine, 1988. Letter in possession of Gabriela Schonbach.

TOWARD THE FUTURE

Cover design by Erwin Fabian for *The Castle*, 1957

In the early 1950s Erwin Fabian left Australia for London, where he found work as an illustrator and graphic designer. He designed covers for Allen Lane's Penguin Books, including its 1957 edition of *The Castle* by Franz Kafka. Fabian used cubist forms to present the nightmare vision of the Czech writer as an undecipherable puzzle.

Copyright: Penguin Random House, United Kingdom.

TOWARD THE FUTURE

Walter Kaufmann under surveillance, 1955–1956

These photographs of Walter Kaufmann come from a file ASIO kept on him. The top photograph was taken in front of the ship *Neptunia* at Fremantle on 27 June 1955. It shows delegates en route to the fifth World Festival of Youth in Warsaw. Walter is standing, third from left. A note with the photograph in the ASIO file identifies Walter as the author of *Voices in the Storm* and a member of Frank Hardy's Realist Writers' Group, which was linked to the Communist Party of Australia. The bottom photograph probably was taken during the Melbourne Olympic Games of 1956, when Walter (centre, with glasses) was part of the combined German delegation. The van in the background is adorned with the Olympic rings.

Source: National Archives of Australia, A9626, 544, Kaufmann, Walter, 1955–1956. Copyright: National Archives of Australia.

Walter and Barbara Kaufmann, Berlin, 1956

This is the moment when Barbara Kaufmann arrived in East Berlin after travelling from Sydney to join Walter in 1956.

The East German Ministry of State Security (Stasi) kept a file on Walter for 40 years: its secret agents monitored carefully this writer who was fluent in English and in possession of an Australian passport. The Stasi's interest in Walter did not harm his career, which appears to have flourished in the German Democratic Republic.

Source: Walter Kaufmann, via Volker Dittrich.

'New visions in photography', 1953

Wolfgang Sievers, a photographer of Jewish descent from Berlin, fled Nazi Germany and migrated to Australia in 1938. He established a photography studio in Melbourne in 1939. Sievers had studied at the Contempora School for Applied Arts in Berlin, an institution associated with the Bauhaus. His work was innovative and modernist.

Helmut Newton, also a Jew from Berlin, shared some of Sievers' ideas and ambitions for photography; Newton too sought to embrace 'new visions' in his work. In 1946 he opened a studio on Flinders Lane in Melbourne. Initially business was slow, but gradually he won more regular and profitable commissions.

Sievers and Newton held a joint exhibition at the Federal Hotel in Collins Street in May 1953. It was Newton's first joint exhibition, and the biggest exhibition he had been involved in to that time.

National Library of Australia. Wolfgang Sievers Photographic Archive. *Poster designed by Gerard Herbst for the Wolfgang Sievers/Helmut Newton New Visions in Photography Exhibition in Melbourne, 1953.* Copyright: Daniel Herbst and Stephen Herbst.

References

Guy Featherstone, 'Helmut Newton's Australian Years', *The LaTrobe Journal*, no. 76, spring 2005.

Jooste, A., (2012) *Wolfgang Georg Sievers, Photographer (1913-2007)* in Museums Victoria Collections https://collections.museumvictoria.com.au/articles/2586. Accessed 18 September 2017.

Helmut Newton, c. 1957

This portrait of Newton, inscrutable and embracing a sleepy cat, was taken by fellow photographer Athol Shmith. It differs from Newton's own photographic work. Sometimes referred to as exhibiting the *Neue Sachlichkeit*, or the new objectivity, his portraits, mostly of women, were sharply focussed, full of black and white contrasts, with a glossy surface embodying what came to be called glamour.

This term captured a form of photography allied to the fashion industry, which presents a kind of cold beauty enhanced by the clothes and accoutrements of the wealthy. Newton's style prepared the way for Louis Vuitton, Armani and a host of other global companies just getting started in the 1950s. Some of the women in his photographs had androgynous qualities, further enhancing the distinctive features of his later work in the magazine *Vogue* and elsewhere.

Athol Shmith, *Portrait of Helmut Newton* (c. 1957), gelatin silver photograph, 36.7 x 29.3 cm (image). National Gallery of Victoria, Melbourne. Purchased through The Art Foundation of Victoria with the assistance of The Ian Potter Foundation, Governor, 1989 (PH20-1989). Copyright: Estate of Athol Shmith.

TOWARD THE FUTURE

Fashion image for Sportscraft, Princes Bridge, Melbourne, 1961

In 1956 Helmut Newton invited Henry Talbot to join his studio as an advertising and fashion photographer. The two men had become friends during their internment at Tatura. In 1957 Newton and his wife June Browne, who later changed her name to Alice Springs, left Australia and moved to London, leaving Talbot to run the Flinders Lane studio. The firm became known as Helmut Newton and Henry Talbot Pty Ltd.

    Henry Talbot's photograph of a model posing by Princes Bridge locates fashion photography in the boom years of post-war Australia.

Henry Talbot, *No title (Fashion illustration for Sportscraft, on location Yarra River, Melbourne, near Princes Bridge)* 1961, gelatin silver photograph, 24.4 x19.0. National Gallery of Victoria, Melbourne. Copyright: Lynette Anne Talbot.

The Dana Nasvytis Modern Dance Group, October 1956

Loretta Forsey (nee Seefeld, at right) poses with members of the Dana Nasvytis Modern Dance Group. Loretta first danced as a young girl in Singapore in the 1930s. After the Second World War, she trained in creative dance and classical ballet in Melbourne. She performed with the Dana Nasvytis group for several years before joining the Victorian State Opera.

Dana Nasvytis was originally from Latvia. Her ballets presented anti-war and anti-Russian themes. Rehearsals and performances took place with the dancers in bare feet, in the manner of the school of Isadora Duncan.

The photograph was taken by Henry Talbot at the studio he shared with Helmut Newton in Melbourne's Flinders Lane.

Source: Loretta Forsey. Copyright: Lynette Anne Talbot.

'Emily Gap, Central Australia', by Leonhard Adam, 1955

In 1955 Leonhard Adam embarked on a field trip to central Australia to study Aboriginal rock paintings. As always, he took his brushes and paints with him.

On this journey he stayed in Alice Springs at the home of Douglas Boerner, his unofficial research assistant. The two men had been friends since meeting on the *Dunera*.

Source: Tatura Irrigation and Wartime Camps Museum. Copyright: Mary-Clare Adam and Tatura Irrigation and Wartime Camps Museum.

'Sydney harbour from Hotel Manhattan, Potts Point', by Leonhard Adam, September 1959

This is one of Leonhard Adam's last paintings. In 1960 he travelled to Europe, representing the University of Melbourne at the International Anthropological Congress. He died in Bonn on 9 September that year from a heart attack.

Source: Tatura Irrigation and Wartime Camps Museum. Copyright: Mary-Clare Adam and Tatura Irrigation and Wartime Camps Museum.

TOWARD THE FUTURE

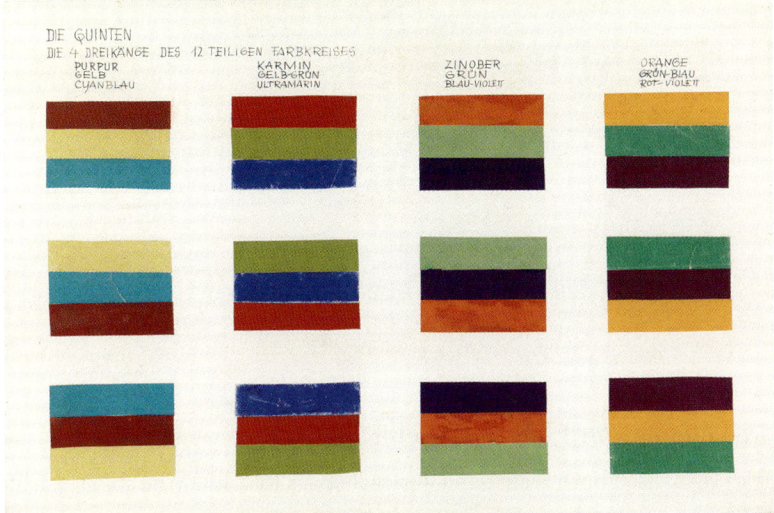

'Yellow landscape with trees' and 'Colour chart' by Ludwig Hirschfeld-Mack

Hirschfeld-Mack's fascination with abstraction and colour theory is evident 40 years after he first entered the Bauhaus in 1919. 'Yellow landscape' (above) was drawn in 1958. The colour chart (below) is undated.

Above: Source: Geelong Grammar School. Copyright: Chris Bell.

Below: Ludwig Hirschfeld-Mack (1893–1965), *Colour Chart* (n.d.), watercolour. The University of Melbourne Art Collection. Gift of Mrs Olive Hirschfeld 1982. 1982.0128.010. Copyright: Chris Bell.

'Kangaroo jumping' by Ludwig Hirschfeld-Mack

Hirschfeld-Mack used both realist and abstract styles to convey the colours, features and peculiarities of his adopted land. In this 1958 work, the European modernist turned to abstractionism to depict the movement of a kangaroo.

Source: Geelong Grammar School. Copyright: Chris Bell.

TOWARD THE FUTURE

Ludwig Hirschfeld-Mack and Olive Hirschfeld, with his daughter Ellinor (Ello), West Germany, 1958

Ludwig Hirschfeld-Mack retired from Geelong Grammar School in 1957. The next year, he and Olive, his second wife, embarked on a European trip. Their travels took them to West Germany, where they visited family and friends. At left is Ello, one of three daughters from Hirschfeld-Mack's first marriage to Elenor Wirth. When he left Germany in 1936, Elenor was bed-ridden with multiple sclerosis and could not leave with him. She died in Germany in 1953.

Many *Dunera* internees had no wish to see Germany again. Hirschfeld-Mack, like Leonhard Adam, felt differently.

Source and copyright: Chris Bell.

Ludwig Hirschfeld-Mack, Ferny Creek, c. 1960

When Hirschfeld-Mack retired from Geelong Grammar School, he and Olive moved to Ferny Creek in Victoria's Dandenong Ranges.

Source: Felicity Renowden and Resi Schwarzbauer.

TOWARD THE FUTURE

Heine Brothers staff, Melbourne, c. 1958

Walter Heine was born into a prosperous German Jewish family in 1916. The family operated Gebrüder Heine (Heine Brothers), a textile firm with headquarters in Leipzig and branches throughout Germany. In 1938 the Nazi party took control of the family business, and in September that year Walter made for Britain, part of the Jewish exodus from Germany.

Walter established Heine Brothers in Melbourne in 1945. Initially his company traded in army surplus goods. Later, as a major import-export business, the company traded in iron and steel, grains and other foodstuffs, machinery and technology. Walter established shipping lines to foster business between Australia and new and promising markets, including in Asia and South America. He had a talent for spotting opportunities and was willing to take bold and potentially unpopular decisions. His company was one of the first in Australia to trade with Japan after the war, while other trading partners included West Germany, East Germany, the Soviet Union, and, after 1949, communist China.

Heine Brothers employed a number of former *Dunera* internees. Initially, they made up all the staff. In this photograph Mike Sondheim is in the back row, second from left. Charles Ehrlich is sixth from left in the same row. Also in the back row is Fred Levy, sixth from right. Jimmy King is at left in the front row, sporting a bow tie. Wally Weyl is third from right in the same row.

The bald man at the centre of the photograph is George Milton, a partner in Heine Brothers. He was soon to leave for Tokyo to run the company's operations in Japan.

Gert Silver, survivor of Auschwitz, stands to the right of Fred Levy. He became chairman and chief executive officer of Heine Brothers after Walter Heine's death in 1978.

The photograph was taken and developed by Harry Jay, formerly Harry Jeidels, *Dunera* internee. Jay ran the Studio for Theatre and Commercial Photography on Collins Street, Melbourne.

Source: Janet Coffman.

Walter Heine with sons Leslie and Michael, c. late 1960s

Walter Heine is pictured between his sons, Leslie and Michael. Leslie is on his father's right, Michael on his left. This Australian scene at Howqua Dale, near Mansfield in Victoria, was far removed from Grossdeuben, near Leipzig, where Walter was born.

The Howqua Valley is part of Victoria's High Country, home to horse riders of legendary skill.

Source: Leslie Heine and Michael Heine.

The Castles family in Britain, c. 1960

In January 1947, Heinz Schlösser changed his name to Henry Castles, though he continued to use Heinz as his first name. His choice of Anglicised surname was a nod to his heritage, Schloss being German for castle.

Two months later, in March 1947, Heinz, Fay and their two sons, Francis, 3, and Stephen, 2, sailed for England. Heinz and Fay returned to their pre-war occupations, working as youth hostel wardens. They ran the hostel at Crockham Hill in Kent until 1959 when they retired to Oxted, Surrey.

From left to right are Fay, Francis (Frank), Flash the dog, Heinz, and Stephen Castles. The picture was taken either at Crockham Hill in the late 1950s, or at Oxted about 1960.

Source: Frank Castles and Stephen Castles.

Franz Philipp, c. 1960

Franz Philipp was born in 1914 to a Viennese Jewish family of mixed Czech and Hungarian origins. Franz attended the University of Vienna, and trained in art history, working on a doctoral dissertation on Italian mannerist painting until he was expelled for being a Jew.

After *Kristallnacht* he and his brother were arrested and imprisoned in Dachau for six months. A bribe secured their release, and they escaped to Britain. His mother and sister were not so fortunate, and were murdered during the war.

In Britain Franz worked as a farm labourer. Deported on the *Dunera*, he was interned at Hay and Tatura. He joined the army in early 1942.

In 1943, while still a soldier, he enrolled to study history at the University of Melbourne. He received his Bachelor of Arts in 1946, topping the Honours list in History, and became a senior tutor at the university the following year. In 1948 he married June Rowley, a fellow tutor and historian. In 1950 he moved to the university's Department of Fine Arts.

Philipp was a legendary teacher, helping to bring the fruits of Viennese scholarship on art history to a generation of Australian students. His friendship with and championing of the work of the artist Arthur Boyd reflected the degree to which Philipp blended Austrian and Australian currents in the field of fine arts. His 1967 book *Arthur Boyd* was a landmark in Australian biography and art history scholarship.

Philipp is pictured at 'The Grange' at Harkaway near Berwick, Victoria. The house had been owned by members of the Boyd family, and in it Arthur had painted the 'Harkaway mural'. Philipp was there to photograph this artwork.

Philipp died in 1970.

Source: Visual Cultures Resource Centre, University of Melbourne. Copyright: Jaynie Anderson.

TOWARD THE FUTURE

Herbert Baer, c. 1960

Herbert Baer was born to a Jewish family in Cologne in 1924. His father was a proud German who had served in the Great War. Herbert played the violin and sang as a child, and the family observed the Sabbath and the Jewish calendar.

A week after *Kristallnacht* and the ransacking of the Baer home, Herbert's parents sent him to Amsterdam. He was 14. He took his violin with him. In 1939, his parents arranged for him to travel to Britain on a *Kindertransport*. He went to school in Bournemouth and learned English, retaining an educated English accent. In July 1940 he was deported to Australia on the *Dunera*.

The visit of Major Julian Layton to Hay marked the start of Herbert's new life. From Layton, who was a relative on his father's side, Herbert learned of the disappearance of his family. He never lost his hatred of Germany. He refused to consider applying for reparations, which would have meant being interrogated by Germans.

He married in 1952, became a chartered accountant, and in 1960 was the first Jew admitted to the Melbourne Stock Exchange. He was a man of wide philosophical and literary interests, which he explored after retirement. He died in 2015.

Baer is pictured around the time of his admission to the Stock Exchange.

Source and copyright: David Baer.

Rainer Radok, 1964

From 1962 Rainer Radok taught mathematics at the University of Adelaide. In 1967 he moved to Flinders University, where he served as foundation professor of applied mathematics. In 1971 he became the university's foundation professor of oceanography and founded the Horace Lamb Institute of Oceanography. He left Flinders soon after, taking the institute with him. He worked as a consultant on projects across Australia until 1981, when he left Adelaide to teach at the Asian Institute of Technology in Bangkok.

Radok was a pioneer in the field of oceanography. His work and publications, including *Australia's Coast: An Environmental Atlas Guide With Base-lines* (1976) and *Capes and Captains: A Comprehensive Study of the Australian Coast* (1990), told Australians much about their coastline and how the seas might be used and protected. He took an inclusive approach to academic work, once conducting field research with a group of primary school students. He believed that knowledge was most powerful when applied practically and shared widely.

Family members and colleagues remember him as intelligent, original and very volatile. Some staff at Flinders knew him as the 'Wild One'. Radok lived in Thailand until his death in 2004.

Courtesy of the University of Adelaide Archives.

Ilse and Erwin Lamm with Menachem Begin, Melbourne, May 1963

Erwin Lamm and Ilse Stock, whose families had known each other in Vienna, married in January 1946 in Carlton, Melbourne. They became fervent Zionists.

In this photograph they flank nationalist Israeli politician Menachem Begin. The Lamms dined with Begin when he was in Melbourne in 1963. Fourteen years later Begin became Israel's Prime Minister.

Source: Ilse Lamm.

Heinz Eggebrecht and friends

Heinrich Joachim Ferdinand (Heinz) Eggebrecht was born to Lutheran parents in Berlin in 1910. His mother and father were bakers, and he too learnt this trade. He was a committed Communist from the 1920s and engaged in street fighting against the Nazis. In the mid-1920s, his parents committed suicide, victims of the failing German economy. Heinz found them dead in their bakery, gas pipes in mouths.

In 1936 Heinz was imprisoned in Esterwegen concentration camp near Bremen. After being moved to Czechoslovakia, he escaped and fled to England, just before the German annexation of the Sudetenland. His wife and child remained in Germany.

Heinz was detained in Manchester on 29 June 1940. After deportation on the *Dunera* and internment at Hay and Tatura, he joined the Australian army in July 1942. He was discharged in November 1945 and left Australia for Britain in January 1946 on the *Athlone Castle*. He lived in London for a year, during which time his partner Elfriede Altmann, who had followed him from Australia to London, gave birth to their daughter, Karin. Elfriede had been married to Bernie Taft, a member of the Communist Party of Australia. In early 1947 Heinz, Elfriede and Karin moved to the Soviet sector of Berlin. Heinz and Elfriede's relationship soured and in 1951 Elfriede and Karin returned to Australia. Heinz remained in East Germany.

Heinz worked for the East German regime, serving on its Afro-Asian Solidarity Committee. For a time he lived in Egypt, where he was responsible for marshalling East German support for the revolution in Angola (1961–1974). It was through his role with the Afro-Asian Solidarity Committee that he met President Abeid Karume (top), leader of the Revolutionary Government of Zanzibar, and Yasser Arafat (bottom). The Karume photograph was taken in Zanzibar, probably in 1969. The Arafat photograph was taken in December 1974, probably in East Berlin. Eggebrecht and Arafat were close, as their warm greeting suggests.

Heinz died in East Germany in December 1989, a month after the fall of the Berlin Wall. He remained a committed communist to his death.

Source: Karin Altmann and Frank Schumacher.

TOWARD THE FUTURE

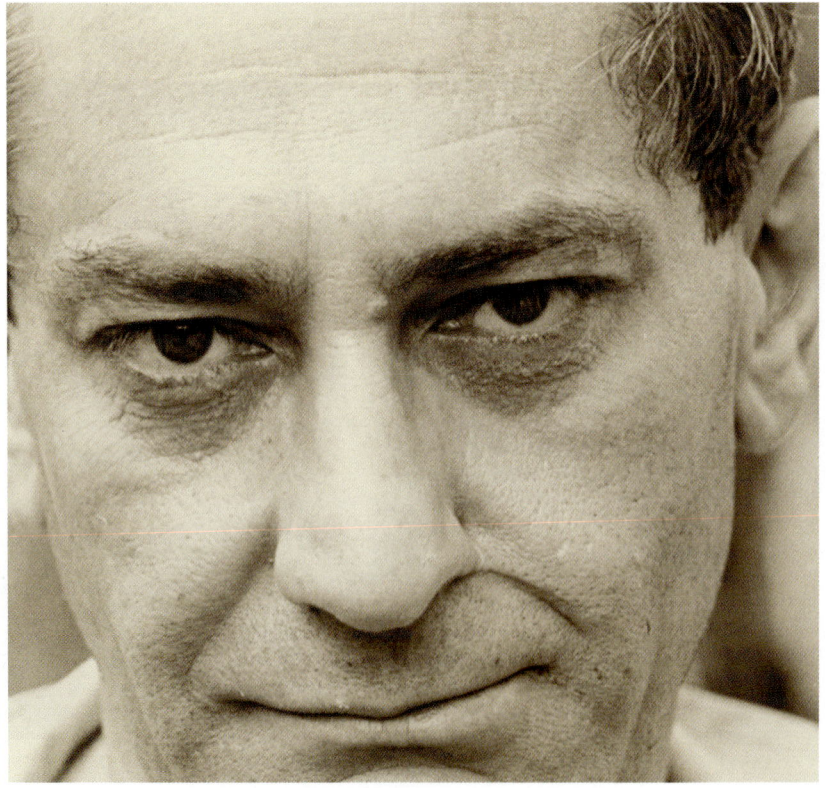

Henry Mayer, 1965

Henry Mayer was born in Mannheim in 1919 to a Jewish father and a Catholic mother. He was educated at Millfield school in Somerset, England. Financial support for his education came from his uncle Sir Robert Mayer, a banker and philanthropist.

In 1940 Henry was deported to Australia on the *Dunera*. After service in the army, in 1947 he enrolled as a Political Science student at the University of Melbourne, a step which marked the start of a stellar academic career. In 1949 he co-edited *Melbourne University Magazine* with Max Corden.

In 1950 Mayer moved to the University of Sydney, where he taught politics. His academic work was wide-ranging and seminal.

The photograph was taken in Sydney in 1965 by Henry's friend Hugo Wolfsohn, also a former *Dunera* internee. Elaine Mayer, Henry's widow, treasures this photograph; in it she sees the 'quintessential humanity and integrity which drove his rigorous work.'

Henry Mayer, 1965, by Hugo Wolfsohn, gelatin silver photograph. Collection: National Portrait Gallery, Canberra. Gift of Mrs Elaine Mayer and Ms Vicky Mayer, 2011. Copyright: Ilse Wolfsohn.

Reference

Email from Elaine Mayer to Seumas Spark, 20 September 2017.

TOWARD THE FUTURE

Klaus and Uyen Loewald, Canberra, 1967

In 1945 Klaus Loewald left Australia to return to Britain. The next year he emigrated to the United States, where he took American citizenship and built an academic career. In 1962 he left Berkeley for Saigon to teach American politics and history at the university and to serve as United States cultural attache. In 1967 the American State Department posted him to Australia to serve as cultural attache in Canberra.

Klaus and Uyen met in Saigon in 1963 and married the following year.

Source: Uyen Loewald and Tonio Loewald.

Franz Stampfl, 1969

Franz Stampfl was born in Vienna in 1913 to a Catholic family. An accomplished skier and javelin thrower, he served as assistant to the chief coach of the Austrian Olympic team in Berlin in 1936.

In 1937 he left Austria for Britain. He was coaching athletes in Northern Ireland when the Second World War began. His passion for athletics and exercise continued through the conflict: at Hay and Tatura he organised physical activities for his fellow internees.

After returning to the United Kingdom in early 1946, Stampfl worked in Belfast as coach of the Northern Ireland athletics team, then in England where he trained athletes on a freelance basis. He was coach to Roger Bannister when he broke the four-minute mark for the mile in Oxford in 1954.

Stampfl emigrated permanently to Australia in 1955. He taught physical education at the University of Melbourne and led its athletics team. His training methods, detailed in his 1955 book *On Running*, were demanding, revolutionary and successful. The Australian athlete Ralph Doubell, who won a gold medal at the Mexico Olympics in 1968, was one of many in Stampfl's training stable who benefitted from his guidance. Stampfl continued to coach even after he was paralysed in a traffic accident in 1980.

This photograph was taken by Henry Talbot.

Talbot, Henry, 1920–1999, *Athletics Coach Franz Stampfl, 1969*. National Library of Australia. Copyright: Lynette Anne Talbot.

TOWARD THE FUTURE

Gough Whitlam and Fred Gruen

In 1972 Fred Gruen was appointed Professor of Economics in the Research School of Social Sciences at the Australian National University. Gough Whitlam, Prime Minister from late 1972, asked Gruen to advise the Prime Minister's department on economic matters. Until 1976, Gruen divided his time between the university and the Prime Minister's office.

This photograph was taken in a restaurant in Cambridge, England, in late 1977 or early 1978. Fred was once again a full time scholar, and with his wife Ann was spending the 1977–1978 academic year at Cambridge. Whitlam was no longer Prime Minister, though he remained a Member of Parliament.

Source and copyright: David Gruen and Jenny Wilkinson.

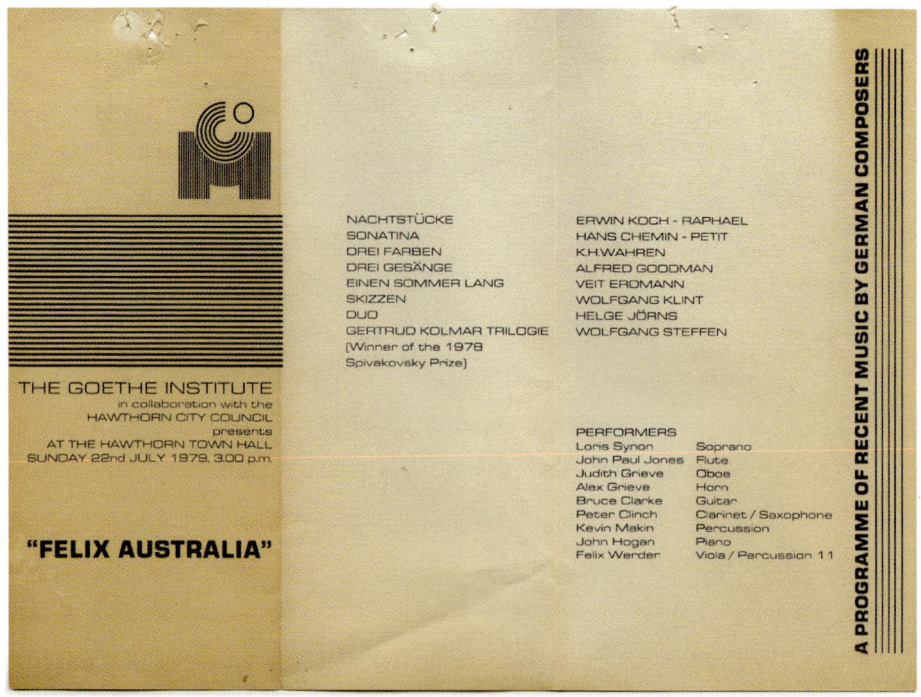

Programme for 'Felix Australia' performance

On being discharged from the army in 1946, Felix Werder embarked on a career as a musician and composer. Initially he had little success. His luck turned in 1948 when he received a letter from Eugene Goossens promising to play one of his works. Goossens, conductor of the Sydney Symphony Orchestra and director of the New South Wales State Conservatorium of Music, wielded heavy influence in the Australian music world. Werder was on his way.

Werder was an experimental composer whose music was not to wide popular taste. He had a parallel career as a music critic for Melbourne newspaper *The Age*, for which he wrote witty and often provocative articles.

Werder always felt an outsider in Australia, in music and life. He was more at home in Germany, and his music was better received there. He formed the ensemble 'Felix Australia' as a reaction against what he saw as an Australian music clique. The programme shown here is for a performance in Melbourne in 1979.

Source: Vera Werder.

Fred Carter at Government House, Melbourne, c. 1980

Fritz Werner Weidenbaum was born in Bonn in 1923.

After the Second World War he worked at the opulent Windsor Hotel in Melbourne, then for five years as a butler to the Governor of Victoria. This photograph was taken at Government House. He died in 1982.

Around 1963 Weidenbaum changed his name to Frederick (Fred) Carter. In 2006 his son Joseph adopted his father's original surname, changing Carter to Weidenbaum.

Source: Joseph Weidenbaum.

Steven Strauss, QC and judge, 1980s

Steven Strauss was born Siegfried Strauss to a Jewish family in Lauterbach in central Germany in 1921. In July 1939 he escaped from Nazi Germany on a *Kindertransport*, leaving behind his mother and sister, who were later murdered. He was interned at Hay and Tatura, joined the Australian army in early 1942, and was discharged in February 1946.

After the war he studied at the University of Melbourne, receiving his Master in Laws in 1949. The next year he became the first lawyer born outside Australia to gain admission to the Victorian Bar. He practised as a barrister, specialising in family law. He was made a Queen's Counsel in 1965, a judge of the Family Court of Victoria in 1976, and a judge of the appeals division of the Family Court in 1985. He continued to practise law after he stepped down from the bench in 1994. He died in 2010.

Source: Hay Internment and Prisoner of War Camps Interpretive Centre. Gift of the Strauss family.

TOWARD THE FUTURE

Fredy Fisher with other editors of the *Financial Times*, London, c. 1991–1993

Max Hermann Fischer, known as Fredy, was born in Berlin 1922 to a Jewish family. His family left Nazi Germany for Switzerland, and Fredy was sent to school in England. He was later arrested, deported on the *Dunera*, and interned at Hay and Tatura. After returning to Britain in October 1941 on the *Stirling Castle*, he joined the British army and served in Europe.

After demobilisation came Oxford, followed by the British Foreign Office, where he edited German documents. In 1956 he returned to Australia for a year, lecturing in the University of Melbourne's history department and researching 'Problems in the study of diplomatic archives'.

In 1957 he joined the *Financial Times* and over a span of 23 years rose from reporter to foreign editor, to deputy editor, to assistant editor, to editor. After editing the *Financial Times* from 1973 to 1980, he became a merchant banker with S. G. Warburg, a firm with Hamburg origins.

This photograph shows four editors of the *Financial Times*. From left to right are Fredy Fisher, Richard Lambert, Sir Geoff Owen, and Sir Gordon Newton.

Source and copyright: *Financial Times*, London. Photograph by Trevor Humphries. Taken from David Kynaston, *The Financial Times: A Centenary History*, (London: Viking, 1988).

Gerald Cunningham, c. 2007

Gerhard Kuppenheim was born in Pforzheim in 1922 to a Protestant family. One great grandfather was Jewish, but Gerhard's family never identified as such.

Gerhard's father was a fine horseman and member of the Baden-Baden horse racing committee. Deprived of a livelihood by the Nazis, he committed suicide when Gerhard was 14. His son shared his love of horses.

Gerhard escaped to England on a *Kindertransport*. After deportation on the *Dunera* and internment at Hay and Tatura, he joined the army in early 1942. At this time he took the name Gerald Cunningham.

Initially Gerald worked in the field of radio engineering, and later in housing construction. All the while he indulged his passion for horses, which he bought and raced successfully. In 1987 he was elected by public vote to the committee of the Victoria Racing Club. It was a significant moment in Melbourne history; an outsider was to join a committee long the preserve of the city's establishment.

Gerald married his wife Eileen in 1951. Their first date had been to the Melbourne Cup.

Source and copyright: Eileen Cunningham.

TOWARD THE FUTURE

Coffs Harbour, New South Wales, 2016

In the centre of this photograph is Park Beach Plaza, a commercial centre which opened in Coffs Harbour in 1979. Max Naumburger, developer of the plaza, played a pivotal role in transforming Coffs Harbour from a fishing village into a major regional centre.

The Bachrach Naumberger Group, a property development company he led, operated along the east coast of Australia.

Naumburger was born to Jewish parents in Fürth, Bavaria, in 1922. He was a student when deported to Australia on the *Dunera*. He died in 2013.

Source and copyright: Peter Tanner.

Section 8

BETWEEN MEMORY AND HISTORY

INTRODUCTION

The *Dunera* and *Queen Mary* internees were as varied a population as any of their generation. They included artists and scholars, cynics and mystics, and a few charlatans. All shared an administrative fate: collectively they were judged a potential threat to the British war effort and arrested, interned and deported to Australia. What else did they share?

While four out of five were of Jewish origin, only a small minority followed Jewish customs and practices. To call the *Dunera* story a Jewish one is both true and misleading. To be sure, a majority of those interned were of Jewish origin, but some were Jewish only in the sense defined by the perverted Nazi racial categories of the day; they had a grandmother or grandfather who was or was deemed to have been Jewish. Of the 'Jews' on board the *Dunera* were hundreds who lived lives utterly remote from the ways of observant Jews.

It is more helpful to see this population as having come from the German and Austrian middle classes, sharing their language, upbringing, tastes and habits. There were men from working class and farming families, but most were city dwellers, whose parents, often bourgeois, had lived through a period of economic growth at the turn of the century, then war and economic instability. In Germany and Austria, they enjoyed the fruits of the Enlightenment: if they chose to practise Judaism, many adopted a liberal outlook. There were communists, socialists, liberals, and conservatives. They were modern Europeans, and history had made them very different from the great masses of Jews living in Eastern Europe and Russia.

The first sub-section presents images of *Dunera* internees some decades after their incarceration. Their faces are as Australian as those of neighbours born in Melbourne or Sydney. Some led public lives; others were less well known. Each life had its own shape, its own signature.

Second, we show how the stories of these internees and their families were shaped as a collective narrative; the tale of a group of people badly treated by Germany and Britain, and again on the *Dunera*, who transcended hardship to endure internment as best they could and then build new lives. The *Dunera* generation was a self-fashioned one, carving out a place for itself in Australian history.

As such the *Dunera* generation was like many other groups throughout the world which came together to tell a collective story from the 1960s on. Thanks to the wonders of technology, they were able to preserve their memories on audio and video cassettes, and later on computers and through the internet. In the 1980s, many of these people joined what we now call the 'memory boom', in passing on to their children and grandchildren, and then to later generations, the story of their persecution, imprisonment, and liberation. Some objected to the location of the *Dunera* story within the history of the Holocaust; others insisted that the Nazis were responsible for all they had endured.

The phenomenon of the 'memory boom' went beyond the Nazis and their prey to include all victims of war and dictatorship, and the *Dunera* internees were certainly among that population. The public fascination, at times obsession, with memory was worldwide. It was determined by the spread of higher education, by the appearance of a popular human rights movement, by the prosecution of war criminals and others in trials in which victims told their own stories. Those who knew these hard times became more than casualties of the war – they became witnesses, who spoke on their own behalf and for those who had perished. Most of those who were on the *Dunera* or the *Queen Mary* lost members of their families. Some lost everyone. They spoke for the disappeared.

The *Dunera* survivors form a kind of fictive kinship group, a family of experience rather than of blood lines. This helps to account for the strength of the bonds these men and women forged and continue to forge in the process of together remembering the past.

Memory activists made the memory boom possible. In the case of the *Dunera* story, a number of people took a special interest in organising reunions, meetings, and publications. Some of their children and grandchildren took up the work when their elders were no longer alive. We see the faces of some of these memory activists in this second sub-section.

A particular difficulty disturbed some memory activists. Former 8th Employment Company servicemen were not eligible for membership of the Returned and Services League on the basis that they had not served overseas. This separated them from groups of Australians whose pride in their military service was displayed in marches on Anzac Day.

As with many people entering their later years, *Dunera* and *Queen Mary* survivors have taken to mulling over their legacy. We introduce this theme in the third sub-section. Some of our subjects have seen parallels between the treatment they received and the experience of refugees today. The *Dunera* and *Queen Mary* internees were prisoners, not refugees, yet they were wanderers in a world at war, people without rights. Other former internees see no parallels. Here we see evidence of their incorporation into Australian society, divided on how to treat today's boat people. On this matter and others, the surviving *Dunera* population holds diverse views.

The story of their lives – which we tell in visual form in this volume and in profile form in the second – is part of their legacy. Through the internees' own words and images, we learn that becoming free took a long time. No one knew what to do with them, and, in any case, political leaders faced more urgent questions than how to correct a political mistake which took these internees far from the battlefields of the Second World War. Accidental though callous benevolence is one way to describe the unintended consequences of their internment in camps at Hay and Tatura from 1940 to 1945. After internment, some of these men were the recipients of what the Russian writer Vasily Grossman called irrational kindness, manifest in the warmth Captain Broughton showed to the men under his command in the 8th Employment Company. Others were helped to find their way into civilian life by men and women moved by their story. Not everyone welcomed them, but once out of camp and out of uniform, many chose to become naturalised

Britons or, after 1949, Australians: citizenship was a precious gift to those who had been deprived of it in Nazi Europe. They became citizens of a buoyant Australian democracy, marked though it was by its own forms of racial prejudice which placed Europeans above Asians and Aborigines. They turned away from Britain and Europe, where they had lost so much, and plunged into new Australian lives, aided by the porous character of Australian society.

These ordinary men, women and children shaped decent and creative lives in internment and in the years after 1945. They did not allow themselves to be defined by the injustices of wartime. This is possibly their greatest legacy.

SECTION 8A

AUSTRALIAN FACES

Kurt Lewinski

Max Bruch

Fred Lowen

Half a century on

In 1989 June Orford, a student photographer, shot a series of black and white portraits for an assignment suggested by her teacher Francis Reiss, whose relatives Peter Turkheim and Hans Heymann had been on the *Dunera*. She photographed Kurt Lewinski, Max Bruch, Fred Lowen, Felix Werder, Horst Jacobs, Jimmy King and Leo Strom. The portraits show ageing and accomplished Australian men in various poses. They are entering Australian history.

Felix Werder

Horst Jacobs

Jimmy King

Leo Strom

Some of these men were well known, others not. Possibly the best known was the actor Max Bruch, who was the only former *Dunera* internee to appear in the telemovie 'The *Dunera* Boys' shown on Australian television in 1985. His German accent limited the roles he could play, and he earned a living as a jewellery assessor. He died in Melbourne in 2012.

Kurt Lewinski was born in Marienwerder, Prussia, in 1921. His birthplace is now part of modern Poland. Lewinski was a mechanical engineer with a gift for wood-turning, a skill which served him well. After the war, his proficiency with wood led to a job crafting furniture at FLER, the company founded by Fred Lowen and Ernest Rodeck. Lewinski died in Melbourne in 2005.

Horst Jacobs was born to a Jewish family in Stuttgart in 1922. He was working as a dental mechanic in Manchester when he was arrested and deported on the *Dunera*. After the war he enrolled in dentistry at the University of Queensland, and following the completion of his studies enjoyed a long career as a dentist in Victoria. In 1988 he was elected the first president of the Hay-Tatura Association. He cautioned against the view that all the *Dunera* internees 'became professors, judges, academics, entered the professions or ended up millionaires.' Most, he declared, 'made their way through life doing the best they could for their families and their new homeland.' Jacobs died in Melbourne in 2009.

Jimmy King was born in Vienna to a Catholic family in 1923. After the war he worked as a pastry cook and then entered the import-export business, doing well with Texta coloured pencils. He joined Heine Brothers, the firm built by Walter Heine, also a former *Dunera* internee. Mike Sondheim and Jimmy helped organise the reunions that led to the formation of the Dunera Association. Jimmy, who died in 2009, had a keen interest in *Dunera* art. He donated many of the treasures in the collection of the Jewish Museum of Australia.

Leo Strom was born to a Jewish family in Wielka Wies in Poland in 1899. When interned in 1940, he was a widower with one child. He served with the Austrian army in the First World War, and the Australian army in the Second. He died in Melbourne in 1993.

Lowen and Werder we have read about through this book.

Source: June Orford via Anna Wolf. Copyright: June Orford.

Quotation from *Dunera News*, 20, November 1991.

Uwe and Anita Radok on holiday, Goondiwindi, Queensland, 1986

Uwe Radok, a *Dunera* internee, and Anita Holper, a *Queen Mary* internee, first met at Tatura (page 256). She spoke Russian and Italian. He spoke German. Their common language was English. Uwe felt fortunate to have survived the war and found a new home in Australia, even if he did not always fit in. His daughter remembers the contrast between her friends' 'jolly' Australian fathers and her 'German academic' father.

Uwe was a meteorologist and glaciologist whose academic work advanced understanding of Australia's weather patterns. He conducted pioneering research in Antarctica, where a glacial lake is named for him. In the 1970s he warned of anthropogenic climate change, though he predicted the earth would become colder rather than warmer.

For many years Anita worked at the Royal Women's Hospital in Melbourne as an Italian translator.

After a long academic career spent in Australia and the United States, Uwe retired with Anita to Coffs Harbour on the New South Wales coast. Uwe died in 2009 and Anita in 2014. Uwe's ashes were scattered in Antarctica.

Source and copyright: Radok family collection.

Reference

Interview with Jacquie Houlden conducted by Ken Inglis and Seumas Spark, Melbourne, 12 July 2017.

Felix Werder, 7 December 2002

In 2002 the University of Melbourne awarded Felix Werder an honorary doctorate in music. He had been reluctant to accept the award, but was persuaded by his wife. Ian Renard, Deputy Chancellor of the university, is at right.

Source: Vera Werder.

Roy Thalheimer discovers sushi, 2006

In July 2006, at the age of 84, Roy Thalheimer tried sushi for the first time.

In Australia Roy worked as a forester. He was the son of August Thalheimer, a founder of the German Communist party. To the end of his life Roy remained curious about the world around him, and his curiosity extended to trying new foods. He died in 2012.

Source and copyright: Liz Zetzmann.

Ernest and Sheila Rodeck, November 2011

Ernest Rodeck and Fred Lowen sold FLER in 1967. Rodeck became a business consultant, Managing Director and Deputy Chairman of Pacific Dunlop, and a passionate advocate for Australian manufacturing. In 1993 he was made a Member of the Order of Australia (AM). He died in Melbourne in 2013, aged 93.

Source and copyright: Anna Wolf.

Erwin Fabian, 2013

Erwin Fabian is pictured in his North Melbourne studio in 2013, the year he turned 98.

From the 1960s on, the work of David Smith and others opened up the field of sculpture in heavy metals. Erwin Fabian began to explore this domain after the age of 60. At the age of 102 in 2017, his creative energy remained undimmed, and he continued to hold exhibitions in Australia and Europe.

Source: Emil Toonen. Copyright: Viki Petherbridge.

Bern Brent, 2015

Bern Brent relaxes in his Canberra home. He has a prodigious memory and a historian's passion for accuracy, which he combines to scrutinise myths associated with the *Dunera* story. He retains a clear sense of what he lost in leaving a close family in Germany, while cherishing the good fortune he enjoys in Australia. He has written two volumes of memoirs.

Source and copyright: Seumas Spark.

SECTION 8B

COMMEMORATION

Dunera reunion, South Yarra, Melbourne, 1963

This is the best known image of a *Dunera* reunion. Copies of this photograph are preserved in a number of collections of *Dunera* memorabilia. The photographer was Henry Talbot, who is at far left (glasses and moustache).

The early 1960s marked the first stages of a worldwide memory boom, in part generated by anniversaries of the two world wars and celebrated war crimes trials in Israel and in Germany, in part a function of the appearance of audio and video recording technologies that enabled anyone to preserve and disseminate the voices and faces of twentieth-century people.

Talbot, Henry, 1920–1999, *Dunera boys reunion, Melbourne, 1963*. National Library of Australia. Copyright: Lynette Anne Talbot.

COMMEMORATION

Framing the story: Benzion Patkin

The Dunera Internees by Benzion Patkin was published in 1979. The presence of the Israeli flag at the launch signalled an attachment to Zionism and the state of Israel which is reflected in the book. Patkin is in the middle of the front row, legs crossed.

The Dunera Internees book launch, c. 1979. Jewish Museum of Australia collection 4438.

Framing the story: Cyril Pearl

The Dunera Scandal by Cyril Pearl, published in 1983, was a severe critique of British government policy on internment and the maltreatment of the *Dunera* internees. The book was generally well received by its subjects.

Pearl had tried repeatedly to gain access to relevant Home Office records held in London. He was convinced he was denied access because the records contained embarrassing revelations.

Through a Freedom of Information request, the authors of this book secured access to the Home Office records, which otherwise remain under embargo. Contrary to Pearl's suspicions, they do not tell of a desire to cover up a spectacular story of British malevolence. The records reveal little that is not already known.

FXB277202: Ronald Stewart/Fairfax Syndication.

Framing the story: Ben Lewin

The telemovie 'The *Dunera* Boys' directed by Ben Lewin was first shown on Australian commercial television (Channel 10) in 1985. Cliff Green's script blended fact and fiction, and brought the story to a wider audience than any previous depiction of the *Dunera* experience. The series gave currency to the term '*Dunera* boys', which was now embraced by the former internees and the public.

Source: Judi Levine.

Framing the story: Paul Bartrop and *The Dunera Affair*

The Dunera Affair: A Documentary Resource Book, edited by Paul Bartrop with Gabrielle Eisen, drew on a wider range of official and unofficial sources than any previous study.

The book, published in 1990, accompanied an exhibition at the Jewish Museum of Australia in Melbourne to mark the fiftieth anniversary of the landing of the *Dunera*. Both the exhibition and the book helped move the *Dunera* narrative from the domain of personal memory into the field of contemporary history.

Image at left: Paul Bartrop. *Image at right*: Jewish Museum of Australia.

COMMEMORATION

Framing the story: Judy Menczel

'When Friends Were Enemies', a television documentary written and directed by Judy Menczel, aired in 1991. It was commissioned and shown by SBS television.

Produced for the fiftieth anniversary of the *Dunera's* voyage, the programme was an exuberant celebration of the *Dunera* boys' experience.

Source: Judy Menczel.

Dunera News, Sydney, September 1984

This is the first page of the first edition of the *Dunera News*, Sydney, September 1984. Pictured is the actor Bob Hoskins, who played the lead character in 'The *Dunera* Boys' telemovie.

Here is another aspect of the memory boom: groups of survivors reinforcing their sense of a collective identity by editing their own newspapers and publications. The first edition of the *Dunera News* was a collection of A4 pages stapled together.

Source: Anna Wolf.

COMMEMORATION

Henry Lippmann: memory activist, c. 1984

Lippmann played a pivotal role in the formation of the Dunera Association and the inauguration of the *Dunera News*. He was the quintessential memory activist, prepared to devote time and energy to preserving and disseminating the *Dunera* story.

In 2004 Lippmann was awarded the Medal of the Order of Australia (OAM) for his work in recording *Dunera* history.

Source: Australian National Maritime Museum, ANMS0222[002].

Mike Sondheim: memory activist, 1990

Mike Sondheim was another memory activist who preserved important elements of the *Dunera* story. In 1991 he succeeded Horst Jacobs as president of the Hay-Tatura Association. In that role he amassed documents about the *Dunera* internees that have been invaluable in writing this book. He retired as president of the Dunera Association in 2011 at the age of 95.

The Hay-Tatura Association was renamed the Dunera Association in 2008. The original name implied recognition of the *Queen Mary* internees from Singapore. The dwindling number of Singaporeans cordially accepted their incorporation into the *Dunera* community.

Source: Anna Wolf. Copyright: June Orford.

COMMEMORATION

Dunera boys at Hay, 1–2 September 1990 (1)

Eric Eckstein (left) and Walter Kaufmann, who had travelled from Berlin, are shown on arrival at Hay for the 1990 *Dunera* reunion. Bungah Creek is on the edge of Hay.

Source: David Eckstein.

Dunera boys at Hay, 1–2 September 1990 (2)

Few *Dunera* boys at the 1990 reunion had visited Hay in fifty years. The townspeople made them welcome, as they have done each September since.

Dunera boys cherish in memory the contrast between their treatment at sea and their reception in Australia, beginning with the soldiers assigned to guard them on the train from Sydney to Hay. One striking image recurs; of a soldier asking a captive to mind his rifle while he rolls himself a smoke. Walter Kaufmann told the story vividly at the 1990 reunion: 'Jesus', says the digger, 'I thought you were enemies, but you're friends. Jews! Jesus Christ!' In some versions of the story the guard then teaches the internees how to roll their own. In another, the guard is off to the toilet, not rolling a cigarette.

Kaufmann and Eric Eckstein were among *Dunera* boys interviewed by local school students at the reunion. Eckstein told them he witnessed the 'mind my rifle' episode, having been in the carriage in which it occurred.

Source and copyright: Eileen Cunningham.

Reference

[Caroline and Ian Merrylees,] *The Dunera Tapes: Conversations on a Windy Day in Hay* (Carrathool: I. F. and C. A. Merrylees, 1991), p. 62.

COMMEMORATION

Dust storm at Hay

A dust storm swept through Hay on the weekend of the 1990 reunion, reminding *Dunera* boys of the one that struck them on arrival fifty years earlier.

Source and copyright: Eileen Cunningham.

Dunera reunion, Beverly Crest Hotel, St Kilda, Melbourne, 4 September 1990

The man in the front row holds a print of an image that appears in this book: the camp at Hay depicted in a Ludwig Hirschfeld-Mack lithograph (page 193).

By the 1990s the *Dunera* boys were seen as Holocaust survivors: many, though not all, had been victims of the Nazis. They represented the transcendence of those who, despite suffering under the Nazis, led varied and productive lives after the Second World War.

Source: Anna Wolf. Copyright: June Orford.

COMMEMORATION

Dunera reunion, Pyrmont Wharf, Sydney, 6 September 1990

On 6 September 1990, fifty years after the arrival of the *Dunera* in Sydney, a reunion was held at Pyrmont Wharf, where the *Dunera* docked. Speakers included the Governor-General, Bill Hayden; Horst Jacobs, president of the Hay-Tatura Association; and Fred Gruen.

Hayden said that the *Dunera* internees had made a profound contribution to the cultural, social, political and economic life of this country. He counselled sympathy toward contemporary refugees and reminded his audience 'of the absolute necessity to resist hysteria and propaganda even at times of national conflict, but always to judge people as individuals and not on the basis of some notion of collective national identity'.

Jacobs too spoke of 'contributions' and achievements, but not Gruen, who expressly avoided any note of triumphalism. He spoke of thanksgiving, of gratitude at finding a welcome and a home in Australia.

Some *Dunera* boys at the reunion found the talk of 'contributions' too close to self-congratulation. Peter Herbst wrote of the fiftieth anniversary commemorations to his friend Gerd Buchdahl: 'Many of our old mates have persuaded themselves that they are the elect, because they suffered on the *Dunera*, but it doesn't follow that all the world loves us. I think people's sentiments vis a vis relative strangers are likely to be more guarded.'

The picture shows Klaus Loewald (right) and Hans Marcus in conversation at the reunion. Loewald, master of ceremonies for the day, was both a participant and historian of the *Dunera* experience.

Source: Rebecca Silk.

References

Dunera News, 20, November 1991.

Ken Inglis, 'The *Dunera* Boys in History and Memory', *Australian Jewish Historical Society Journal*, vol. 21, no. 3, November 2013, 287-305.

Letter from Peter Herbst to Gerd Buchdahl, 3 November 1990. Letter in possession of Kit Buchdahl.

Peter Huppert

Peter Huppert is shown reading Cyril Pearl's *The Dunera Scandal*.

Huppert was born in Vienna in 1914, a Protestant of Jewish extraction. In the late 1930s he and his brother Harold escaped to England. Both were interned and deported on the *Dunera*. Peter, a medical student, returned to England in 1941 on the *Stirling Castle*. After the war he qualified as a doctor, then as a psychiatrist. In 1962 he returned, with his wife Nora and their children, to Australia. They spent three years in Tasmania before settling in Sydney. Peter suffered from depression for much of his adult life, and in 1987 committed suicide. This photograph was taken in the same year.

Nora, who escaped Europe on a *Kindertransport*, recorded her memories in her book *Home Without a Homeland* (2012).

When the *Dunera* docked in Sydney in September 1940, Harold was sent directly to hospital and then to Waterfall Sanatorium on account of tuberculosis. He remained in the sanatorium until August 1945 when he returned to Britain. He died in the United States in 2005.

Source and copyright: Rebecca Silk.

Rebecca Silk: memory activist, 2016

Rebecca Silk became a prominent keeper of the memory of the *Dunera* generation. She is the daughter of Peter and Nora Huppert.

Rebecca, who has made a career in social work, health administration and education, succeeded Mike Sondheim as president of the Dunera Association in 2011. She has done much to cherish and extend the *Dunera* story beyond the generation of those who lived through it. Erwin Fabian relished the fact that the Dunera Association was now led by a woman.

Source: Rebecca Silk. Copyright: Margie McClelland.

Dunera reunion, Hay, September 2015

Werner Haarburger (standing) and Bernhard Rothschild pose for photographs at Hay train station, September 2015. *Dunera* internees filed across this platform when they arrived at Hay in 1940. The old suitcases are props, a historical touch arranged by the organisers of the Hay reunion.

Haarburger and Rothschild were the only *Dunera* boys at the reunion that year. Few now make the long journey to Hay. Haarburger died suddenly just after the reunion.

Anton Stampfl, son of Franz, took public transport from Sydney to Hay to help simulate his father's journey 75 years before.

Source and copyright: Anna Wolf.

COMMEMORATION

Dunera reunion, Melbourne, November 2015

Ben Lewin was the special guest at the 2015 annual reunion in Melbourne. He spoke via Skype from his home in Los Angeles. Leaning on the pillar, at left, is Adrian Bruch, son of Max Bruch, whom Lewin directed in the telemovie 'The *Dunera* Boys'.

Source and copyright: Anna Wolf.

Albert Meyer

Four *Dunera* reunions are now held every year. *Dunera* family and friends gather at Tatura in April or May, at Hay and Sydney in September, and at Melbourne, heartland or *Heimat* of the *Dunera* community, in November.

This picture of Albert Meyer, *Dunera* boy, was taken at the Melbourne reunion in 2012. He holds a photograph of his younger self.

Source and copyright: Anna Wolf.

COMMEMORATION

Dunera reunion, Melbourne, November 2016

Linda Dessau, the first Jewish governor of Victoria, and the first woman governor, was the guest of honour at the 2016 Melbourne reunion. She and her husband, Anthony Howard QC, pose with Rebecca Silk and the four *Dunera* boys who attended.

Left to right: Bernhard Rothschild, Harry Unger, Anthony Howard, Albert Meyer, Rebecca Silk, Linda Dessau, Henry Hirsch.

Source and copyright: Anna Wolf.

SECTION 8C

LEGACIES

'Happy 2016' card

This new year's card was drawn by Erwin Fabian, aged 100. The *Dunera* legacy was ecumenical: Father Christmas is represented by his beard on the number 1.

Source: Ken Inglis. Copyright: Erwin Fabian.

Erwin and Ilse Lamm, St Thomas's Primary School, Sale, Victoria, 2008

Erwin and Ilse Lamm were determined to bring their family history to the attention of schoolchildren. In this effort they followed many others who mixed stories of family history with tragic narratives of the Holocaust.

They are pictured with students from St Thomas's Primary School. This Catholic school was an ideal venue for the Lamms' ecumenical project to preserve the *Dunera* story.

Source: Ilse Lamm.

Erwin and Danny Lamm

Above, Erwin Lamm and his son Danny meet former Prime Minister Julia Gillard in Melbourne in November 2013. Below, father and son are shown at the inauguration of the Lamm Jewish Library of Australia in 2012. The library is named for Erwin's parents, who died in the Holocaust. Danny and Rolene Lamm, and their son Rafi, donated generously to the library, which has become an educational and cultural centre for Melbourne's Jewish community. The library's collection of literature on Jews and Judaism is the largest in the southern hemisphere.

Erwin Lamm grew up as an Orthodox Jew in Vienna without a commitment to Zionism. After the war and the Holocaust, he changed his mind, and became a major figure in Australian Zionism. His son has followed the same path. Danny has served as president of the Zionist Federation of Australia, and president of the Executive Council of Australian Jewry.

Erwin was a director of a company that manufactured women's clothing, and then worked as an energy consultant for the American firm NUS International. He died in 2015.

Image above: Source: Zionist Council of Victoria. Copyright: Dean Schmideg.

Image below: Source: Zionist Council of Victoria. Copyright: Peter Haskin.

***Dunera* boys at the grave of Captain Broughton, September 2006**

Many stories preserved during the memory boom have sacred elements. In the *Dunera* narrative, a kind of redemption from prejudice, denigration and poor treatment came from a Maori soldier who understood how dignity was a property all human beings shared. For many former internees, their commander in the 8th Employment Company restored their faith in the future.

Edward Broughton died in 1955. Half a century later, some of the men who served under his command were disappointed that his grave had become neglected. They determined to set that right.

The event pictured is the dedication of Broughton's gravesite in Melbourne's Fawkner cemetery. Major General David McLachlan, president of the Victorian Returned and Services League, lays a wreath. The soldier in the background is in New Zealand army uniform. Here, for a moment, the *Dunera* and Anzac legends meet.

The three *Dunera* men at the centre of the image are, from left, Albert Meyer, Ernst Wolf and Fred Katz. The friendship between Katz (originally Albert) and Wolf dated to the *Dunera*. They are pictured together in army uniform on page 356.

FXB276741: Angela Wylie/Fairfax Syndication.

Plaque honouring Franz Stampfl

Set in the footpath outside the Baillieu Library at the University of Melbourne are plaques honouring distinguished service to the university. The makers have chosen not to mention Franz Stampfl's passage on the *Dunera*.

Source and copyright: Seumas Spark.

Murray Williams, October 2015

Dr Murray Williams, 88, is pictured in his home in Canberra. He stands in front of two Ludwig Hirschfeld-Mack paintings, and one of his own works. One of the Hirschfeld-Mack paintings was a gift from the artist and the other Williams bought cheaply at a fete. These paintings are among his most prized possessions.

Williams was school doctor at Geelong Grammar in 1953–1954. He treasures the time he spent with Hirschfeld-Mack, who, he says, taught him much about art and life. To Williams he was a saintly figure.

Source and copyright: Seumas Spark.

Art school gates, Geelong Grammar School

These gates, outside the art school at Geelong Grammar, were designed by Ludwig Hirschfeld-Mack. Wrought iron figures hold hands, in the gesture he added to the last of his wall paintings of the life of Christ in the art school, which now bears Hirschfeld-Mack's name. These days his small flat in the art school is occupied by visiting artists.

Source and copyright: Peter Bajer.

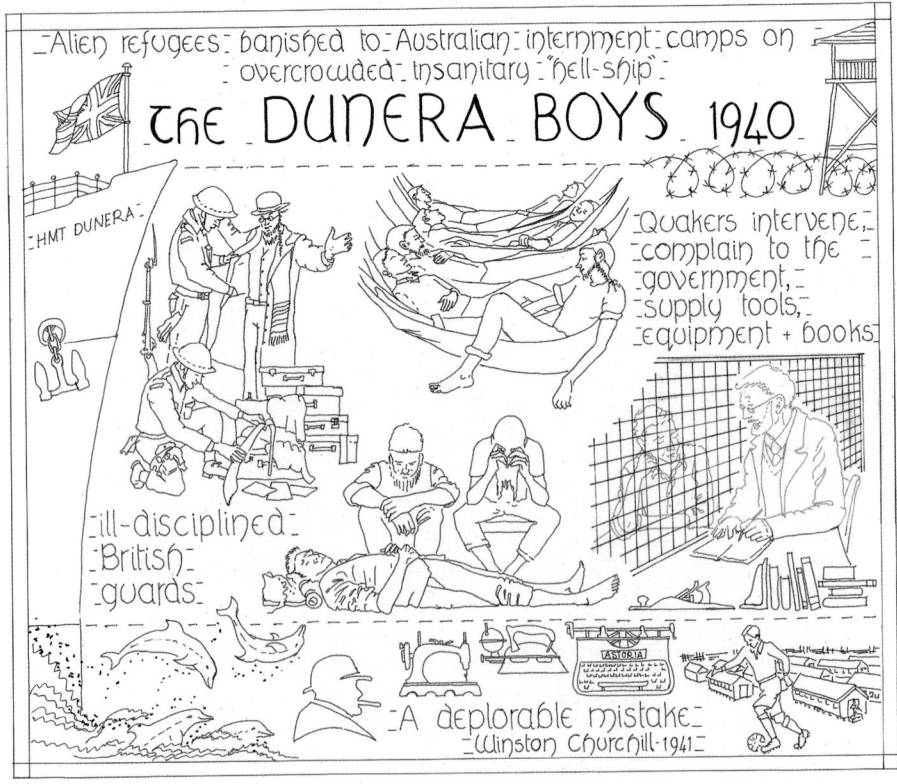

'The *Dunera* boys' tapestry panel

Quakers were active in improving the material conditions of the *Dunera* internees and arguing against their internment. This is the design for a tapestry panel celebrating these efforts. Volunteers at the Quaker Tapestry Museum in Kendal, Britain, where the panel was conceived, are embroidering a coloured tapestry that follows the design shown here. When 'The *Dunera* boys' panel is finished in 2018, it will be presented to the Australian Quaker Tapestry Project, which will include it in a forty-panel tapestry telling the history of Quakers in Australia.

'The Dunera Boys'. Design for an embroidered panel by Bridget Guest and Roy Wilcock. Further information about the project is available at: https://www.quaker-tapestry.co.uk/embroidery/the-dunera-boys-story/ Source: Bridget Guest, Quaker Tapestry Museum.

Remembering the *Dunera*, National Library of Australia, 2010

The seventieth anniversary of the arrival of the *Dunera* in Australia was marked by an exhibition held at the National Library in Canberra. The Ludwig Hirschfeld-Mack print used on the exhibition poster is perhaps the most famous *Dunera* image: a man looking through a fence at the stars of the Southern Cross. The poster reproduces a version of the print made at Orange in 1941.

The exhibition proved to be more popular than its makers had expected, both among *Dunera* boys and a wider public.

Courtesy of Chris Bell and the National Library of Australia. Copyright: Chris Bell.

Eva de Jong-Duldig, Duldig Studio, 2014

Eva de Jong-Duldig founded the Duldig Studio, a gallery and museum dedicated to the art and memory of her parents. The studio is housed in her parents' former home in the Melbourne suburb of Malvern East.

In 2017 she published a memoir entitled *Driftwood: Escape and Survival Through Art*.

Eva de Jong-Duldig – The Duldig Studio 2014. Photographer Philip Betts – Murray Betts Group. Copyright: The Duldig Studio.

LEGACIES

The Hay Internment and Prisoner of War Camps Interpretive Centre

The *Dunera* museum at Hay, formally the Hay Internment and Prisoner of War Camps Interpretive Centre, is housed in railway carriages at the town's now defunct train station.

Source and copyright: Anna Wolf.

The site of camps 7 and 8, Hay, 2015

These photographs, taken at the edge of Hay town, show where camp 7 (above) and camp 8 (below) once stood. The photographs were taken in September and the foliage of early spring hides some of the realities of Hay's harsh climate. No traces of the camps remain on this land.

Source and copyright: Seumas Spark.

Grave of Menasche Bodner, Hay

Menasche Bodner, one of the older *Dunera* internees, was born in the town of Wisnicz in south-eastern Poland to a Jewish family in 1886. He was a watchmaker by trade, and a Polish nationalist by conviction. He managed to get to Britain, but was interned and deported – 'mistakenly' the commemorative plaque says – on the *Dunera*. Affected by the extreme climate in Hay, he suffered a heart attack and died there in November 1940.

Kurt Lewinski, Bert Andjel and an armed guard buried Bodner. Lewinski and Andjel were friends, but did not share Bodner's origins or occupation. Andjel was born in Constantinople in 1914, and had worked in the textile trades. Lewinski was born in 1921 in Brandenburg and received ORT training as an engineer.

Bodner's grave (near the pole) points to Jerusalem. The plaque on his grave was erected by members of the Dunera Association in 1998. The original tombstone made no reference to his Jewish faith. The plaque includes the Hebrew acronym 'May his soul be bound up in the bond of life eternal', rendered as the English acronym M.H.D.S.R.I.P. ('May his departed soul rest in peace').

Source and copyright: Seumas Spark.

Hut at 'Torriganny'

This hut, one of those that housed internees at Hay, is on the 'Torriganny' property, 80 kilometres north of Hay. It was taken there after the war to serve as a shearing shed, though it was never used for this purpose. The graffiti of *Dunera* internees scribbled in pencil on the inside walls has faded.

Source: Alison Crossley and Ed Crossley.

Telling *Dunera* history as Hay history

Mick Beckwith, a former mayor of Hay, and David Houston, a grazier in the district, have worked tirelessly to keep alive the *Dunera* story in Hay. They have helped their town remember and celebrate its part in *Dunera* history. Mick helped organise the 1990 Hay reunion, and was a prominent advocate for the establishment of the Hay Internment and Prisoner of War Camps Interpretive Centre. David is president of this museum.

The photograph was taken at the Melbourne *Dunera* reunion in November 2013, when Mick, and David and his wife Coleen, were made honorary life members of the Dunera Association.

From left to right: Alice Beckwith, Mick Beckwith, Mike Sondheim, Coleen Houston, David Houston, and Lurline and Arthur Knee of the Tatura Irrigation and Wartime Camps Museum.

Source and copyright: Anna Wolf.

Arthur and Lurline Knee, *Dunera* reunion, Tatura, 7 May 2017

Arthur, 92 when the photograph was taken, and Lurline Knee, 89, stand outside the museum at Tatura they have done much to develop. They have been essential to the emergence of a narrative of the *Dunera* boys. The Knees' collection of testimonies, *Marched In*, adds another dimension to the objects they display in the Tatura Irrigation and Wartime Camps Museum, which opened in 1988. Their interest extends to the period after 1945, when Tatura was the site of a hostel for migrants.

Source and copyright: Seumas Spark.

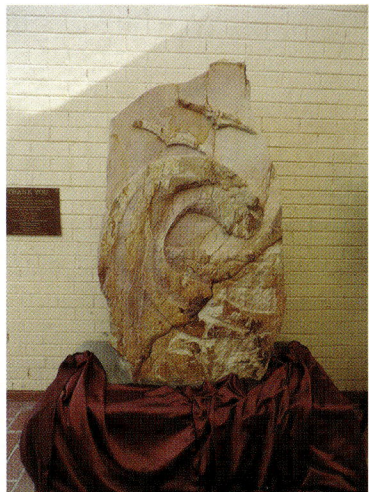

Bern Brent unveiling a new *Arandora Star* memorial, 7 May 2017

The tragic story of the extensive loss of life among internees on board the *Arandora Star*, a week before the *Dunera* set sail in July 1940, was commemorated in a sculpture by *Dunera* internee Robert Braun (page 200). His work, unveiled at Tatura in July 1941, was destroyed in 1947 or 1948.

In 2017 the Dunera Association launched an appeal for $15,000 to fund a new memorial, modelled on the earlier sculpture. The commission went to Jason Huntley. His sculpture, which stands outside the Tatura Irrigation and Wartime Camps Museum, was unveiled at the Tatura reunion in May 2017. Bern Brent was the only person present at the unveiling of both memorials.

Source and copyright: Rhiannon Tanner.

'Dunera' property, Tatura

Camp 2 once stood on this land just outside the town. The current owner, unlike some others in the district, is interested in the *Dunera* story and welcomes visitors. He named the property 'Dunera'.

Source and copyright: Seumas Spark.

Traces of the past, 'Dunera' property, Tatura

Some traces remain of camp 2 at Tatura; cells, ovens, long-drop latrines. Above is a coil of barbed wire, never removed from the site of the camp, and latrines. The bullet holes in the latrines suggest they have since been used for target practice.

Source and copyright: Seumas Spark.

Gum tree, 'Dunera' property, Tatura, with Waranga Basin in the distance
Is this the tree Leonhard Adam sketched in 1942 (see next image)?
Source and copyright: Seumas Spark.

Leonhard Adam, gum tree, Tatura, 6 January 1942

Adam caught what many *Dunera* internees saw: a strange land which through the upheavals of war became their home.

Sketchbook: drawings and paintings of Tatura Internment Camp and University of Melbourne, Leonhard Adam collection, University of Melbourne Archives, 1994.0060.00001, p. 27.

Copyright: Mary-Clare Adam.

CONCLUSION

Images of injustice and its aftermath

One great advantage contemporary historians have over scholars who specialise in earlier periods is access to a cornucopia of images and photographs bringing vividly to the reader the contours of recent events. We have presented a wide array of such images, all the while aware of the way visual history can distort the past if not used with care.

A potential danger here is the framing of the image. All photographers make editorial choices: they choose to show this and not that. We cannot go back to the scene of the snapshot and retake it in such a way as to include contextual elements, which might change the meaning of the photograph entirely. Another source of distortion is that we unconsciously locate images in a visual library we all carry with us.

Scholars of the visual image, following Roland Barthes, contend that we read photographs using a visual grammar, which affects the way we perceive images and which yields a common body of knowledge, or received wisdom.[1] Thus, when we see Gerd Bernstein (Bern Brent) at age 15 toasting his family before his departure from Germany on a *Kindertransport* in December 1938 (page 16), we place this fairly ordinary happening in a cultural setting of family photography found all over the world. But when we see images of the events which helped precipitate the departure of Bernstein and most of those whose lives we trace in this book, then our gaze is arrested. Our sense of what is normal is troubled, puzzled, upset; our gaze is 'pierced', in Barthes' language, and we enter another space marked by uncertainty or disorientation. Why is the Boemestrasse synagogue in Frankfurt on fire on 10 November 1938? Why are ordinary people in Vienna on their hands and knees scrubbing the streets of their city on 13 March 1938, much to the amusement of those watching them?

CONCLUSION

This book is a visual history of the move from the 'common knowledge' of family images in the 1930s to the strangeness of images of human displacement which accompanied the rise of the Nazis and the outbreak and early stages of the Second World War. There is nothing ordinary about the way 2,000 or so German and Austrian nationals ranging in age from 16 to 66 were forced to board the transport ship the *Dunera* on 10 July 1940. The deportation from the Straits Settlements of Singapore of about 265 German and Austrian men, women and children was similarly strange; they were deported on the *Queen Mary*, a luxury liner turned troop ship. More bizarre still is the chilling story of the more than 800 lives lost when the *Arandora Star*, a troop ship, was torpedoed and sunk on 2 July. Survivors of that disaster boarded the *Dunera* and wound up not in Canada, their original destination, but in Australia.

The same sense of strangeness accompanies the visual history of the life these internees led once they arrived in Australia. What were these mostly middle-class, law-abiding people doing in camps in the Australian outback, assailed by dust storms and enduring the rigours of the antipodean summer of 1940? Why were artists and physicians and poets and ordinary citizens imprisoned on the other side of the world, far from their original homes and from the lodgings they occupied in search of a safe haven?

Our sense of estrangement or puzzlement is inevitable when we gaze at visual representations of their fate. But eventually the accumulating visual record moves back to a revised version of what we understand as received wisdom. Many, though not all, of these internees managed to normalise the abnormal circumstances in which they found themselves, as the images in Volume 1 show. They created art schools and music schools, organised concerts and sporting events. On board the *Dunera*, three of them wrote a constitution to guide the self-governing committees they would create to manage their affairs once on dry land. They created a new kind of normality, a way of living with dignity despite the indignity of internment.

After internment, there were other incongruities to be faced. Consider the unlikelihood of German and Austrian-born internees joining the Australian army without Australian citizenship, and forming something like a better-educated, and unarmed, branch of the French Foreign Legion. The 8th Employment Company was made up of men who did not have the right to bear arms or to use them in combat. This applied also to those who returned to Britain to join the British army's Pioneer Corps. And yet, over time, even hide-bound British staff officers recognised that the former internees spoke fluent German and could be useful behind enemy lines. One of those who volunteered for this dangerous assignment was Anton Walter Freud, Sigmund Freud's grandson. He was urged to change his name to hide his Jewish origins. He refused to do so. If captured, he said, he wanted the Nazis to know who he was, and that he and his people were coming for them.

Dunera and *Queen Mary* internees, once released, benefitted from the openness of Australian society at a moment of unprecedented economic and demographic expansion. As seen in Volume 1, images of the oddities of fate give way to images belonging to a canon of normality. While many of the former internees would surely have made their way anywhere, others thrived thanks specifically to the relatively tolerant and liberal culture of post-1945 Australian society. They built families and careers, and many contributed to the general well-being of their new home. To be sure, there were crooks and con men among them, and political zealots, including communists who returned to build the new Germany, East Germany. There are many *Dunera* and *Queen Mary* stories, each configured in its own distinct fashion.

In this first volume of our study, we have tried to outline visually the history of this cohort of refugees turned internees turned soldiers or civilians. What is missing is the 'thick description', to use Clifford Geertz's celebrated term, of individual trajectories. The sheer number and variety of endings precludes generalisation about how and why individuals emerged from the desert of internment. Thus, in the second volume we offer a selection of national – indeed, transnational – profiles of the lives of wartime internees.

CONCLUSION

We hope the individual chapters bring to life the dazzling array of strategies of adaptation they brought to a world turned upside down. We invite you to enter these *Dunera Lives*, to understand better the challenges of displacement and injustice, and to consider the matter of resilience.

One way of expressing the difference between the thrust of the two volumes is to note that the first is based on images, which are rooted in space, showing what happened 'here', while the second, a longitudinal history, tells what happened when, 'at this time', and if possible, why.

Our two volumes also differ in other ways. In the structure of our visual history is a kind of progression from the bad days of the 1930s to the limbo of internment, deportation, and incarceration in the early 1940s, to release and the creative years of the later 1940s and after. This tends to make the history of the *Dunera* and its human cargo a success story, a tale of righteousness triumphant. This kind of heroism is the stuff of myth, not history. Nothing was certain in the trajectories we describe through the visual imagery of Volume 1. In Volume 2 we chart individual histories, with all their stops and starts, misdirection and risks. No one knows the shape of our lives while we live them; neither did the men and women whose lives we glimpse in Volume 1. The individual profiles of Volume 2 break down the collective into its vivid, and at times messy, human stories.

In Volume 2, we spend more time on comparison than in Volume 1. We have profiles of those who chose not to stay in Australia but to return to Britain or elsewhere. We have profiles of those who lived Jewish lives, those who left their Jewish heritage behind them, and those who never were Jewish. Ours is not a uniquely Jewish story, but a human story in which Jews and others were trapped.

Still the Jewish component of the *Dunera* story has shaped the way it has been remembered. In the later chapters of Volume 1, we describe the emergence of a collective memory of the *Dunera* experience. A collective memory is the memory of a collective, at a certain point in time. The memory of the *Dunera* emerged at the extended moment from the late 1960s to the 1990s when the history of the Second World War was rewritten to incorporate the Holocaust as a central – for some, the central – element of the disaster.

Those who sailed to Australia on the *Dunera* and the *Queen Mary* were not victims of the Holocaust. But they were victims of the regime that perpetrated that crime. They were also victims of the panic and blindness of Churchill and his generals in the European spring of 1940 when the invasion of Britain was a real possibility. By arresting and deporting them, Churchill added insult to the injury already inflicted by the Nazis in persecuting Jews and other enemies of the regime. The collective memory of the *Dunera* thus became infused with the same moral significance as that of other victims of the Nazis. In other words, their story mattered morally, and was worth elaborating as a tale of collective injustice and survival.

At this time a human rights movement and consciousness emerged throughout the world; the *Dunera* story is part of that universal human rights narrative.[2] The creation of institutions of memory, like the Dunera Association, alongside the dissemination of the story through television, books and film, added resonance to the narrative. Certain individuals acted as memory agents, preservers of a tale worth telling and remembering.

Now that most of the population that lived through the war is gone, we are at a point when collective memory can be preserved through collective history. The two volumes of *Dunera Lives* show different facets of the move from the history of the 1930s and 1940s to the shared memory of those years to a history of post-war lives. The volumes present the voices and faces of people trapped in the shifting contours of war. All over the world there were *Dunera Lives*, those of men and women who passed through the varied upheavals of the Second World War. Many survived to tell the tale. Here are some of their stories.

Notes

1. Roland Barthes, *Camera Lucida. Reflections on Photography* (New York: Hill & Wang, 1981).
2. Sam Moyn, *The Last Utopia* (New York: Oxford University Press, 2007).

APPENDIX 1

THE END OF INTERNMENT

Appendix 1 contains two figures compiled by Carol Bunyan. The figures describe the chronological history of the end of the internment for the men and boys sent from England to Australia on the *Dunera* in July 1940. We do not have similar information for the internees who were sent from Singapore to Australia on the *Queen Mary* in September 1940.

Figure 1 shows that internees were freed in distinct groups over time. The first departures – fewer than a dozen men – took place before Major Layton arrived in Australia in late March 1941. 198 men were freed in June 1941, and 440 in October 1941. In 1942, there were three occasions when substantial numbers of internees left the camps. In January, 285 internees departed. 88 were freed in March 1942, and nearly four times that number left the camps in July of that year. From then on, internees left the camps (and internment) in smaller groups. The 41 men released between May and the end of July 1945 were the last non-Fascist *Dunera* internees to regain their freedom.

There were several pathways to liberation. Internees could return to Britain, either to serve in non-combatant units in the British army, or to request a review of their case with the aim of securing release. This latter pathway was not open to all internees equally, with officials favouring those who were sick or whose wives were in Britain. Some men had their cases reviewed while in Australia, and were able to return to Britain as free men. Internees who wished to stay in Australia, at least for the duration of the war, could volunteer for the 8th Employment Company, formed in April 1942, or find work deemed important to the war effort in Australia. Some internees secured their release by migrating to countries other than Britain, some left internment on the basis of illness or age, and others followed different pathways again. Figure 2 explains why internees left camp.

More internees chose to return to Britain than to join the Australian army; initially, a return to Britain was the only choice open to those who wanted to leave internment. It took until the Japanese attack on Pearl Harbor for the Australian government to recognise that the men interned at Tatura could help the Australian war effort, both in the military and civilian spheres. It also took time for internees to develop contacts with potential employers who could use their services. There were intermediaries, particularly in church organisations, who put internees and employers together. These liaisons were effective in bringing internees into the urban labour market and the civil society it served.

Some refugees, in the hope of migrating to the United States, opted to remain in camp. This was a futile strategy as American officials would not process the visa applications of interned men. They had to secure their freedom first. And even then, visas tended to be given only to men whose wives were already living in the United States.

These two figures support another way of looking at the end of the history of internment. By early 1943, most *Dunera* internees – about 1800 of 2000, excluding enemy sympathisers – had left internment. Over the next two years releases continued, though irregularly and at a slower pace. It is possible, therefore, to divide the history of internment into three main phases. The first covers the period from the arrival of the *Dunera* in September 1940 to the arrival of Major Layton in the spring of 1941. Few men left internment during this time. The second is from April until December 1941, when the most effective way out of the camp was to accept the offer of transport back to Britain to join the British army. Roughly 400 men took this option. The third is from January 1942 onward, when men could join the British army, the Australian army, or, skills permitting, the civilian workforce. In this period, 553 men enlisted in the Australian army, 511 of them before December 1942. Nearly half of the *Dunera* internees chose to serve in one or other army. 394 were released to civil society, 258 in Australia and 134 in Britain.

Why did some remain interned? There were many reasons. Some were not interested in joining either army. Some were confined to camp because authorities had suspicions about their loyalties. Some did not want to risk a sea passage to Britain, a hazardous journey given the threat posed by U-boats. Others had no idea where to go: they had no relatives in Britain; they could not gain entry to the United States, where immigration rules were stringent; and Australian society was full of unknowns. Furthermore, the outcome of the war was unclear as late as 1944. Going back to Europe might mean going back to the Nazis. British and Australian officials had to find solutions for individuals with very different profiles. The question of what to do with the *Dunera* internees occupied officials for the duration of the war.

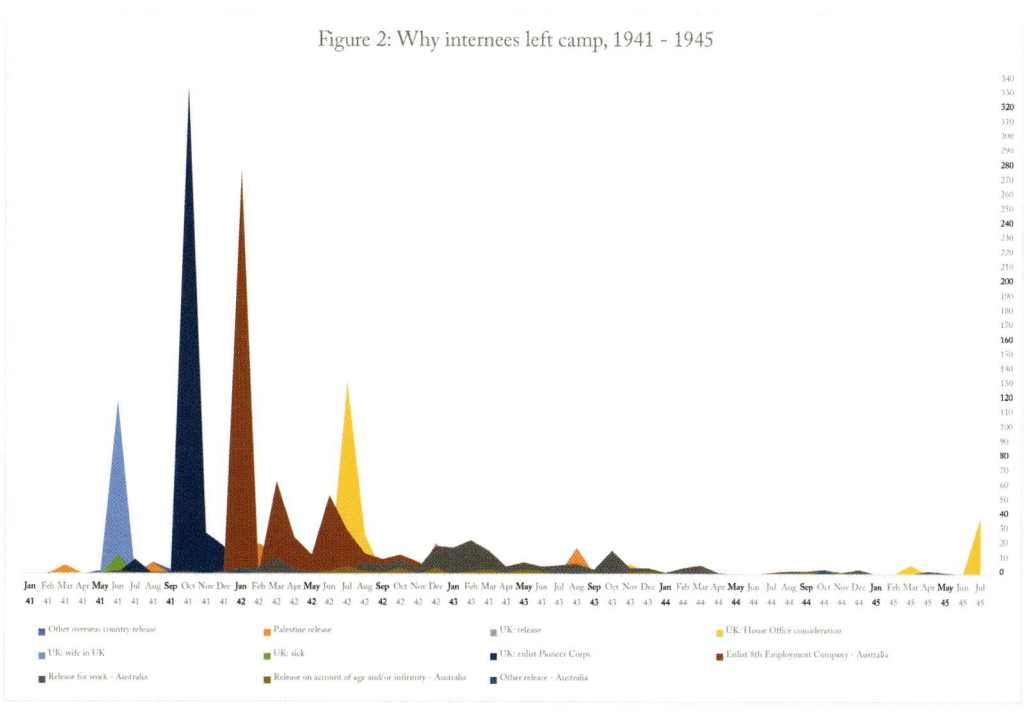

Figure 1: When internees left camp, 1941-1945

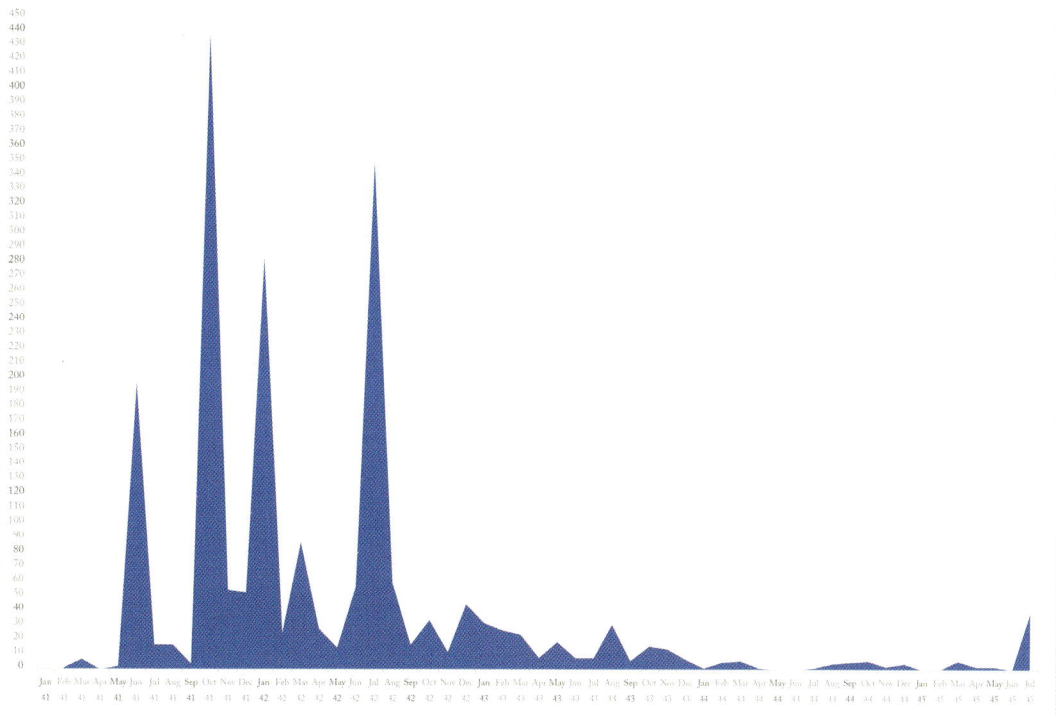

Figure 2: Why internees left camp, 1941 - 1945

APPENDIX 2

Ships on which *Dunera* internees returned to Britain, 1941–1945

Ship	Month sailed from Australia	Number of internees
Largs Bay	June 1941	138
Themistocles	June 1941	58
Gleniffer	July 1941	16
Ceramic	October 1941	56
Ceramic/Stirling Castle	October 1941	50
Stirling Castle	October 1941	328
Rangitiki	November 1941	50
Largs Bay	December 1941	51
Themistocles	July 1942	281
*Westernland/**Abosso***	August 1942	36
Desirade	October 1942	7
Waroonga	January 1943	7
Themistocles	November 1943	7
Dominion Monarch	March 1945	7
Dominion Monarch	July 1945	39
TOTAL		1131

This list includes only those internees who left Hay and Tatura directly for Britain. It excludes a small number of men who were released in Australia and then chose to return to Britain in wartime. Bold type indicates the ship was sunk by enemy action. Where two ships are listed, the internees left Australia on the first then transferred to the second at a port en route. This list is the work of Carol Bunyan.

APPENDIX 3

Name changes

This list of *Dunera* internees who changed their names was compiled by Carol Bunyan. In the first five chapters of this book we use the names internees had before and during the Second World War. In the final three chapters of this book, covering the post-1945 period, we use the names former internees adopted during and after the war. Those who did not change their names are not listed here, nor are those with unidentified name variations. A full list of the names of all internees on the *Dunera* and on the *Queen Mary* appears at the end of Volume 2.

In Australia, as elsewhere, changing names was part of the self-fashioning of former internees during and after the Second World War. Many had lost their families and their homes. Some wanted nothing more than to escape the horrors of war. Choosing an Anglo-Saxon name made life easier in the Anglophone world. At the same time, discarding a German name was one way of having as little as possible to do with the language of Hitler and the Nazis. The compulsory Israel or Sarah was often the first name to disappear. Choosing a Hebrew name was useful for those in Israel or intending to go there. Others fled the stigma, real and imagined, of Jewish identity by taking a name without any association with the Jewish world.

Each man made his own choice. While whimsy and accident applied in some cases, others had their reasons. Many chose an entirely new name, others adopted a name that shared something with their old name, and some simply adjusted the spelling of their birth name. They were ready to seize a second chance in life.

Notes:
Names where the only change was the removal of an umlaut are not included in this list.
An underlined name indicates it was used in lieu of the person's first name.
A name in parentheses indicates the person was known by that name.
'Also known as' [aka] is used when it is thought the person retained their original name but was known by another name.
ß, the symbol for double 's' in Germanic languages, is not used.

DUNERA LIVES

From	To
ABEL (ABEL-OPPENHEIM) Fritz Nachmann Veit	ABEL Fred
ABRAHAMOWICZ Richard	served as ARLEN Richard George
ABRAHAMSOHN Kurt	AMBROSE Kenneth (Ken)
ADAM Siegfried James	ADAM James Stanley
ADLER Hans Ludwig	ALLAN Henry John
ADLER Josef	ALDER Joseph
ALTBACH Ludwig	ALLAN Louis
ANSBACHER Joseph	ASHER Joseph
ARENDT Gerhard Kurt Max	ARENDT Gerald
ARNDT Hans Günther	ARNDT Hartley Graeme
ARNSDORF Alfred	ARNOTT Alfred Sidney (Alf)
ARNSDORF Max Israel	ARNOTT Max Victor
ARNSDORF Selmar Israel	ARNOTT Stanley Frank (Steve)
ARON Waldemar Wolf	ARON Ze'ev Akiva
ASCHER Artur	ASCHER Arthur
ASCHER Ernst	ASCHER Ernest Isaac
ASCHER Josef	ASCHER Joseph
AUFRICHT Helmut	ALFORD Harold
AUFRICHTIG Robert	AUSTIN Robert
AUG Hersch	aka Harry
AXELRAD Hans Gustav	AXEL Hans Gustav
BABBEL Franz Otto	aka BABBEL Francis Oswald
BAER Hermann Herbert	BAER Herbert Hermann
BAERWALD Werner Bruno Richard	BARWOOD Vernon Bruno Richard
BÄHR Hans Ludwig	ARMSTRONG Alexander
BALBIERER Emanuel	BALBIER Emanuel (Manny)
BALL Raphael	aka Ralph
BALNEMONES Walter Mandel	HILL Walter
BAMBERGER Rudolph Max	BAMBER Rudolph Max
BÄNDEL Georg	BANDEL George Jehuda
BANDEL Josef Moses	BANDEL Joseph Moses
BANK Lothar	BANKS Laurence
BARON Max Erich	BARON Max Eric
BASS Robert	BASS Robert E
BASWITZ Heinz Ludwig	BASSETT Harry Lewis
BASWITZ Herbert	aka BASWICK Herbert
BAUMGARTEN Horst Norbert	BARRETT Horace Norbert (Norbert)

APPENDIX 3

BAUMWOLLSPINNER Gotthard	BARNES Robert Gerald
BEER Franz Joseph	BEER Francis James
BEER Friedrich	BEER Frederick (Fred)
BEGACH Klaus Eberhard	BEACH Claude
BEHN Hans Max	BEHN Hans Max Wilhelm
BELLAK Alfons Heinz	BELLAC Alphonse Heinz
BELLAK Otto	BELL Leslie Otto
BELOCERKOWSKI Bernhard	BELTON Bernard
BENJAMIN Heinz Adalbert	BENJAMIN Henry Adalbert
BENJAMINI Stefan Rafael	BENJAMIN Stefan (reverted to original surname, c. 1946)
BENSINGER Fritz	BENSINGER Frank
BERGER Bernhard Isidor	BERGER Bernard Ben
BERGER Walter Hermann	BENNETT Walter Leslie
BERGFELD Hans Hermann	MOUNTFIELD John Hugh
BERGMANN Bernhard	FREEMAN George Bernard
BERGMANN Ferdinand	BERGMAN Ferdinand Anthony
BERNHARDT Lutz Kurst	BERNHARDT Lawrence
BERNSTEIN Gerd	BRENT Bern aka Bern Gerald
BERNSTEIN Hellmut Michael	BRENT Michael
BIER Günter Heinz	BIER Gunter aka Shimshon
BIERMANN Gerd	BIERMANN Gerhard Johannes (reverted to birth name)
BILD Viktor	BELL Joseph Victor
BILLITZER Wolfgang Erhardt Rouland Anton	BILLITZER Anthony Wolfgang
BISCHOFSWERDER Bojas	BISCHOFSWERDER Boaz
BISCHOFSWERDER Felix	WERDER Felix
BLANK Georg	BLANK George
BLAUHORN Friedrich Otto	BALLARD Derek
BLEDI Paul	BELL Paul Henry
BLEICHRÖDER Adolph	served as BLEACH Timothy Alexander
BLOMBERG Harald Kurt	BLOMBERG Harold Kurt
BLUMENTHAL Heinz Joachim	BARLOW Henry John
BLUMENTHAL Horst Adolf	BARNETT Horace Abraham (Barney)
BLUMENTHAL Wolfgang	GILLARD Stephen
BOCK Heinz Joachim	BOCK Jacob
BÖHM Heinrich Samuel	BOEHM Henry Samuel aka Tony
BÖHME Ernst Gerhard	BOEHME Ernest Gerald
BÖTTCHER Gottwald	BOETTCHER Franz Gottwald
BOXER Heiner (Harry)	LATIMER Harold Stewart

BRAININ Mordouch	BRAININ Max
BRANDEIS Jürgen Fritz	BRANDON Brian Frederick
BREINER Egon	BREINER John Egon
BRENNER Adolf	BRENNER Dolf
BRESLAU Heinz	aka Henry
BRETLER Moshe	BRETLER Max
BRETTHOLZ Juda Wolf	BRETTHOLZ Wolf Juda (Willie)
BREUER Jacob	aka Yakov
BRIEFWECHSLER Simon	BRIEFWECHSLER Shimon
BRITZMANN Rudolf Manfred	BRYAN Roger
BRUCH Herbert	BRUCH Herbert Max (Max)
BRUCK Heinz Werner	BROOKE Harry Walter
BRUMMER Leo Manfred	aka Fred
BRUNNER Alfred	BAR-NIR Aharon
BÜCHENBACHER Otto	BUCKENBY Otto
BUCHTHAL Arnold	WHITE Arnold (reverted to original surname c. 1947)
BUCHTHAL Wolfgang Heinrich Albert	BUCKNALL Wilfred Henry Albert
BUKOWITZ Stefan Hans	BUKOWITZ Stephen
CAHN Franz Robert	CAREY Francis Robert
CAHN Fritz	CAHN Derek
CAHN Richard Otto	COLLINS Richard
CALLOMON Walter Hugo	GODFREY Walter Hugh
CARLEBACH Peter Andreas	CARSON Peter Andrew
CARSTENS Günther Werner	CARSON Frederick Edgar
CASSIRER Ulrich	CASS Eric Victor
CHLUMECKY-BAUER Johannes	CHLUMECKY John Bauer
CHONE Fritz	CHOWN Fred
CHONE Herbert	CHOWN Herbert later VAN DYCK Herbert Chown
CLUSMANN Gustav Heinrich	HENGHES Heinz
COHEN Alfred	COOPER Alfred
COHEN Erich	COOPER Eric Herbert
COHN Friedrich Falk Gerhard (Gerd)	COLLIN Gerard Fredric C
COHN Fritz	COHN Frederick
COHN Gerhard Norbert	PRESTON Gerald Norbert
COHN Hans Hermann	COLLINS John
COHN Joachim Werner	CONWAY Joachim Werner
COHN Klaus Peter	COLLINS Keith Peter
COHN Sally	COHN Sol Sally

APPENDIX 3

COSSMANN Gerhard Hermann Karl	CRAWFORD Peter
CZARNIKOW Hearst Günter	CARRINGTON Hearst George
DAHL Eduard	DAHL Edward
DAMM Heinrich	DAMM Henry
DANZIGER Gerhard	DUNN Gerald
DANZIGER Heinz Georg	DUNN Henry George
DANZIGER Peter Fred	DANBY Peter Freddy
DANZIGER Rudolf Walter	DUNN Rudolf Walter
DARNBACHER Felix Hellmut	DARNELL Fritz Herbert aka DARNELL Felix
DAVIDS Hans	DAVIDS John Heath
DAVIDSOHN Otto	DAVIDSON Otto
DAVIDSON Hans	DAVIDSON Harley Hans
DEUTSCH Eduard Johann	DEUTSCH Edward John
DEUTSCH Friedrich Michael (Fritz)	DEUTSCH Frederick Michael
DEUTSCH Heinrich (Henry)	DEUTSCH Henry
DEUTSCH Johann	aka Hans
DEUTSCH Josef	DODGE Joseph
DIAMAND Leo	DIAMOND Harold Leo
DIETRICH Emil _Alfred_	DIETRICH Alfred
DRACH Georg	DARELL George Robert Michael
DRACH Otto	DRAKE Owen James
DRECHSLER Heinrich	DRAKE Henry
DRESSING Herbert	DRESSING Bill
DRESSING Louis	aka Louie
DREXLER Heinz	TURNER Henry Peter
DRIELS Hans Jürgen	DREELS Johnny
DRIELS Norbert	DRIELS Norman
DSCHENFFZIG Klaus _Peter_	DANE Peter
DÜMMLER Joachim	DUNCAN John Gordon
DÜRRHEIM Georg Erich	DUERRHEIM George Eric
ECKES Franz	ECKES Frank
EDELHOFER Friedrich	EDEN Fred
EHRENBOTH Henri	EHRENBOTH Henry
EHRENWERTH Hermann Hirsch	EHRENWERTH Herman Hirsch
EHRLICH Josef Johann	served as EAGER J. T. aka EHRLICH John Josef
EHRLICH Karl Wolfgang	EHRLICH Charles
EIBUSCHITZ Hans Bernhard	EDWARDS Harry Bernard
EICHBAUM Ludwig Ernst (Lutz)	EVERETT Leslie Ernest (Ernie)

EICHENBERG Friedrich Franz	EATON Frank Frederick
EICHENGRUN Ernst	GREEN Ernest Edward
EICHNER Fritz	OAKES Francis
EIRICH Friedrich Roland Otto	EIRICH Frederick Roland (Fred)
EISEMANN Justin	EISEMAN Justin
EISIG Konrad Theodor	ELSDON Konrad Theodor
EISINGER Erich	EISINGER Eric
EISMANN Jakob	EISMAN Jack
ELTING Günter	ELTING John Gordon
EMDEN Walter Heymann	EMDEN Walter Harold
ENGEL Werner Adolf	EDEN Peter Wilfred
ENGELMANN Max Julius Hermann	ENGELMANN Max Julius Herman
EPHRAIM Eduard Alexander	EPHRAIM Edward Alexander
EPHRAIM Kurt Helmuth	FRAME Eric Kurt
EPPENSTEIN Andreas Hans Heinrich	ELLIOTT Andrew Hilary
EPPENSTEIN Richard Otto Julius	ELLIOTT Richard
ERDÖS Erich Karl	FORESTER Eric
ERLANGER Franz	EARLE Francis Robert
ETTLINGER Hermann	ETTLINGER Harry
FACHON Hans Heinz	FACHON John Robert
FACKENHEIM Wolfgang Amadeus	FRASER William Alan
FALK Sigbert	FALK Somer
FALTER Karl	FALTER Charles
FASS Oskar	FONTAIN Anthony
FAST Walter	FOSTER Walter Jonathon
FEDER Hans Werner	FEDER John Warner
FEDERBUSCH Markus Abraham	FEDERBUSCH Marcus Abraham
FEDERER Heinz Rudolph	aka Henry R
FEDERN Karl Peter Ilmari	SPRAGUE Charles Edgar
FEHL Paul	FRASER Paul
FEIBES Fritz Heinrich	aka Fred Henry
FEIGELSTOCK Siegfried	FEIGELSTOCK Kurt?
FEISTMANN Heinz Peter	FEISTMAN Peter
FELDAN Siegmund	FENTON Sydney Trevor
FELDER Adolf	aka Adi
FELDER Hansheinz (Henry)	FELDER Henry
FELDMANN Erich Horowitz	FELDMAN Eric Horowitz
FELDMANN Hans	FELDMAN Hans
FELSENSTEIN Jakob	FELTON Jacob or Yacob

APPENDIX 3

FESTBERG Alfred	aka Alfred Nicholas
FEUCHTWANGER Oscar	aka Asher
FEUERSTEIN Franz Wolfgang	FIRESTONE Frank Wilfred
FEUERSTEIN Hanns Gerhard	FIRESTONE John Gerald
FICHMANN Hans	FICHMANN John Hans later FISS John Hans c. 1951
FINK Ernst	FINCH Ernest
FISCHER Emmerich	FISCHER Erich
FISCHER Hugo	FISHER Hugh
FISCHER Max Hermann	FISHER Max Henry (Fredy)
FISCHL Eugen	FISCHL Eugene
FLATAU Gert	FLATAU Gerald
FLEISCH Walter Josef	FLETCHER Walter Josef
FLEISCHER Hans Ernst	FLETCHER John Ernest
FOKSCHANER Friederich (Fritz)	ALLAN Frederick
FORELL Gotthold Karl Johannes	FORELL John
FRAENKEL Heinz Martin	FRANKLIN Harold Martin
FRAENKEL Herbert Max	FRAENKEL Herbert
FRANK Emil	JIZHAK Zvi
FRANK Rudolf Adolf Walther	FRANK Rudolf Adolf Walter
FRANKEN Ludwig Heinrich	FRANKLIN Lewis Henry
FRANKENSTEIN Hans	FRANKENSTEIN Hanan
FREIER Eli	DROR Eli
FREIER Fritz	DROR Shlomo
FREILICH Karl Friedrich	FRASER Charles Frederick
FREITAG Fritz Karl	FREITAG Frederick (Fred)
FREUDENSTEIN Georg Gerson	FREUDENSTEIN George Gerson
FREUND Emil	FRIEND Edward
FREUND Heinrich Alexander	FREUND Henry Alexander
FREUND-HALLER Hanns Heinz Günther Gerhard	HALLER Hal
FREUTHAL Gerhard	FIELD Gerard
FREY Peter Hans	FRY Peter Howard
FRIEDENHEIM Curt Paul	FRIEDENHEIM Paul Curt
FRIEDHEIM Heinrich Oskar Felix	LONGFELLOW Thomas Henry (reverted to birth name)
FRIEDHOFER Arnold	DE MARIGNY Harold
FRIEDLÄNDER Bruno Ernst	FERELL Bruce Ernest
FRIEDLÄNDER Erich	FRIEDLANDER Erich aka Eric
FRIEDLÄNDER Hermann	FREEMAN Howard Roger (Roger)
FRIEDLÄNDER Ignaz	FREEMAN James Robert (Jimmy)

FRÖHLICH Ernst Friedrich	FROHLICH Ernest Fredrick
FRÖHLICH Peter Emerich	FOREST Peter Eric
FRÜHLING Manfred Joachim	FAULKNER Michael John
FRYMERMAN Haim Simche	FERNLEY Henry Steven
FUCHS Ernst Martin	FUCHS Ernest Martin
FUCHS Josef	FOX Joseph Richard
FUKS Jakob	FOX Jacob
FÜRNBERG Robert	FARNBOROUGH Robert
FÜRSTENBERG Paul Phillip Hans	FORBES Paul Phillip
FÜRTH Hans Georg	FIRTH Anthony (Tony)
GEIER Franz	GEIER Francis
GEIRINGER Rudolf	aka Rudolph
GEISENBERG Hans Hermann	GEISENBERG Chanan
GEISMAR Erich Julius	GARSON Eric Julius
GELBEIN Paul	GILBOA Paul
GELLER Hans Georg	GELLER Jack George
GERSTEL Richard	GARSTON Richard
GIEPEN Wilhelm Alexander	GIEPEN William Alexander
GIESENER Horst	GILBERT Harry
GIRKE Franz	GIRKE Francis
GLASER Hans Gerson	GLAZER John Gerald
GLAUNERT Gerhard Erich	GLAUNERT Erich
GLÜCKSMANN Ernst	GLUECKSMANN Eliezer/Eliyahu
GOLD Ernst	GOLD Ernest
GOLD Josef	GOLD Joseph
GOLDENBERG Friedrich Wilhelm	GILLARD Frederick William (Fred)
GOLDMANN Bernhard (Ben)	GOLDMAN Bernhard aka Ben
GOLDMANN Ernst Ludwig	GOLDMAN Ernest Ludwig
GOLDMANN Leo Werner	GOLDMAN Leo Werner
GOLDMANN Wilhelm	GOLDMAN William
GOLDSCHMIDT Erich	GOLDSCHMIDT Eric
GOLDSCHMIDT Herbert	GOLDSMITH Herbert
GOLDSCHMIDT Kurt Edwin	GOLDSCHMIDT Edwin Curt
GOLDSCHMIDT Kurt Max	GOLLARD Curtis Maurice
GOLDSCHMIDT Werner	DWELLY Vernon Ian
GOLDSTEIN Joachim	GOLLDSTONE Jack robert
GONSENHÄUSER Hans Wolfgang	GRANT Peter
GORBULSKI Abrascha	GORDON Alexander
GRAETZER Friedrich	aka Fred

APPENDIX 3

GRAFFUNDER Horst Otto Robert	aka Robert Horst Otto
GRAUPNER Felix	BARDEN Felix
GREIF Walter	GORDON Walter
GREILSHEIMER Hans	GRESHAM Henry John (John)
GREVE Walter Franz Bernhard	GREVE Werner Walter
GRIESHABER Adolf	SANDS Tom
GRIESHABER Julius	SANDS John
GRINDLINGER Pinkas Chaim	GRINDLINGER Chaim Pinkas aka GRANT Chaim
GROCH Josef	GROCH Joseph
GRODSZINSKY Hans Werner	GRODIE John
GROSS Hugo	GROSS David
GROSSBARD Jakob	GROSSBARD Jacob
GROSSBARD Julius	GORDON Julius
GROSSBARD Siegfried	GORDON Steven
GRÜN Fritz Heinz Georg	GRUEN Fred Henry Georg
GRÜNBAUM Kurt	GREEN Ken
GRÜNBERGER Fritz	GLANVILLE Fred
GRÜNEBAUM Kurt Max	GRIERSON Robert Max
GRÜNHUT Ignatz Andor	GREENHUT Andrew
GRÜNHUT Simon	GREENHUT Simon
GRUNWALDT Karl Heinrich (Heinz)	GRUNWALDT Heinz
GUMPERZ Ernst	GUEST Ernest Bernard
GUSSMANN Viktor Bernhard	GUSSMAN Victor
GUTFREUND Paul	GODFREY Gordon Paul
GUTMANN Gerhard Ottmar/Otmar	GUTMAN Gerard Otmar (Gerry)
GUTMANN Hermann	GOODMAN Dennis John
GUTTENBERG Fritz	GORDON Frederick (Fred)
GUTTMANN Hans Julius	GILBERT Ronald
GUTTMANN Rudolf (Rudi)	GORDON Ralph Anthony
GUTTSMANN Wilhelm Leo	aka GUTTSMAN
HACKENBROCH Wilhelm Leon	HACKENBROCH Shimon Wilhelm
HALBERSTADT Felix Isaak	HALBERSTADT Isaac Hakohen aka Yizchak
HALBERSTADT Herz Hermann	HALBERSTADT Herman
HALLE Samuel	HALLE Sam
HAMBURGER Friedrich	HAMBER Frederick Charles
HAMBURGER Ulrich Wilfred	HAMBURGER U Wilfred
HAMMER Jakob Jesua	HAMMOND Jeffrey Joshua
HAMMERSTEIN Hans Herbert	SHILONI Yisrael

HARTWICH Günter Julius	HARTWICK Guenter Julius
HECHT Josef Otto	HENDERSON Joseph Pepo
HECKROTH Heinrich George	HECKROTH Hein
HEIDORN Wilhelm	HANSEN Werner
HEILBRUNN Sigmar	HEILBRUNN Shlomo
HEILBUT Rolf Max Günter	HEYWOOD Ralph Max Graham
HEIMANN Erich	HEIMANN Shraga
HEIMANN Friedrich <u>Albert</u>	HEIMANN Frederick Albert
HEINEMANN Karl Heinz	HEINEMANN Charles Henry
HEINSHEIMER Hugo	HEINS Hugo
HELI Manfred	HELI Moshe
HELLER Samuel	HELLER Samuel Abraham
HELLER Walter Oskar	HELLIER Walter Oscar
HELLER Werner Alfred	HELLIER John Alfred
HEMER <u>Nikolaus</u> Georg Peter	Hemer Georg Peter Nikolaus later Nicholas George & aka Nikolaus
HEMMERDINGER Ludwig	AMIR Jehuda or possibly HEMMERDINGER-AMIR Ludwig Jehuda
HENLE Kurt Siegbert	HENLEY Keith Stuart
HEPPNER Herbert	BRIGHT Herbert
HERBST Philip Günther	HERBST David Philip Gunter
HERMANN Kurt	HARRIMAN Louis Joseph
HERR Wilhelm David	HERR William David (Bill)
HERRMANN Gangolf Ernst	HERMAN Gangolf Ernest
HERRMANN Josef	HERMAN Joseph
HERRMANNSOHN Heinz Robert	HENDERSON Henry (Harry)
HERSCH Emil Emmanuel	HURST Eric Ronald
HERSCHAFT Hans Joachim	HARTLEY John
HERZ Ralph Alexis Vernon	FLEMING Ralph Alexis Vernon
HERZ Sophoni	HERZ Yitzhak/Yitzchok Sophoni
HERZOG Georg Friedrich	HERZOG George Friedrich
HESZEL Israel	HESCHEL Israel
HEUSER Josef	aka Joe
HEYMANN Fritz	HEYMANN Frank
HEYMANN Hans Peter	served as HEATON Hugh Peter
HEYNEMANN Jim Günther	HEYNEMANN James Guy
HILLEL Alfred	HILLEL Alfred James
HIRSCH Ernst Hermann	HIRSCH Ernest Hermann
HIRSCH Heinz	HIRSCH Henry

APPENDIX 3

HIRSCH Leopold	HIRSCH Leo
HIRSCHBERG Hans Ulrich	HOWARD Peter John
HIRSCHFELD Artur Kurt	HIRST Arthur Kurt
HIRSCHFELD Ludwig	aka HIRSCHFELD-MACK Ludwig
HIRSCHFELD Willy	FIELD William (Willy)
HIRSCHFELDT Hans Julius Walter	HARTFORD Huntley Julian Lewis
HIRSCHHORN Sandor Josef	HORNE Joseph
HOCHBERG Siegfried	HOCHBERG Fred Stanley
HÖCHSTER Emil	HOCHSTER Eliezer aka Emil
HOFFMANN Hans Ernst	HOUSEMAN John Ernest
HOFSTÄDTER Walter	HOFSTADTER later HARWOOD Walter
HOLLÄNDER Siegfried	HOLLAENDER Shimon
HONY Oskar	HONY Oscar
HULISCH Heinz Alfred	HULTON Henry Alfred
HUMBERG Rolf	JEHUDA Shmuel Ben
HUTTENBACH Alfred Heinrich	HUTTEN Alfred Henry
HUZENLAUB Frank Erich Gustav Adolf	CALVERT-HUGHES Frank Erich Gustav Adolf
ISAY Max Artur	ISAY Max Arthur
ISRAELS Franz Alexander	FRANK Franz Alexander
ITALIENER Curt	TALLEY Curt
JABLONSKY Alfred	JASON Alfred
JACOBINSKI Horst	JACOBS Richard Horst
JACOBIUS Heinz	JAMES Henry
JACOBOWITZ Josef	JACOBOWITZ Joseph
JACOBS Otto	JACOBS Jack Otto
JACOBSOHN Peter Max Wilhelm Schiffer	JACOBSOHN Peter Max Wilhelm
JACOBY Franz Victor Günther	aka JACOBY Frank Viktor Gunther
JASKULEWICZ Gerhard	HANDS Geoffrey
JEIDELS Harry	JAY Harry
JOACHIM Fritz Siegfried	JOCELYN Frank Steven
JONTOFSOHN Aron Harry	aka Harry
JONTOFSOHN Fritz	JOHNSON Frank
JOSEPH Bernhard	JOSEPH Bernard
JOSEPH Otto Moritz Aby	JOSEPH Asher
JOSEPHS Wolfgang	JOHNSON Peter William
JOSEPHY Hans Hermann	JACKSON Harold (Hans)
JOSTEN Franz Josef	JOSTEN Francis Joseph
JUDENBERG Heinz Werner	DENBY Werner John

JULIUSBERG Franz Siegmund Ignatz	BERG Frank
KADDEN Gerd	aka Gary
KADRITZKI Leo	KAYE Leo
KAHAN Siegfried (Sigi)	KAHANA Shaul
KAHANE Jakob Isak	KAHANE Jacob Isaac
KAHN Josef	KENT Joseph
KAHN Rudolf Anselm	KAHN Ralph Anselm
KALB Norbert	GRAY Robert
KANDELMANN Richard	KANE Richard Allan
KANTOROWICZ Manfred	KAY Manfred
KANTOROWICZ Walter Heinz Edgar	KANTOR Walter
KAPLAN Alfred Aron	KAPLAN Aharon
KAPPIUS Josef	KAPPIUS Josef (Jupp)
KAROLYI Albert Ferdinand	KAROLY Albert Ferdinand
KARPOWITZ Heinz Manfred	KARPOWITZ Henry Manfred
KASSNER Eduard	KASSNER Edward
KATSCHKE Heinrich	KATSCHKE Henry
KATZ Albert	KATZ Albert Frederick
KATZ Ernst	KATZ Ernest (Ernie)
KATZ Gerhard Hermann	KATZ Gerhard Herman
KATZ Rudolf Max	KARRELL Rudy
KATZENSTEIN Heinz Egon	KENLEY Henry David
KAUFMANN Hans Werner	KAUFMANN John
KAUFTHEIL Paul	KENT Paul Dwight
KAYSER Emil Karl	KAYSER Emil Carl or Carl Emil
KEIL Hans Jürgen	KEEL George
KEMPNER Bernhard	KEMPNER Benny
KERBES Chaim Wolf (Willi/Willy)	KENDALL William Randolph
KERESZTES Adalbert or Bela	KERESZTES Albert
KERNEK Erich Hugo	KENNETH Eric Hugh
KESSLER Alfred Hans Egon	PARKINSON Fred
KIRCHHAUSEN Julius	KIRK Julius
KIRSCHNER Günter	KIRSNER Gordon
KLAK Emil	CLARKE Emil
KLAUSNER Hans Stephan	KLAUSNER H Stephan
KLEIN Georg	KLEIN George
KLEIN Manfred Martin	aka Mike
KNOPP Siegfried	KNOPP Fred
KNOTHE Hans Walter	KNOTHE John Walter

APPENDIX 3

KOBLITZ Fritz Andre	KOBLITZ Frederick Andre (Fred)
KOCH Bernhard	KOCH Bernard
KÖHLER Willi Friederich	KOHLER Willi (Willy)
KOHN Adolf	KOHN Adolf Harry
KOHN Josef	KERRY Joseph George
KOHN Kurt	HARWOOD Burton Frank
KOHN Kurt	MARTIN Raymond Stuart (Ray)
KOHN Leopold	KING James Leopold (Jimmy)
KOHN Walter	KEATS Walter
KOLM Friedrich Valentin Emil (Fritz)	KOLM Frederick Valentin
KÖLZ Johannes Matthäus	KOELZ John Matthew aka KELTS Matthew
KONIARSKY Walter Eduard	KONIARSKY Walter Edward
KÖNIG Hans Peter	KENT Henry Peter
KÖNIG Karel Josef	KOENIG Karel Joseph
KÖNIGSBERGER Hans Clemens Alfred	KONIGSBERG Hans Clemens Alfred
KÖNIGSBERGER Hans Eduard	KONIGSBERGER Hans Edward aka KONIGSBERRY aka KONISBERRY
KÖNIGSBERGER Hans-Peter	KINGSHILL Peter
KÖNIGSBERGER Heinz Martin	KINGSLEY Henry
KÖNIGSBERGER Josef Reinhard Rolf Erich	KOENIGSBERGER-MAASSEN Rolf Erich
KORN Fritz	PENNELLS Frank
KOSSMANN Heinz Moritz	KOSSMAN Heinz Moritz (Henry)
KOWALIK Alexander	KENT Alexander
KRIEGSMANN Herbert	KRIEGSMAN Herbert
KRIPSTAEDT Gerhard Paul Erich	KRIPSTEAD Gerrard Paul Eric
KRUK Walter Mayer	COLLINS Anthony Henry
KUFFNER Stefan von	KUFFNER Stephan
KUH Georg Alfred Ritter von	KUH George Alfred later DE KUH
KUPPENHEIM Gerhard Louis Bruno Alexander	CUNNINGHAM Gerald Alexander
KUTSCHER Hans Dodi	KUTSCHER Hans
LADEWIG Paul Erwin	LAWRIE Paul Edward
LAMPL Wilhelm Wolfgang (Willi)	LAMPLE William Wolfgang (Bill)
LANCZI Eduard Rudolf	LANCZI Edward Rudolf
LANDAUER Rudolf	LANDERS Ralph Steven
LANDBERGER Wilhelm	LANDBERGER Zev
LANDESMANN Heinrich	LANDESMAN Henry
LANGMEIER Johannes Carl Paul	LANG John Charles Paul
LASKE Peter Georg	LASKY Peter George

LEDERER Georg Julius	LEDERER George Julius
LEESER Rolf Severin	HAMILTON Rodney Stuart
LEHMANN Ernst Elias	LAYTON Peter Anthony
LEHMANN Ernst Peter Dietrich	LAYTON Peter Ernest
LEHMANN Siegfried	LEHMAN Sidney
LEHR Arthur	LAMDAN Aharon
LEICHT Norbert Wilfred Helmut	LESTER Norman
LEICHT Peter Karl	LEIGH Peter Charles
LEIDERT Wolfgang Josef	LEIGHTON Peter Warren Joseph
LEISER Hans Georg Wilhelm	LEISER George
LESCHNITZER Walter	LESH Walter
LESER Ernst	LESER Ernest
LESSMANN Hans Siegfried	LINDSAY Henry
LEUFER Albert	LANGLEY Albert
LEVENBACH Kurt Jakob/Jacob	LYNTON Roger Kenneth
LEVI Ernst Justin	LENNEY Ernst Justin
LEVIN Jakob Michael	LEVIN Michael Jacob
LEVIN Leonhard	LEVIN Elieser
LEVY Adolf	LESS Adolf
LEVY Ernst	LESTER Ernest Manfred (Ernie)
LEVY Fritz	LEVY Fred
LEVY Hermann	LEVY Herman
LEWEN Werner	WARNER Lawrence Lewen
LEWIN Georg	LEWIN George
LEWIN Oskar	LEWIN Oscar
LEWIN Rudolf Martin	LEWIN Rudolf Martin (Rudi)
LEWINSKY Max Werner	served as LADDY Max
LEWINSOHN Max	served as LEWIS Michael
LEWINZON Juda Lejb Leo	LEWINSON Juda Lejb Leo
LEWKONJA Hans	LEFF Hans
LEWKOWICZ Moses	LEVINSON Morris
LEWY Artur	LEWY Arthur
LICHTHEIM Ludwig	LAYTON Louis
LIEBSCHÜTZ Leser	LIEBSCHUETZ Eliezer
LIEBSTER Alfred	COOPER Alfred Peter
LIND Josef	LIND Joseph Elias
LINDAU Johannes Fritz Otto (Hans)	aka Hans
LINDEMANN Alfred	LINDEMAN Alfred
LINDEMEYER Wolfgang Karl Gustav	LINDSEY John Wilfred

APPENDIX 3

LINDHEIMER Paul Peter Theodor	LAND Peter Paul
LINDHEIMER Walter	LIND Walter
LION Ernst Max	LION Ernest
LIPPMANN Heinz	LIPPMANN Henry Heinz
LITWIN Franz Georg	LITWIN Franz George (Frank)
LÖBL Emmerich	LOEBL Israel
LÖBL Paul	LOBL Paul
LOCK Hermann	LOK Herman (reverted to original surname)
LOEBENSTEIN Eli	LOEBENSTEIN Eli Leo
LOEBENSTEIN Heinemann	LOEBENSTEIN Elchanan
LOEWE Arnold Joachim	LOEWE Yizhak
LOEWE Hans Hermann Adolf	LOEWE Herman Hans Adolf
LOHDE Sigismund aka LOHDE Sigurd	LODER Sydney (Syd) & LOHDE-Loder Sigurd
LOMNITZ Wolfgang Peter	LOMNITZ Peter
LOPATKA Heinz Hermann	LAWSON Heinz
LOPATKA Klaus	LAWSON Klaus
LÖWENSTEIN Fritz Karl Heinz	LOWEN Fritz Karl Heinz (Fred)
LÖWENSTEIN Hans	LORRAINE Hans John
LÖWENSTEIN Helmut	LIVINGSTON Harold
LÖWENSTEIN Kurt	LIND Kenneth Kurt
LÖWENSTEIN Werner	LANGTON Peter Werner
LÖWENTHAL Georg Kurt Alexander	LANGLEN George
LÖWENTHAL Siegbert	LOWENTHAL Bert Siegbert
LUCA Hans Günther	LENNARD Harold George
LUSTIG Walter	LOGAN Walter
MAASS Herbert Adolf	MARSDEN Edward Arthur
MACHEZOW Max	MANNING Max Richard Nicholas
MACHOL Helmut	MACHOL Henry
MAJEWSKY Leonhard Norbert	MEINHARDT Leonard
MAMMA-MANHART Leopold	MARLOW Leo
MANASSE Gustav	MASSEY Geoffrey
MANDL Peter Leo	MARSHALL Peter
MANG Johann	MANG John
MANNHEIM Hans	MANNHEIM Jack H
MANSFELDT Walter Wolfgang	MANSFIELD Walter
MARCUS Fritz	MARCUS Frederick James
MARCUS Siegfried	MARCUS Stephen John

MARCZYNSKI Egon Karl Maria	MARBERG E Marczynski aka Egon Karl
MARGULIES Heinz Werner	MARGATE Heinz Werner
MAROWILSKY Heinz	MARLOW Henry
MARX Karl	MURRAY Charles
MARX Moses	aka Moe
MASCHLER Fred Robert	aka Bob
MASSARIK Franz	MASSARIK Frank
MAUTNER Georg	MARTIN George
MAY Gerd	MAY Gerald
MAYER Edfried	HOWARD Anthony
MAYER Heinz Adolf	MAYER Heinz Nicola
MAYER Helmut	MAYER Henry
MAYER Wolfgang Joseph	MAYER William Joseph
MEHRLÄNDER Wolfgang Bernhard	LANDER Peter
MEIER Bernhard	MEYER Bernard (Bernie)
MEIER Bertold	MYER Bertold Irving (Bim/BIM)
MEIER Gerhard Hermann	MEIER Gerhard Herman
MERTES Willi	MERTES William
MERZBACH Hanns Martin	MERZBACH H Martin
MESSERSCHMIDT Heinz Hartwig Hindenburg (Heino)	MESSERSCHMIDT Heino
METH Rudolf Karl Heinrich (Rudi)	METH Karl Rudolf Heinrich later Rudolf Carl Heinrich (Rudi)
MEYER Albert Ernst	MEYER Ernst Albert (Albert)
MEYER Friedrich Victor Emil Gotthelf Josef	MEYER Frederick Victor
MEYERSON Gerd	MEYERSON George
MEZULIANIK Paul	JULIAN Paul
MIEDZWINSKI Gerhard	MITCHELL Gerhard
MILLET Josef	MILLET Joseph (Joe)
MINZ Joseph	MILTON Joseph Peter
MISCHKOWSKI Leopold	MITCHELL Leopold (Leo)
MOHR Heinrich	MOHR Henry
MOHR Rudolf Jakob	MOHR Rudolph Jacob
MOHRENWITZ Martin Bernhard	MOORE Martin Bernard
MONDSCHEIN Ernst	MORTON Ernst Fred
MORGENSTERN Bob Wolfgang	MORTON Bob William
MORGENSTERN Curt Peter	MORTON Charles Peter
MORGENSTERN Siegfried Fritz	MORTON Frederick Charles
MOSES Gerhard Arnold	MOORE Gerald Stephen
MOSES Viktor	MOSES Victor

APPENDIX 3

MUGDAN Francis Lewis Robert	MUGDAN Robert Francis Louis (Bob)
MÜHLHAUS Johannes Oskar (Hans)	MUHLHAUS Johannes Oscar Hans
MÜHLIG Georg	MILTON George
MUNDSTEIN Josef	MUNSON Joseph George
MURMANN Carl	MURMAN Carl
NAGLER Isidor	NAGLER Irving Isidor
NATHANSOHN Walter	NAPIER Walter Michael
NAWRATZKI Max	NEWTON Mickey
NELKEN Eduard	NELSON Edward George
NELL Gerhard Heinz Hermann	NICHOLS Gerald Peter
NEUFELD Ernst	NEUFELD Simha Bunim
NEUGEBOREN Samuel Wolf	NEUGEBOREN Wolf Samuel
NEUWAHL Hans	NEWALL John (Johnny)
NÖHLE Eduard Otto	NOEHLE Edward Otto
NUSSBAUM Adolf	NUSSBAUM Adolph Isaac (Eddie)
NUSSBAUM Ozyasz	NUSSBAUM Jehoshua
OBERLÄNDER Leopold	OSBORNE Leonard
OESTERREICHER Hans Joachim	ONSLOW Ian Howard
OFFENBURG Joseph	OFFENBURG Josef
OPPENHEIM Hans Siegfried	OSBORNE Harold Stephen
OPPENHEIM Kurt Albert	OSBORNE Kenneth Albert
OPPENHEIM Werner	OAKFIELD William (Bill)
OPPENHEIMER Hans Max	OLIVER John Max
OSCHINSKY Friedrich Heinz	OSBORNE Frederick Heinz
OTTO Willy	OTWELL Peter
OVERHOFF Wilhelm	OVERHOFF Willy Moritz Julius aka William
PAIS Berthold	PRESTON Robert Kenneth
PAPE Eduard Ludwig Otto Moritz	PAPE Edward Ludwig Otto Moritz aka Adolph
PAUSON Adolf	
PERGER Gustav Rudolf Imre Julius	PERGER Gustav Rudolph
PERITZ Werner Siegmund	PEARCE Vernon
PERLE Wolfgang Walter	PEARL Walter
PETÖ Stefan	PETO Stephen
PETRUSCHKA Leo	PETERS Leonard
PFEFFER Fritz	SPENCER Frederick
PHIEBIG Heinz	PHILLIPS Henry
PIEKARZ Jakob Jankel	PIEKARZ Jakob Jankiel aka Jacob
PINNER Hans Moritz	PINNER Henry Maurice
PISKI Paul	PIERCE Paul Israel

PITSCHENEDER Karl Richard	PITSCHENEDER Peter
PODBIELSKI Gerhard Rene	PODBIELSKI Rene Gerhard
POLATSCHEK Kornel	PAGET Cornel
POLLAK Rafael Felix	PARKER Felix
POLLAK Walter Paul	POLLOCK Walter Paul
POSNER Leonhard	POSNER Leonard
PRAGER Georg Joseph	BRUCE George Michael
PRINZ Ernst	PATERSON Ernie
PROBST Henry August Peter Adolph	PROBST Henry August Peter Adolf
RABI Moses	aka Max
RATNER Bernhard	RATNER Peretz
RAUCH Artur	RAUCH Arthur
RECHELMANN Georg	aka George
REICH Hanns Herbert	REECH Herbert Henry
REICHENBERGER Hans	RICKENBERG Howard Vincent
REICHMANN Klaus	RICHMOND Alan James
REICHMANN Kurt	RIMON Moshe
REIHER Erich	REIHER Eric
REIHL Karl Alfred Theodor	aka REIHL Charles Alfred
REINMANN Hans	REINMAN John
REISER Adrian Gillian	RIDELL Adrian
REISNER Franz Wilhelm	REISNER Frank W
REISS Fritz Otto	REES Frederick
REISSNER Alexander Nicolai	REISSNER Alexander
REITER Erich	REED Eric James
REITER Maximilian	REID Robert Maximilian
RESCH Wilhelm Josef	RESCH William Joseph
RIEGELHAUPT Erwin	RIEGELHAUPT Naftali
RINDSBERG Alfred Siegbert	RENTON Alfred R
RITTERMANN Friedrich Michael Emil	RITTERMANN Michael
RODECK Ernst	RODECK Ernest
ROGOSCHANSKI Jakob	ROGOSCHANSKI Jacob
ROM Günter Ernst	ROMNEY George Ernest
ROSE Siegfried Heinz	ROSE Frederick
ROSEN Werner Georg	RIGBY William George
ROSENBAUM Gerhard Werner	RUSSELL Gerald Werner
ROSENBAUM Günter Heinz	RUSSELL Gunter Henry
ROSENBAUM Otto	FLEMING David Christopher
ROSENBERG Heinz Hermann	ROSENBERG Heinz Herman
ROSENBERG Herbert	served as RUSSELL Robert

APPENDIX 3

ROSENBLÜTH Eli	served as HOWELL Michael Aley
ROSENBLÜTH Ernst Emanuel	ROSENBLUTH Menahem
ROSENBLÜTH Hans Carl	ROSS John Caryl
ROSENFELD Manfred	RESSLER Michael
ROSENSTIEL Hans	BRYANT John Michael
ROSENSTIEL Karl Ludwig	BRYANT Charles Leslie
ROSENTAL Abram Sziya	ROSENTHAL Abraham
ROSENTHAL Arthur	WEST Arthur
ROSENTHAL Georg	ROSENTHAL George
ROSENTHAL Hans	ROSENTHAL Harry
ROSENTHAL Hans Ewald	RANK Hugh Eric
ROSENTHAL Rudolf	ROGERS Randolph (Roy)
ROSINSKI Karl Friedrich	ROSINSKI Charles Friedrich
ROTH Josef	RODGERS Joseph Leslie (Joe)
ROTH Kurt	ROWLAND Kenneth Francis
ROTHE Johann Joseph (Hans)	ROTHE Hans Joseph
ROTHENBERG Konrad Akiba	ROTHENBERG Conrad Akiba Michael
ROTHHOLZ Heinz	REDWOOD Harry
ROTHMANN James Oliver	O'ROURKE James Oliver
ROTHSCHILD Bernhard	ROTHSCHILD Bernard
ROTHSCHILD Gottfried Walther	ROTHSCHILD Walter
RUBEN Georg Walter	RUBEN George Walter
RUHSTADT Kurt Julius	ROSS Kenneth Julian
RUPPIN Max Fritz Gerhard	MATTHEWS Gerald Max
SACHS Siegmund Wolfgang Erich Lukas	SACHS Wolfgang Eric
SALOMON Otto Erich	HUNTER Peter aka Hunter-Salomon or Salomon-Hunter
SALOMON Walter Ernst	SEYMOUR Walter Ernest
SALOMONIS Hans Joachim	SELWYN Hans John
SAMUEL Konrad	SAMUEL Conrad
SAURSTROM Leib Werner	STROM Leopold (Leo)
SCHÄCHTER Otto	SHERWIN Steven Otto
SCHÄCHTER Walther	SCHAECHTER Walter
SCHÄDLICH Kurt Hermann	THOMAS Kenneth Conway
SCHÄFFER Johann	SCHÄFFER John
SCHAFFER Siegfried	SCHAFFER Shaul
SCHAFRANEK Karl Peter	SELWYN Peter Charles
SCHAPIRO Izek	SCHAPIRO John
SCHAPS Hans Peter	aka Peter

SCHICK Ernst	SCHICK Ernest
SCHIDLOF Georg	TURNER George
SCHIEHSEL Augustin Anton	SCHIESSEL Augustin Anthony
SCHIFF Max	KENNING Max
SCHIFRIN Leo	SIMMONS Leo
SCHILLER Paul Eugen	aka Paul-Eugen
SCHINBACH Samuel	SCHINBACH Zevulun
SCHINDLER Gustav	SHEPHERD George
SCHISCHA Adolf	SCHISCHA Abraham
SCHISCHA Mayer	SCHISCHA Meir
SCHLACHCIC Martin	SANDERS Martin
SCHLESINGER Erich	SCHLESINGER Eric
SCHLOSSER Hans Emil Robert	ALLEN John
SCHLÖSSER Heinz Hans	CASTLES Henry
SCHMIDT Siegfried	SCHMIDT Shimon
SCHMITT Alfons Andreas	SCHMITT Alfons Andrew
SCHMITZ Karl Alfred Elmar Peter	SCHMITZ Alfred Peter (Peter)
SCHNABL Alexander	SHAW Alexander
SCHNEIDER Ulrich Johannes Wolfgang	TAYLOR John
SCHNEIER David	SNOWER David
SCHÖNBACH Friedrich (Fritz)	SCHONBACH Friedrich (Fred)
SCHÖNEFELD Alfred Max	SCHONEFELD Max
SCHÖNEMANN Gerd Albert	SHERMAN Jack Geoffrey
SCHÖNFELD Ernst Adolf	SCHONFELD Ernest Adolf
SCHÖNLICHT Martin Max	SHENLEY Martin Michael
SCHÖNTHAL Martin	SHELTON Martin Morris
SCHOR Heinrich	SHORE Henry Peter
SCHOR Salo Fanger	SHORE Sidney
SCHOTT Julius	SCOTT Jay
SCHRAML Albin Eugene	SCHRAML Alvin Eugene
SCHREUER Rudolf Wilhelm	SHERMAN Rudolph William
SCHRÖDER Friedrich August Johannes	aka Frederick August Johannes
SCHRÖN George Robert Erhard	MILLAR George Robert Erhard
SCHUCKARDT Erich Leo	SCHUCKARDT Eric Leo
SCHÜFTAN Heinz Hanns	SEAMAN Henry Harold
SCHÜFTAN Herbert	SCHUFTAN Herbert
SCHWAB Heinz	SCHWAB Henry
SCHWABE Helmut Robert Hermann	SCHWABE Helmut Robert Herman
SCHWARCZ Julius	SANDERS John Julian (Jack?)

APPENDIX 3

SCHWARZ Herbert	SHAW Herbert
SCHWARZ Julius	aka Joe
SCHWARZ Kurt	BARZVI Yacob
SCHWARZTHAL Ludwig	PICK Ludwig
SCHWEINBURG Konrad Ludwig	SCHWEINBURG Kurt Ludwig
SCHWERINER Heinz Werner	SPENCER Henry
SEELIG Siegfried	SEELIG George Siegfried
SELIGMANN Walter	SELBY Walter Colin
SELTMANN Gerhard Richard	aka Joe
SENDER Rudi	SHELDON Ralph (British army) later SANDERS Rueven (Rudi)
SHOLNA Benno	STUART Barry
SILBERMANN Herbert	SILBERMAN Herbert
SILBERMANN Martin	SILBERMAN Martin
SILBERSTEIN Gerhard	MARSHALL Frank Gerald
SILBERSTEIN Leopold	SILBERSTEIN Leopold D
SILBERSTEIN Moses Moshek	SILBERSTEIN Marshall
SILBERSTEIN Otmar	SILVERSTEIN Otto
SIMON Bernd Maximilian Leopold	SIMON Bernard
SIMON Karl Heinz	SIMON Karl Henry
SINGER Erik	CRANLY Eric Ronald aka CRANLEY
SINGER Ludwig	SINCLAIR Lewis
SKALLER Friedrich (Fred)	SKALLER Frederick (Fred)
SKIBBE Ernst August	SKIBBE Ernest
SOBELMANN Samuel	SOBELMAN Samuel
SOHN Hans	SOHN Robert Hans
SOKAL Friedrich Jakob (Fritz)	MANSELL Frederick
SOLF Wilhelm Hermann Arnolt George Theobald	SOLF William Herman Arnold George Theobald
SOLMITZ Carl Felix	SOMERS Carl Felix aka Charles Felix
SOMMERFELD Alfred	SUMMERFIELD Steven Alfred
SONDHEIM Günter	SONDHEIM Gunter Michael (Mike)
SONNEWALD Gerhard Heinz	SONNEWALD Gerd
SOSTHEIM Gerd Salli	SOSTHEIM Gary
SPAGAT Erich	SPARK Eric
SPANGLET Heinz Günther	DALE Stephen Patrick
SPIEGEL Ernst	SPIEGEL Ernest
SPIEGEL Otto	CURTIN Gary Randolph aka Randolph Gary
SPIEGEL Walter	CURTIN Walter Anthony

SPIER Julius	SANDERS John (reverted to birth name c. 1970s)
STADLEN Erich Otto Gottfried Max	STADLEN Eric
STAHL Günther Werner Peter	STEELE Peter Gunter
STAHL Werner Joseph	STAHL Josef
STAHR Joachim Georg Ferdinand Adolf	STAHR John George
STEIN Hermann	aka Zvi
STEINBERG Walter	STANLEY Walter
STEINDLER Ernst	STEINDLER Ernest
STEINFELD Gerhard	STANTON Gerald
STEINFELS Wolfgang Curt	STONLEY Charles Walter
STEINHART Oskar Karl	STEINHART Oscar Karl
STEINMETZ Heinz Wolfgang Emil	STEINMETZ Walter (Wally)
STEKEL Wolfgang Johannes	STEKEL William James
STEPHAN Paul Johann	STEPHAN Paul John
STERN Alfred	STANLEY Alfred
STERN Alfred Isak Jacob	STERN Alfred Jacob
STERN Fritz	STERN Fred
STERN Hans	SEATON John David
STERN Hellmut	STERN Harold Helmut
STERN Isidor	STERN Israel
STERN Kurt	STERN Kenneth Charles
STERN Leo Elieser	STERN Elieser
STERN Rolf Alfred	STERN Ralph
STERNBERG Rolf Theobald	STRATTON Ralph Trevor
STERNFELD Norbert Gabriel	STERNFELD Gavriel
STRAUS Emanuel	STRAUS Stanley Emanuel
STRAUS Sali	STRAUS Salli
STRAUSS Erich	STRAUSS Eric
STRAUSS Georg Hermann	STRAUSS George Hermann
STRAUSS Karl Hans Nathan	STRAUSS Charles
STRAUSS Siegfried	STRAUSS Steven
STROHEIM Ernst	STROHEIM Ernest
STROHMAYER Markus	STROHMAYER Marcus
SUFIT Israel Stanislaw	SUFIT Stanislaw (Stan)
SÜSSKIND Herbert	SUTTON Herbert
SÜSSKIND Kurt	SUTTON Ken
SÜSSMANN Alfred	STEVENS Alfred
SÜSSMANN Gerson	SUSSMAN Gerson
TANDLER Heinz Otto	TANDLER Henry Russell

APPENDIX 3

TANDLER Walter	HARVEY Walter Reginald
TEDESCO Fritz <u>Rene</u>	BEVERLEY Rene Ralph
TEICHMANN David Moses	TEICHMAN David Moses
TELTSCHER George Anthony	ADAMS George Anthony
TELTSCHER Heinrich Michael	TELTSCHER Henry Michael
TETELBAUM Mordko Josef	TELSON Joseph
THALHEIMER Ruben Heinrich Markus	THALHEIMER Roy
THIERFELDT Alfred Otto Wilhelm	BARNETT Alfred
TICHAUER Erich	TOWERS Eric Robert
TICHAUER Heinz	TALBOT Henry
TICHAUER Willy Werner	TIRR William (Willy)
TISCH Leo	TAIT Leo
TRAUTNER Eduard Michel	TRAUTNER Edward Michael
TREBITSCH Walter	TRAVERS Walter
TREITEL Kurt Gert	TRENT Gary
TREMESBERGER Josef Anton	TRAVERS Joseph Antony
TÜRK Gustav <u>Werner</u>	TURK Werner
TÜRKISCHER Kohos Karl	TURKISHER Kohos Charles aka Kahat
ULLMANN Michael	ULLMAN Michael
UNGER Heinz	UNGER Harry
VAJDA Stefan	VAJDA Stephen
VALENTIN Albert	VALENTINE Albert Graham
VEIT Georg	VEIT George
VETTER Karl Friedrich	aka Carl Friedrich
VOGEL Egon	served as VILLIERS Ernest Robert
VOGEL Marcel	VERNON Marcel Evelyn
VOLKMANN Oswald Artur Erich	VOLKMANN Oswald Arthur
VOLLMER Heinz	VOLLMER Henry
VOLLWEILER Heinz Siegfried	VOLLWEILER Henry
VON CLAER Horst-Friedrich Josias	LINCOLN John (reverted to birth name, 1986)
VON GRÜNEWALDT Hans Wolter	GRUENEWALDT Gerry von
VON SOMMARUGA Lorenz Johannes Emanuel	VON SOMMARUGA Lorenz aka SUMMERS Laurie
VORGANG Heinz	VORGANG Henry
WACHSMANN Walter	WAXMAN Walter
WALDE Martin Van Der	WOOLTON Charles
WALDSCHMIDT Friedrich Wilhelm Paul Gustav Karl	WALDSCHMIDT Friedrich
WALLACH Herman	WALLACH Zvi

WALLIS Georg	WALLIS George
WALTHER Hans Felix	WALLACE Harry
WANTUCH Julius Otto	WANTUCK Julius Otto
WARSCHAUER Friedrich Franz	WARSCHAUER Frederick Francis (Fred)
WARSZAWSKI Fritz (Fred) Nathan	WARD Fred Nathan
WARZECHA Josef	WARZECHA Joseph Paul
WEBER Jan August Fritz Heinrich	WEBBER Ian Alan
WEHSELY Johann Peter (Hans)	WEHSELY John Peter
WEIDENBAUM Fritz Werner	STONE later CARTER Frederick (Fred)
WEIHS Kurt	WHYTE Keith
WEIL Franz Phillipp (Frank)	WEIL Frank Phillipp
WEINBERG Alfred	WEINBERG Uri
WEINBERG Franz Stefan Max	WYNNE Stephen Max
WEINBERG Hans Hermann	WEBB Harold Howard (reverted to original surname, c. 1954)
WEINBERG Hans Robert	WELDON Hugh Robert
WEINGEIST Julius	GUEST Julius
WEISER Fritz	WEISER Fred Paul
WEISS Günter Maximilian	WYANT Gordon Michael
WEISS Leopold	WEELER John
WEISS Richard Erich Johann Josef Anton Maria	aka WEIHS Richard (original surname c. 1950s)
WEISS Robert Martin	COOPER Randolph Anthony
WEISZ Eduard	WEISZ Edward
WEISZ Hans August	WHITE Robert Hans
WEISZ Heinrich	WEISZ Henry
WELLNER Artur	WELLNER Arthur (Turl)
WELNER Aron	WELNER Aaron
WIENER Alfred	WINGHAM Alfred George
WIESELMANN Viktor	WIESELMANN Victor
WIKOWSKI Manfred Gerhard	WESTERN Fred Gerald
WILDE Hans	SPENCER Eric John
WILDE Werner Berthold	SPENCER Ronald
WINKLER Hans	WINKLER Henry
WISCH Arthur Hermann	WISH Arthur
WITTENBERG Emil	WITTEN Edward Geoffrey (Emil)
WITTGENSTEIN Louis Werner/Werner Louis	DEWITT Vernon Louis
WOHLFELD Heinrich	WOHLFELD Henry

WOHLGEMUTH Gotthilf Ludwig	WILMONT Gotthilf Ludwig
WOHLGEMUTH Leon Eduard	WOHLGEMUTH Leon Edward aka WILMONT Leslie
WOLFFSBERG Heinz Albert	WOLFSBERG Heinz Albert
WOLFSHEIMER Hans Heinz	WOLHAM John Henry
WOLFSOHN Hugo Adolf	WOLF Hugo
WOLFSTEIN Erich	WINTON Eric
WOLKENSTEIN Christoph Franz von	WOLKENSTEIN Christopher Francis
WOLKENSTEIN Oswald Veit von	WOLKENSTEIN Oswald Veit
WOLLSTEIN Manfred	WELDON Stanley Frederick
WOYTHALER Erwin Belmont	WAINWRIGHT Irvine Belmont
WUNDSCH Paul Karl Hans Harro	POWELL Harold John
ZACHARIAS Walter Baruch Joel	ANSON Walter James
ZADEK Arthur	GRANT Arthur Peter
ZAJAC Abram	ZAJAC Abraham
ZEILINGER David Josef	NIZAN David
ZEITZ Wolfgang	GORDON John
ZELMANOWICZ Isidor	TALMON Jizhak
ZENTNER Hermann	CHANDLER Henry
ZIMMELS Hersch Jakob	ZIMMELS Hirsch Jacob
ZITTWITZ Günter Benno	SEATON Gunter Benno
ZUCKER Josef	ZUCKER Joseph
ZUCKERMANN Chiel Schulem	ZUCKERMANN Chiel Scholem
ZUTRAUEN Ernst Rudolf	SEATON Ernest
ZWICKER Robert	VICKERS Robert

This list was compiled using naturalisation, probate and cemetery records; information taken from the *Dunera News*, Ancestry and other genealogical sites; death notices; and personal knowledge.

Hebrew names are, for the most part, based on a list published in the *Dunera News*, 52, June 2001.

INDEX

Abosso (ship) 217, 304, 315
Adam, Leonhard 11, 69, 199, 211, 224, 262, 263, 316, 508
    on Tatura 197, 198, 249, 250, 251, 259, 267, 509
    post-internment life 370, 371, 374, 427, 428
Agamben, Giorgio 71
Alcorn, Franklin 177, 178, 179
Altmann, Elfriede 440
Altmann, Karin 440
Altschul, Franz 365
Andjel, Bert 501
Ansbacher, Joseph 238, 239
Arafat, Yasser 440-1
Arandora Star (ship) 44, 60, 61, 63, 70, 195, 229
    memorials 200, 505
Arndt, Kurt 23, 24, 25, 105, 106
Arndt, Wally 23, 24, 25, 105, 106
Aron, Raymond 401

Baer, Herbert 437
Baer, Walther 268
Baier, Kurt 130, 281, 394
Bannister, Roger 444
Barber, Herbert 373
Barnett, Barney 317, 318
Barthes, Roland 510
Bartrop, Paul xxi-xxii, 472
Baruch, Ludwig 110
Bassett, Ian 377
Bauhaus, the 58, 131, 182, 376, 377, 423
Beckwith, Alice 503
Beckwith, Mick 503
Begin, Menachem 439
Berlin 5, 20, 59, 112
Berlin, Isaiah 401
Bernstein, Gerd *see* Brent, Bern
Besch, Gerhard Leopold xxii, xxiv
Bildungsbürgertum 4, 12, 111
Bischofswerder, Boaz 34, 392
Bischofswerder, Felix *see* Werder, Felix
Bischofswerder, Fred 34
Blair, Hans 205
Blau, Hans *see* Blair, Hans
Bleiweiss, Norman 288
Blumenthal, Hans 177
Blumenthal, Horst *see* Barnett, Barney
Bodner, Menasche 113 n. 4, 501
Boerner, Douglas 408-9, 427
Boerner, Herbert 409
Boomerang (newspaper) 173, 308

Borkenau, Franz 69
Bowles, C. A. 71
Boyd, Arthur 351, 436
Brand, Walter 137, 138
Braun, Robert Felix Emil 200, 505
Brent, Bern 16, 196, 358, 359, 363, 365, 510
    post-war life 398, 399, 466, 505
Breyer, Bruno 262
Broughton, Capt. Edward 341, 343, 349, 353, 354, 365, 455
    admired by soldiers 337, 339
    remembering 338, 492
Browne, June 425
Bruch, Adrian 485
Bruch, Herbert *see* Bruch, Max
Bruch, Max 147, 458-9, 485
Buchdahl, Gerd 35, 69, 86, 127, 128, 374, 406-7, 481
Buchdahl, Hans 35, 374, 405, 406-7
Buchdahl, Nancy 406-7
Buchdahl, Pamela 405, 406-7
Buchenwald concentration camp 13, 30, 35
Buenos Aires 414-15, 417
Bunce Court 51
Bunyan, Carol xxi, xxvi, 515, 520, 521

Calwell, Arthur xxi
camp constitution 69, 86-98, 127-8
camp currency 129-33
Canada 44, 68, 79, 418-19
Carter, Fred 345, 447
Castles, Fay 33, 311, 435
Castles, Francis (Frank) 435
Castles, Heinz 33, 311, 435
Castles, Stephen 435
Chaplin, Charlie 342
Chifley, Ben 110
Churchill, Winston xvii, xx, 42-3, 45, 48, 49, 71, 514
Civil Alien Corps 409
Coffs Harbour 451
Cohn, Sally 287
Collegium Taturense 112, 262-3
compensation 71
Corden, Max xviii, 401, 442
Court, John 377
Cunningham, Eileen 450
Cunningham, Gerald 450
Curtin, John 110, 310
Czech internees/Czechoslovakia 28, 42, 44, 53, 372, 440